THE COMMERCIAL USES OF TRUSTS

This book provides a systematic and critical analysis of the role trusts play in modern commercial markets.

Commercial trusts are complex and ever-evolving, and a reassessment of the traditional legal norms relating to them is much needed in order to provide new doctrinal insights. The book does just that: focusing on trusts in the UK, while drawing on developments in European jurisdictions and in China. It presents a thought-provoking assessment and a unified understanding of commercial trusts.

Volume 49 in the series Hart Studies in Private Law

The Commercial Uses of Trusts

Rethinking the Traditional Approach

Ruiqiao Zhang

•HART•
OXFORD • LONDON • NEW YORK • NEW DELHI • SYDNEY

HART PUBLISHING

Bloomsbury Publishing Plc

Kemp House, Chawley Park, Cumnor Hill, Oxford, OX2 9PH, UK

1385 Broadway, New York, NY 10018, USA

29 Earlsfort Terrace, Dublin 2, Ireland

HART PUBLISHING, the Hart/Stag logo, BLOOMSBURY and the Diana logo are trademarks of Bloomsbury Publishing Plc

First published in Great Britain 2024

A catalogue record for this book is available from the British Library.

A catalogue record for this book is available from the Library of Congress.

Library of Congress Control Number: 2024944006

ISBN: HB: 978-1-50997-405-4
ePDF: 978-1-50997-407-8
ePub: 978-1-50997-406-1

Typeset by Compuscript Ltd, Shannon

FOREWORD

Trusts have been used in commercial applications since at least the nineteenth century. Indisputably, however, their appearance in that context now dominates the worlds of the trust. Pensions and other collective investment structures, securitisations, trading trusts, and trusts for debenture holders are only some of the many manifestations of the rise of the commercial trust. Some recent decisions have even caused us to reflect on whether the substantive principles governing such trusts may differ from those that apply to traditional family trusts (*AIB Group (UK) plc v Mark Redler & Co Solicitors* [2014] UKSC 58, [2015] AC 1503, [70]–[71]; cf [136]–[137]).

In the light of this, Ruiqiao Zhang's monograph on commercial trusts is a most welcome addition to our understanding of the law of trusts. Her work reaches beyond the common law to explore also the rise of commercial trusts in civilian jurisdictions. Her study examines how, in all these jurisdictions, the commercial context informs and affects the legal relationships in the trust. In particular, she looks carefully at the nature of the beneficiary's interest, always a challenging point of analysis in comparative trust law. She studies also the role and responsibilities of the trustee, which can be substantially different in the commercial setting. Another feature that is particularly striking in that setting is the systematic presence of creditors, who may appear only incidentally in traditional trusts. The interests of creditors may conflict in complicated ways with those of both the beneficiaries and the trustees, and commercial trusts must be equipped with defensible systems for resolving these conflicts.

The challenge that Ruiqiao Zhang faces is a difficult one. What remains of the basic principles that govern the trust when it arises in the commercial milieu? When the trust is created and regulated by contract, or when it is used as a business organization, or when the settlors are also the only beneficiaries, what needs to change? Must the governing principles be adapted, or is it only that the context may modify their application, as is so often the case in law? Ultimately, she demonstrates that the commercial context must never lead us to think that commercial trusts are somehow less worthy of the name than more traditional trusts.

The publication of this book, which is the fruit of many years of scholarship in comparative trust law, should be a moment of celebration. Dr Zhang is to be congratulated on a formidable achievement.

Professor Lionel Smith
May 2024

ACKNOWLEDGEMENTS

First, I am eternally grateful to Professor Lionel Smith, my doctoral supervisor, who has provided me with inspiration and support throughout my entire academic journey. Professor Smith has provided valuable feedback and advice on both my research and career development; his teaching and guidance, in his role as a world-leading scholar and educator in trust law, has exemplified academic rigour and ethics. It has been the greatest honour to have him write the foreword to my monograph.

I would also like to express my sincerest gratitude to Professor Paul Miller, who is both a teacher and a friend to me. His kindness and intelligence have inspired me at work and in life in general, while his help and support were crucial during difficult times.

I am grateful to all of those with whom I have had the pleasure to work at Edinburgh Law School. I would especially like to thank Professors Claudio Michelon and David Fox, who have both provided professional guidance and pertinent feedback on my career and research.

Nobody has been more supportive to me than the members of my family. I am forever indebted to my parents, Xiang and Wencai, whose love and support have uplifted me in all of my endeavours. A very special thanks goes also to my loving assistance and therapy dog Lang, who has offered unconditional love and been a loyal guardian. I wish all my family a healthy, happy and long life.

Last but not least, I extend my sincere thanks to everyone I have worked with on the Hart Publishing team, who have been forever patient and professional and have helped me in many ways.

CONTENTS

ABBREVIATIONS

ASIC	Australian Securities & Investments Commission
BGBl	Federal Law Gazette of Germany
CBRC	China Banking Regulatory Commission
CBIRC	China Banking and Insurance Regulatory Commission
CIRC	China Insurance Regulatory Commission
CRS	Common Reporting Standard
CSRC	Chinese Securities Regulatory Commission
CLJ	Cambridge Law Journal
FATCA	Foreign Accounts Tax Compliance Act
FCA	Financial Conduct Authority
FSMA 2000	Financial Services and Markets Act 2000
HCCH	Hague Conference on Private International Law
ICLQ	International and Comparative Law Quarterly
LQR	Law Quarterly Review
MOHRSS	Ministry of Human Resources and Social Security of China
OECD	Organisation for Economic Co-operation and Development
OJLS	Oxford Journal of Legal Studies
PAYE	Pay As You Earn
REITs	Real Estate Investment Trusts
UCITS	The European Directive on Undertakings for Collective Investment in Transferable Securities

TABLE OF CASES

TABLE OF LEGISLATION AND OTHER MATERIALS

Introduction

Trusts, which originated in common law and have been used to protect family landholdings over generations, have developed into vehicles that are more often used for commercial purposes. This shift has occurred without any systematic understanding of in what form and to what extent trusts can be adopted in a commercial context. Furthermore, few have considered whether existing trust law can adequately govern commercial trusts or whether the commercial use of trusts requires a redeveloped trust law regime, distinguished from traditional approaches. This book offers a critical analysis of these issues by illustrating how business requirements have shaped the evolution of trusts, categorising the principal forms of commercial trusts, examining the legal transplant of trusts into civil law jurisdictions promoted by the commercial uses of trusts, and analysing the changes and challenges the commercial uses of trusts bring to the rights and obligations of trustees, beneficiaries and trust creditors.[1] It aims to redress the misunderstandings of the new role trusts play in modern financial markets and make a significant contribution to the legal reform of trusts by juxtaposing historical, comparative, theoretical, doctrinal, and interdisciplinary methodologies. This book focuses on the regime of the United Kingdom while adopting comparative studies of other jurisdictions (eg European countries and China) in order to provide a unified understanding of commercial trusts.

Commercial trusts are a complex and ever-evolving area of research. Trusts, which originated in common law and have been used to protect family assets over generations, have developed into vehicles that are more often used for commercial purposes, and this has spurred the introduction of trusts into civil law jurisdictions. Their increasing importance in commercial contexts and their transplant into civil law require a developed understanding of trusts and a rethinking of the traditional approaches to trusts. For example, it is important to understand how business requirements have shaped the evolution of trusts and explored the different settings, distinguished from the traditional approaches, in which commercial trusts are now found. It is also important to know how civil law jurisdictions have interpreted the essence of trusts, accommodated traditional common law norms (eg dual ownership), and transplanted trusts into their own systems. Finally, it is

[1] The role of a settlor is neither a key factor nor an independent discussion in this monograph. This is because settlors are often also the beneficiaries in commercial trusts (especially in trusts for investment purposes) and/or take a minor position in a trust after its creation, with their contribution enclosed in trust instruments and the ownership of trust property transferred to a trustee (which is the case in most jurisdictions).

necessary to grasp how the commercial uses of trusts have developed the rights and obligations of trustees, beneficiaries and trust creditors, which differ from the traditional understanding of such roles, and whether or not these uses separate commercial trusts from other trusts. However, there is a dearth of systematic scholarly literature on these topics and a delay in legislation in response to the speedy expansion of commercial uses of trusts, which may result in confusion or misuse of trusts in practice.

This book aims to fills the gap in legal research on UK commercial trusts and provides advice on trust law reforms by juxtaposing historical, interdisciplinary, comparative, theoretical and doctrinal methodologies. Chapter one examines how business has shaped the evolution of trusts from a historical background, in order to address misunderstanding of the new role that trusts play in commercial contexts or remove mystery around this role. It also critically analyses the reasons for this evolution and answers the question of what makes a trust attractive for commercial uses. Chapter two continues to explore the specific types of commercial trusts that currently exist, focusing on the UK regime. It analyses hypotheses concerning the economics of trust relationship from a disciplinary perspective, and argues that, given the different settings and contexts in which commercial trusts are found, trust law should be developed to serve the way in which trusts are now used in a commercial context. After discussing the evolution of trusts, which are considered a common law product, and the principal forms of commercial trusts in the UK and other common law countries, chapter three examines the introduction of the trust into civilian jurisdictions (both mixed jurisdictions and pure civil law systems) and adopts a comparative legal study based on discussion about the essence of trust as the theoretical basis for research on legal transplant of trust. Moving on from the rethinking of traditional approaches of commercial trusts in general, chapter four, chapter five and chapter six focus on examining the changes and challenges of the roles of beneficiaries, trustees and trust creditors respectively from both theoretical and doctrinal perspectives. Those chapters not only illustrate how traditional approaches have adjusted in order to meet commercial demands but also answer the question of whether those changes or challenges suggest separation of commercial trusts from trusts should be considered. As the closing chapter, chapter seven envisages the future of trust law and suggests the need for a reform of trust legislation.

1

The New Role Played by Trusts in Commercial Contexts

This chapter first examines the evolution of trusts, seeking to redress misunderstandings of the new role of trusts and remove the mystery around the trust by placing it within the broader historical context within which trusts evolved.[1] It then critically analyses the reasons for such evolution and attempts to answer the question of what makes a trust attractive for commercial uses.

I. Evolution of Trusts

The trust is often claimed to be the most significant contribution that English law has made to the world of jurisdiction.[2] As a product of Equity, it was essentially an emanation of the willingness of the Chancellor and his courts to side with deserving claimants to circumvent the strictures of the common law and even of statutes.[3] The origins of the trust can be traced back to the thirteenth century, when it was developed from the 'use' and worked as a device to prevent and correct perceived injustices committed by men in connection with privately held land in English feudal times. The trust was adopted as a conveyancing device for the holding of land to avoid financial liability and restrictions on the inheritance of property.[4] As Davies and Virgo explain:

> At its most basic, this device was used to transfer land to people who would hold it for the use of the transferor for life and then for selected family members. In that way, the

[1] Trusts of this evolved form – trusts used in commercial contexts or for commercial purposes – are described as commercial trusts in this book. The expression 'commercial trusts' is not a legal term of art and it is not a category of trust in the traditional taxonomy. The boundaries of commercial trusts have continued to expand as trusts have been deployed across a greater range of commercial contexts. There are claims that a clear distinction between commercial and non-commercial trusts is difficult to articulate; for example, see criticisms of the *Stack v Dowden* approach.

[2] TG Watkin, 'Changing Concepts of Ownership in English Law During the Nineteenth and Twentieth Centuries: The Changing Idea of Beneficial Ownership under the English Trust' in M Dixon and GLLH Griffiths (eds), *Contemporary Perspectives on Property, Equity and Trusts Law* (Oxford, Oxford University Press, 2007) 139, 143.

[3] N D'Angelo, *Commercial Trusts* (Chatswood, LexisNexis Butterworths, 2014) 42.

[4] See especially SFC Milsom, *Historical Foundations of the Common Law*, 2nd edn (Oxford, Oxford University Press, 1981) ch 9; J Baker, *An Introduction to English Legal History*, 5th edn (Oxford, Oxford University Press, 2019) 309–11 and ch 14.

> transferor could ensure that the land was inherited by a member of his family rather than forfeited to a lord. The use was also deployed where a tenant of land was fighting abroad, for example in the Crusades, so that trustees could be appointed to manage the land on his behalf.[5]

Under the traditional trust model, rather than being transferred under a contract, trust property was normally transferred by way of gift to one or more human trustees, who acted gratuitously and managed the property in a conservative and risk-averse manner for the benefit of familial beneficiaries, in order to preserve family capital and look after the interests of the elderly, the young, the incapacitated and the foolhardy.[6] Therefore, the ability of traditional trusts to circumvent unwanted rules and outcomes was applied to achieve private rather than commercial objectives.

Although their original uses were not for commercial purposes, family trusts helped carve out the earliest modern trust law parameters. In the mid-Victorian era, many small to mid-sized families held investments and securities in trusts.[7] The burdens of trusteeship that increased in Victorian England gave rise to more investor-friendly trust law[8] and prompted the development of the notion of a trust as a fund.[9] Trusts were an integral part of commercial dealings in England from at least the early eighteenth century. In the early nineteenth century, before the invention of joint stock companies, they were commonly used as a device to allocate the risk of a commercial party's insolvency and in corporate structures.[10] Following the rise of a wealthy Victorian middle class, the increase in commerce and later changes in tax law in the early twentieth century, trusts came to encompass shifting funds of personal property. These socio-economic changes caused the trust law doctrine to change.[11]

In addition to acting as guardians of family assets, trusts increasingly also became used as business entities. Equity's key innovation, the trust, as well as

[5] PS Davies and G Virgo, *Equity & Trusts: Text, Cases, and Materials*, 3rd edn (Oxford, Oxford University Press, 2019) 24.

[6] See especially D'Angelo (n 3) 6–7 and 45; S Wilson, *Todd & Wilson's Textbook on Trusts & Equity*, 12th edn (Oxford, Oxford University Press, 2015) 447; ME Carn, 'Distinguishing Traditional from Commercial Trusts: A Dangerous Precedent or Necessary Complication?' (2015) 21 *Trusts & Trustees* 868, 879. The core idea of this traditional trust remains important for wealthy families today. Settlors can now arrange to preserve and generate family assets for three or four generations for the benefit of family members. But such an outcome is achieved through economies of scale in the management of the large pool of family assets. See, eg, DJ Hayton, 'English Trusts and Their Commercial Counterparts in Continental Europe' in DJ Hayton (ed), *Extending the Boundaries of Trusts and Similar Ring-Fenced Funds* (London, Kluwer Law International, 2002) 23, 33–34.

[7] This is evidenced in many of the classic Victorian cases on breach of duty by trustees, eg *Re Hallett's Estate* (1880) 13 Ch D 696; *Speight v Gaunt* [1883] UKHL 1.

[8] See C Stebbings, *The Private Trustee in Victorian England* (Cambridge, Cambridge University Press, 2002).

[9] See R Nolan, 'Property in a Fund' (2004) 120 *LQR* 108.

[10] A Televantos, *Capitalism Before Corporations: The Morality of Business Associations and the Roots of Commercial Equity and Law* (Oxford, Oxford University Press, 2021) pt I.2.

[11] ibid 32.

the obligations associated with a trust, can be extremely useful in commercial situations.[12] Although many of the essential components of the modern commercial trust can be traced back to its medieval use, the context in which the trust arose nonetheless is very different from that of medieval use.[13] As society has become more complicated, so too has the commercial trust continuously reacted and adapted. At the heart of complex commercial dealings, the trust becomes a popular structural basis for a range of uses, including investment, protection in insolvency, securitisation and shareholding, and many others.[14] That is, in fast-changing, highly sophisticated and complex environments, the trust serves as an extremely useful mechanism for achieving fair play in a variety of contexts, corresponding with commercial rhetoric and an intent to play fair in the face of the unexpected.[15] A trust is of particular use in international financial markets and is now one of the key indicators of financial law.[16] It permits the legal relationship between persons and assets to remain secure and flexible at the same time, with property or priority rights relating to a changing pool of assets being enjoyed by a changing class of persons and being subject to concurrent interests and/or enforcement restrictions.[17] In financial terms, the most important role a trust plays in today's world is related to the holding of incorporeal wealth.[18]

Trusts nowadays are vastly more important in a commercial context than in family trusts.[19] Although family trusts can still be found today, they are no longer as significant as they were in what was once a far more socially polarised society that featured a much larger aristocratic class.[20] Evidence shows that the trusts that are found in commercial and business contexts nowadays have the most influence on how trust law is adapting; this reflects how trusts are now being used. Trust law cases are becoming increasingly more focused on commercial dealings, rather than familial ones, and the litigation of commercial trust law issues has become more frequent than in the past.[21] The UK Law Commission's 2006 report on Trustee Exemption Clauses[22] confirms the popularity of commercial trusts. The main intention of this consultation paper was to examine the law and practice

[12] Wilson (n 6) 473.

[13] Davies and Virgo (n 5) 25.

[14] A detailed discussion of the principal forms of commercial trusts that are currently employed in the UK can be found in ch 2.

[15] Wilson (n 6) 472.

[16] PR Wood, 'Commercial Trusts in an International Context' (2013) 19 *Trusts & Trustees* 267, 273.

[17] DJ Hayton, H Pigott and J Benjamin, 'The Use of Trusts in International Financial Transactions' (2002) 1 *Journal of International Banking & Financial Law* 23, 29.

[18] M Graziadei, U Mattei and L Smith, 'Commercial Trusts in European Private Law: The Interest and Scope of the Enquiry' in M Graziadei, U Mattei and L Smith (eds), *Commercial Trusts in European Private Law* (Cambridge, Cambridge University Press, 2005) 3, 27, fn 74; see RH Sitkoff, 'An Agency Costs Theory of Trust Law' (2004) 89 *Cornell Law Review* 621, 621–84.

[19] JH Langbein, 'The Secret Life of the Trust: The Trust as an Instrument of Commerce' (1997) 107 *Yale Law Journal* 165, 188.

[20] Wilson (n 6) 28–31.

[21] See Graziadei, Mattei and Smith (n 18) 3.

[22] *Trustee Exemption Clauses* (Law Com No 301, 2006).

relating to trustee exemption clauses in England and Wales and to set out options for reform with the economic implications of the regulation of such clauses in mind.

The diversified uses and increasing prominence of trusts in business and commerce have become the strongest influence on the nature of trust law in the twenty-first century.[23] In response to the special and complex arrangements engaged in the commercial use of trusts, this book claims that a redeveloped trust law regime, distinguished from traditional approaches, is required. Trust law is due for review and reform.

II. Attractiveness of Trusts for Commercial Uses

Having discussed the development of trusts from its role as a guardian of family assets to a commercial vehicle, the question as to the reasons for such evolution arises. What is it about the trust that makes it attractive for commercial use?

The advantage of using trusts in commercial contexts is that trusts grant institutions total flexibility in arranging matters of internal governance, protection of creditors dealing with trustees, and distribution of capital or income by creating fixed or discretionary interests in beneficiaries.[24] Specifically, the reasons for the evolution of trusts and their commercial uses lie in the following elements: the inherent flexibility of the trust device; the independence of trust property – a proprietary element of the trust, which allows the creation, recognition and protection of multiple separate economic interests in property; the segregation of control and the benefits of trust property, which offers inbuilt protections for beneficiaries and contracting third parties through the imposition of personal liabilities on trustees; and an ability of the trust to circumvent legal obstacles and avoid unwanted outcomes otherwise mandated by common law or statute.

A. Inherent Flexibility of Trusts

In contrast to most other commercial vehicles whose formation and governance are to a greater extent controlled by legislation and complex procedures, a trust is created and managed in a simple and private way, leaving flexibilities to its parties: to the settlor, who is more likely to create a trust to manage a property in the way they want; and to the trustee, who has more discretion with fewer procedural barriers to administer the trust property.

[23] Wilson (n 6) 37.
[24] DJ Hayton, 'The Uses of Trusts in the Commercial Context' in A Kaplan (ed), *Trusts in Prime Jurisdictions*, 3rd edn (London, Globe Law and Business, 2010) 611, 623.

A trust can be easily created by an agreement between the settlor and the trustee, or is sometimes even based on the settlor's will with the trustee's acceptance.[25] A commercial trust may be established by nothing more than a trust instrument that satisfies the minimum trust law requirements and the presence of three certainties: intention, subject matter and objects.[26] There is no requirement for the minimum value of trust property.[27] And no registration or other public filing is required for a trust to be legally recognised and properly administered.[28] Therefore, the constitution and operation of a trust may be kept confidential, making it completely invisible to the outside world. This makes trusts particularly attractive to those who require or prefer to manage their assets efficiently and/or secretly.

The value of inherent flexibility of trusts is also reflected in its internal governance. 'There is no law, beyond the general fiduciary overlay imposed on trustees, regulating the decision-making processes within a trust and parties are free to construct whatever governance regime they wish through the trust instrument.'[29] The commercial trust eliminates a layer of regulation, ie the state corporation statute. As Langbein notes:

> The flexibility to eliminate governance procedures that are obligatory under the corporate form has been one great attraction of the trust form. For example, the trust instrument can be drafted to dispense with routine shareholder meetings. As a result, the costs of proxy solicitation and other meeting-related expenses that are mandated under corporation codes can be eliminated.[30]

Additionally, entitling trustees to legal ownership (or proprietary powers in civil law) facilitates a more efficient use of the trust, especially in commercial contexts where prompt and reliable decision-making is essential. This quality gives the trust an advantage over agency because an agent does not have the discretion permitted to the trustee.[31] A trustee, as the legal owner of trust property, has a wide discretion and full decision-making power over the trust property.[32] This degree of discretion enables the trustees to react efficiently to current economic conditions and adapt their contemporary understanding of markets and investments. Investments which were imprudent in the days of the gold standard may be sound and sensible in the case of high inflation, while modern trustees acting within

[25] See WG Hart, 'What is a Trust?' (1899) 15 *LQR* 294.

[26] *Knight v Knight* (1840) 3 Beav 148, 49 ER 58. Every trust, except for charitable trusts, must satisfy the three certainties of intention, subject matter and objects.

[27] This makes a trust easier to be established comparing with a public company, which has a minimum share capital requirement of £50,000. See Companies Act 2006, pt 20 ch 2.

[28] A trustee simply has a reporting obligation to beneficiaries of the trust: a trustee must regularly give beneficiaries accurate and full information and explanations of the state of the trust.

[29] D'Angelo (n 3) 82.

[30] Langbein (n 19) 184.

[31] R Zhang, 'Principal Forms of Commercial Trusts in the UK and the Rethinking of Traditional Approaches' (2022) 28(8) *Trusts & Trustees* 787, 789.

[32] See especially Trustee Act 1925 and Trustee Act 2000.

their investment powers are required and entitled to be judged by the standards of current portfolio theory, which emphasises the risk attaching to each investment taken in isolation.[33]

A trustee's legal ownership also significantly reduces transaction costs, because the trustee can devote the trust's resources to taking advantage of business opportunities, instead of needing to obtain the investor-beneficiaries' consent to the transaction. Consequently, the investors (who are, in most cases, the settlors and the beneficiaries) are able to devote their resources to their principal activity, rather than searching for business opportunities that fall outside of their profession.[34]

Moreover, trust instruments in commercial trusts commonly give investors the right to demand redemption at a price calculated in accordance with a mandated formula. In other words, investments in trusts can easily be returned without a formal process if the trustee and the investors have agreed to do so.[35] It is worth noting that limited companies have rules and provisions that prevent a company from acquiring its own shares.[36] As such, any redemption of a contribution made by a shareholder who has financed the company's own assets since making an investment is restricted by strict conditions.[37] Thus, the ability to easily return investments often makes trusts more attractive to investors than other commercial instruments.

In short, a trust, which is largely regulated by its trust instrument, is considered a more flexible and less complex application than a corporation or other commercial schemes. A modern merchant or investor would hope to choose a vehicle that allows the free transfer of interests and permits the rules governing the scheme to be changed where necessary.

B. Independence of Trust Property

Another element that has contributed to the popularity of trusts for commercial uses is the independence of trust property. That is, since trust property is independent from trustees' personal assets, trusts are well placed to deal with modern banking requirements (which often mandate the separation of managed assets from other assets belonging to managers in a personal capacity). Trusts are ideally placed to take on such a structure and achieve the required segregation of assets.[38]

[33] G Watt and P Todd, *Cases & Materials on Equity & Trusts*, 10th edn (Oxford, Oxford University Press, 2016) 395.

[34] Graziadei, Mattei and Smith (n 18) 3, 41.

[35] D'Angelo (n 3) 81–82.

[36] See Companies Act 2006, s 658.

[37] See especially Companies Act 2006, pt 18 (Acquisition by limited company of its own shares) and pt 17 ch 10 (Reduction of share capital).

[38] Graziadei, Mattei and Smith (n 18) 3, 25.

During the twentieth century, trusts were used throughout Europe to separate assets in the way required of money managers.[39]

Trusts, as financial and investment vehicles, provide both diversification and active asset management on a collective basis. Due to the independence of trust property, a trust can exclude assets that are the result of commercial transactions from a person's balance sheet, either for insolvency risk management or taxation purposes. Trust property must be separated from a trustee's personal assets; this is because, under a trust, the trustee wears the 'two hats' of their fiduciary office and their personal affairs. These two roles are distinct, as is the property that comes under the auspices of each role.[40] Consequently, a trustee's personal creditors have no claim against trust property; they can only claim against the trustee's personal assets.[41]

In addition, the settlors' creditors cannot claim trust property; this is because (unless they retain the right to revoke) creditors lose their ownership of trust property when they transfer the property to the trustees.[42] The beneficiaries' personal creditors do not have any claim on the trust property either, because the beneficiaries hold no legal ownership of the trust property until the trustee transfers it to them (they only hold the equity title that allows them to enjoy the trust benefits). Therefore, the rule of independence of trust property successfully separates trust property from non-trust assets and immunises the trust property from the claims of any personal creditors or trustee spouses, protecting the settlor and beneficiary in the event of bankruptcy or divorce. Trusts achieve this without the need to lodge ownership of the trust property in a distinct entity endowed with juridical personality, such as a corporation. In this way, the independence of trust property successfully separates trust property from non-trust assets and immunises the trust property against the claims of personal creditors or divorced spouses.

A trust does not fail simply 'because no trustee is designated or because the designated trustee declines, is unable, or ceases to act, unless the trust's creation or continuation depends on a specific person serving as trustee'.[43] As a result, even when a trustee goes bankrupt or becomes insolvent, they still retain their interest in the trust. This means that a trust is more likely to be readily accepted by

[39] See ibid fn 63: H Coing, *Treuhand kraft privaten Rechtsgeschäfts* (Munich, Beck, 1973) 62. With the idea of replicating this mode of operation, experiments that took place in the nineteenth century aimed to set up a vehicle that could hold German investments on the New York Stock Exchange.

[40] D Waters, L Smith and M Gillen, *Waters' Law of Trusts in Canada*, 5th edn (Toronto, Carswell, 2021) 13.

[41] It is noted that even trust creditors have no direct claims on the trust property in common law. Professor Smith states that the trust creditor, just like a personal creditor of the trustee, has no direct access to the trust assets (L Smith, 'Trust and Patrimony' (2009) 28 *Estates, Trusts & Pensions Journal* 332, 338). Nevertheless, Smith is careful to mention that in some jurisdictions, the law has changed so as to give creditors direct access to the trust assets. The clearest example is in the US (L Smith, 'Scottish Trusts in the Common Law' (2013) 17 *Edinburgh Law Review* 283, 305).

[42] PH Pettit, *Equity and the Law of Trusts*, 12th edn (Oxford, Oxford University Press, 2012) 45.

[43] Restatement (Third) of the Law of Trusts, § 31 (2001).

beneficiary investors than other financial instruments such as companies (where investment interests and the company's own assets will both be bankrupted should the company become insolvent).

C. Separation of Control and Benefits of Trust Property

In addition to the independence of trust property, trust law's ability to separate the control and benefits of trust property between the trustee and beneficiary is also a key advantage in a commercial context. This becomes especially apparent in cases that involve trustees' fiduciary duties to a beneficiary. While trusts automatically invoke the distinctive protective regime of fiduciary duties to safeguard the interests of investors or other beneficiaries, they also grant considerable powers over the trust property to the trustee. This makes the trust perfectly designed to effectively manage modern financial assets (which often require that a manager be granted extensive powers over property). At the same time, the fiduciary duties implicit within the trust offset and control this power, requiring the trustee to exercise it in the best interests of the trust beneficiaries.[44] In other words, trusts inherently promote both management efficiency and investment safety.

Essentially, a trust is administered and disposed by a trustee, while the trust property is enjoyed by the beneficiary. This is true even in cases where the trust terms allow the beneficiary to enjoy the trust property in specie, ie where they allow the beneficiary to possess the trust property. A trustee possesses the legal rights and powers associated with the property; however, the trustee must act upon these rights and powers in accordance with their personal obligations. That is, they must exercise their ownership of trust property according to the trust terms and thereby ensure the beneficiary's interests are met.[45] Benefits obtained from the trust property (both immediate and deferred) accrue to the trust beneficiary.

This fundamental quality of the trust in Anglo-American law is reflected in the external appearance of the dual ownership of trust property. The concept of dual ownership resulted from the influence of the courts of equity and was rooted in two separate court systems that operated in tandem in England before the development of modern trust law.[46] The common law courts recognised legal ownership in property and considered the *feoffees to uses*; the Chancellor, on the other hand, focused on the enjoyment to property by forcing *feoffees to uses* to hold the property for the benefit of the *cestui que uses* on the basis of conscience. As the Chancellor's intervention became more regular, the Court of Chancery emerged. The common law courts recognised legal ownership in property, but did

[44] Langbein (n 19) 182.
[45] *Westdeutsche Landesbank Girozentrale v Islington London Borough Council* [1996] AC 669, 705.
[46] Watt and Todd (n 33) 10.

not admit the existence of equitable ownership. The Court of Chancery, on the other hand, sprang up to recognise situations where the legal owners of land ought not, in good conscience, be allowed unfettered enjoyment to property owned by them, but instead, ought to be subject to an overriding claim of some other person who had a claim in conscience to the use and enjoyment of the property. The Court of Chancery protected the beneficiary's rights to ensure the achievement of equity or justice.[47] While both courts were merged in 1875, and equitable interests are now recognised by all branches of the court, and may therefore in a sense be considered legal, the distinction in law between legal and equitable ownership persists.[48]

Intrinsic features of the law of trusts make trusts desirable financial and investment vehicles. The division of control and benefits of trust property, for example, offer inbuilt protections for both beneficiaries and contracting third parties through the imposition of personal liabilities on trustees. As a result, trusts suit the needs of both the beneficiaries of the investment and other third parties. Trusts in commercial contexts are commonly alter ego trusts, wherein the settlors and the investors are also the trust beneficiaries. Therefore, the segregation of ownership and right to benefit makes the trust tremendously attractive to investors in this context.[49] The key essence of the trust – the trustees hold and manage the trust property in the beneficiary's interests, rather than their own – makes the trust a better option (ie a safer method) of investing compared to other vehicles such as companies, wherein the invested assets become the company's assets and the investors are no longer the beneficial owners.

D. Ability to Circumvent Legal Obstacles

The history of trusts derived from the circumvention of unwanted legal, regulatory and fiscal burdens. Landowners took advantage of their use before 1535 in order to evade payment of feudal dues. At times, the use of trusts took on a social dimension. In addition to, or as part of, tax saving schemes, family patriarchs would often use trusts to distribute family assets to a mistresses or illegitimate children.[50] Taxation has been a significant factor in the history and evolution of trusts. There is a long history of the trust being used specifically as a device for evading, avoiding or minimising direct and indirect taxes.[51] The ability of a trust to circumvent legal obstacles and avoid taxation and other unwanted outcomes

[47] See Pettit (n 42).

[48] JE Penner, *The Law of Trusts*, 12th edn (Oxford, Oxford University Press, 2022) 13.

[49] R Zhang, 'The New Role Trusts Play in Modern Financial Markets: The Evolution of Trusts from Guardian to Entrepreneur and the Reasons for the Evolution' (2017) 23(4) *Trusts & Trustees* 453, 463–64.

[50] Pettit (n 42) 15.

[51] D'Angelo (n 3) 33.

not only originally gave life to the trust, but has continued into its applications to modern financial markets.[52]

Many trusts are now created as tax planning devices (the accepted euphemism for minimising tax liability through legal avoidance). This has become a dominant reason for the creation of trusts in the modern law of trusts and a driving force behind the growth of the commercial uses of trusts.[53] A trust can be used to achieve tax advantages by passing beneficial interests, which incur tax liabilities, to people who benefit from a low tax rate, or by transferring taxable property to tax havens, or simply by taking advantage of the nature of tax conduits, using the absence of legal personality to avoid entity-level taxes. Unlike a corporation, which attracts entity-level taxation in income tax, a trust is not considered a legal person in most jurisdictions; therefore, no taxation tends to be imposed on the trust itself.

A typical example of a trust used for tax planning purposes is an offshore trust.[54] Generally speaking, offshore trusts (also known as foreign trusts) are trusts that are routinely managed outside the country, in jurisdictions known for their favourable tax regimes,[55] and where all or most of the trustees are not resident or habitually resident in the country.[56] The benefits of adopting an offshore trust ultimately depend on the governing law of the offshore jurisdiction; an obvious, common advantage is that the offshore trust protects trust property from unfavourable tax treatment (eg income or capital gains tax) in home jurisdictions where the tax rate is high (eg the UK or US).[57] Moreover, offshore trusts help people to avoid regulatory or governmental oversight in their home jurisdiction, putting their assets beyond the reach of creditors and allowing them to

[52] A danger in commercial contexts is that if a commercial trust is structured improperly, serious adverse tax consequences can arise. See E Powles and S Mazzier, 'The New Rule against Perpetuities: Hidden Traps for Commercial Trusts' (2009) 8 *Journal of International Banking & Financial Law* 486, 486.

[53] See especially *Prest v Petrodel Resources Ltd* [2013] UKSC 34, [2013] 2 AC 415, a Supreme Court decision that indicated the significance of tax in trust creation; Langbein (n 19) 181.

[54] Offshore trusts can be subclassified into revocable offshore trusts (which may be altered or liquidated at any time or after a certain date by the settlor); irrevocable offshore trusts (which cannot be altered or terminated by the settlor, at any time); discretionary offshore trusts (for which the trustee has the discretion to decide the distribution of the trust profits for different classes of beneficiaries); fixed offshore trusts (for which the distribution of the trust income to beneficiaries is fixed and cannot be altered by the trustee); and hybrid offshore trusts (which are made up of a combination of elements that come from discretionary and fixed trusts).

[55] Examples of the jurisdictions in which offshore trusts are usually established are the British Virgin Islands, Bermuda, Belize, Cayman Islands, Guernsey, Isle of Man, Jersey, Liechtenstein, New Zealand, Seychelles and Switzerland.

[56] See especially Wilson (n 6) 33; J Garton, R Probert and G Bean, *Moffat's Trusts Law: Text and Materials*, 7th edn (Cambridge, Cambridge University Press, 2020) 962–68.

[57] In creating an offshore trust, there are also disadvantages to take into account: this arrangement engages uncertainty or unfamiliarity with the law and economic policies of the offshore jurisdiction, which requires extra time and effort to be spent on research. Also, tax exemption is not always the case. See A Fairpo and D Salter, *Revenue Law: Principles and Practice*, 37th edn (Edinburgh, Bloomsbury Professional, 2019) ch 30, for a detailed statement.

avoid liabilities. Finally, the trust form protects the confidentiality of such an arrangement.[58] Offshore trusts play a significant role in commercial contexts; for example, in debt securitisation and in altering trustees' duties of supervision over company directors when the trust assets consist of a corporate shareholding.

III. Conclusion

This chapter adopts a historical methodology, and examines the evolution of the trust from a guardian of family property to an entrepreneur for commercial uses. In so doing, it attempts to redress misunderstandings of the evolved role of trusts. The concept of the trust has grown gradually over the centuries, adapting with marked flexibility to the demands that society has made upon it, and the trust now plays a significant role in modern financial markets. Trusts cannot be equated with companies,[59] and in contrast to contracts, trusts can offer protection against creditors.[60] A trust's inherent flexibility, its design providing the independence of property and the division of control and benefits of the trust property, and its ability to circumvent legal obstacles makes it a unique vehicle to facilitate business – a role that is unlikely to end in the future.

[58] The decision on the confidentiality of trust was made in *Breakspear v Ackland* [2008] EWHC 220 (Ch), although mainly based on a family context. Whether the confidentiality function applies to commercial trusts in the same way is controversial.

[59] See Companies Act 2006. For example, a company is established and governed following a series of procedures and disclosing obligations. Decision-making on significant issues has to be approved by members through ordinary resolution or special resolution. Return of capital is generally prohibited. See *Trevor v Whitworth* (1887) 12 App Cas 409. The House of Lords held that a company could not acquire its own shares, even though there was an express power to do so in its memorandum, because this would result in a reduction of capital.

[60] Lord President Inglis once asserted in the Scottish court that 'a trust is a contract made up of the two nominate contracts of deposit and mandate' in *Croskery v Gilmour's Trs* (1890) 17 R 697, 700. However, it is worth noting that this explanation is inadequate, as property held in trust cannot be seized by the personal creditors of the trustees. See *Heritable Reversionary Co Ltd v Millar* (1892) 19 R (HL) 43, [1892] AC 598, 600. Where a trustee, the owner of trust property, becomes bankrupt, the trust property is not available to his creditors. See *Sharp v Thomson* 1995 SC 455, 479 (Lord President Hope).

2

The Main Varieties of Commercial Trusts in Common Law: Rethinking Traditional Approaches*

Trusts are ubiquitous across the worldwide economy and society, and they have diverse applications and the ability to adapt to new usages. This chapter first identifies, categorises and examines the principal types of commercial trusts that are currently employed in the UK and then briefly introduces key examples of commercial trusts in the common law jurisdictions of Australia and the US. It concludes that, given the different settings and contexts in which commercial trusts are found, trust law should be developed to serve the way in which trusts are now used in a commercial context.

I. Principal Types of Commercial Trusts in the UK

According to their key different uses or purposes, this chapter broadly divides commercial trusts in the UK into four main varieties: trusts for investment purposes; trusts underpinning commercial loan arrangements; trusts protecting assets in insolvency; and trusts applying to shareholding. Some trusts might come under more than one category, as they have various functions. Such cases will be put into the category that best describes their principal purpose.

A. Trusts for Investment Purposes

At present, investors who wish to own stocks, bonds or other financial assets are showing an increasing preference for buying shares in a pooled fund in which investment professionals select and manage assets according to guidelines while complying with the investment objectives.[1] Such preference makes a trust a well designed tool for investment purposes; it enables investors to invest in a trust

* This chapter draws on previously published work in R Zhang, 'Principal Forms of Commercial Trusts in the UK and the Rethinking of Traditional Approaches ' (2022) 28 (8) *Trusts & Trustees* 787.

[1] JH Langbein, 'The Secret Life of the Trust: The Trust as an Instrument of Commerce' (1997) 107 *Yale Law Journal* 165, 170.

within which a professional trustee and/or manager selects from a pooled investment, managing the investment for the benefit of the trust beneficiaries (who are, in most cases, the investors themselves).[2] In this way, small investors are able to achieve a diversified investment portfolio that is professionally managed by a trustee and by investment experts recruited by the trustee. Investors rely heavily on the rate of return these managers are able to achieve. In other words, the trust offers expertise and diversification superior to what would be obtainable by small investors constructing an individual portfolio.

In the UK, trust-related investment schemes come in two main types: unit trusts and investment trusts. The investment trust, although called a trust, is not viewed as a trust today; rather, it takes the form of a company.

i. Unit Trusts

A unit trust in the UK, defined in s 237(1) of the Financial Services and Markets Act 2000 (FSMA 2000), is 'a collective investment scheme under which the property is held on trust for the participants'.[3] It is usually open-ended, both potentially and in practice, such that new investors are able to add funds at any time, acquiring units and enlarging the pool.[4]

The essential principle behind the unit trust is the entrusting of a property portfolio to a trustee and the sale, to participants (unitholders), of units of interests in this portfolio.[5] The trustee of the unit trust must be a corporation[6] and is usually a well-known bank that legally holds trust assets on behalf of and for the benefit of unitholders. The unitholders are the beneficiaries (and the settlors[7]) of the trust and therefore have beneficial interests in the underlying investment.

The trustee forms a trust deed (which constitutes the unit trust) with a manager, which must also be a corporation.[8] The manager, as an investment expert, is able to identify new areas and asset classes that the trustee may not be aware of due to a lack of sufficient knowledge and expertise in the area.[9] For this reason, the manager takes on a different role from the trustee (which simply holds trust property and provides dividends and capital growth for the unitholder beneficiaries).[10] That is, the manager is responsible for the day-to-day running of the unit trust;

[2] The world's first trust investment fund was the Foreign and Colonial Government Trust in the UK in 1868; and investment funds have since developed rapidly.

[3] ibid s 237(1).

[4] See especially M Graziadei, U Mattei and L Smith (eds), *Commercial Trusts in European Private Law* (Cambridge, Cambridge University Press, 2005) 459; G Thomas and A Hudson, *The Law of Trusts*, 2nd edn (Oxford, Oxford University Press, 2010) part I 53 Unit Trusts.

[5] A unit trust in the UK is regulated in part XVII chapter III of FSMA 2000.

[6] FSMA 2000, s 243(5).

[7] cf KF Sin, *The Legal Nature of the Unit Trust* (Oxford, Oxford University Press, 1997) 55.

[8] FSMA 2000, s 243(5). Also, see FSMA 2000, ss 242(2) and 243(4): the manager and the trustee must be different persons who are independent of each other.

[9] M Wain and M Shenkin, 'Trustee Investment Powers and the Use of Asset Managers' (2009) 15(2) *Trusts & Trustees* 72, 76.

[10] *Smith v Anderson* (1880) 15 Ch D 247.

this includes selecting investments and administering the trust fund. The manager sets a value for units according to a formula and is obliged to buy back units when investors (the unitholders) wish to redeem them.[11]

A unit trust presents a complex and advanced form of the original trust adopted in a family context. First, trusteeship is split and delegated[12] in unit trusts between two legal persons bound by trust deed: a trustee in name, who holds the trust assets, and a manager, who selects and administers the investment fund, and makes decisions on the value of units. Kam Fan Sin argued in *The Legal Nature of the Unit Trust* that a unit trust separates the trust obligation into custody and the management of the trust corpus.[13] That is, the unit trust has two limbs. The primary one is that of the trust fund subject to the deed's provisions and all regulations, which is a trust for a collective purpose rather than a means of disposition. The secondary one arises from the moment of a triggering event for winding up the unit trust. It is a trust for sale or conversion into money for contribution to unitholders on a proportionate basis.[14] The simultaneous appointment of a custodian trustee and a trust manager was fully acknowledged by the Public Trustee Act 1906,[15] facilitating the specialisation of commercial trusts.[16] Furthermore, in the unit trust, the liabilities of the trustee and the manager are limited.[17] This contrasts with the liabilities of the traditional trustee, who bears the burden of personal duties and unlimited personal liability, yet is more likely to be relieved of liability for breaches of trust.[18]

Such complexity in the unit trust both derives from and furthers the challenges that specialised business and diversified commercial uses have brought to trusts. In order to address those challenges, rules and regulations developed and differentiated from traditional approaches are expected. For example, a question that ought to be answered regarding the unit trust is how to define the nature of the manager. Is the manager a co-legal owner of the trust property (the same as the trustee) or simply a delegate of the trustee?[19] Is the manager a fiduciary who is

[11] FSMA 2000, s 243(10).

[12] The general rule is that trustees must act personally, although with exceptions (see, eg, P Matthews and others, *Underhill and Hayton Law of Trusts and Trustees*, 20th edn (London, LexisNexis Butterworths, 2022) art 57), whereas it would be very rare to find a unit trust deed that does not give additional delegation powers to the trustee. A detailed discussion of the delegation of unit trusts is provided in Sin (n 7) 242–52. The manager's beneficial powers are also delegable, whilst its fiduciary powers are non-delegable in the absence of express authorisation. See especially *Re Callen* (1918) 18 SR (NSW) 219; *Re Triffitt's Settlement* [1958] Ch 852.

[13] Sin (n 7) 186–87.

[14] ibid 71–75.

[15] Public Trustee Act 1906.

[16] Sin (n 7) 188, fn 8: Generally, see Stephenson, 'Co-trustees or Several Trustees?' (1942) 16 *Temple ULQ* 249, 250–55; Maurice, 'The Office of Custodian Trustee' (1960) 24 *Conveyance and Property Lawyer* 196.

[17] See, eg, *Cox v Hickman* (1860) 8 HLC 268.

[18] PS Davies and G Virgo, *Equity & Trusts: Text, Cases, and Materials*, 3rd edn (Oxford, Oxford University Press, 2019) 749–52.

[19] This issue is addressed by the author in R Zhang, 'Changes and Challenges of the Role of a Trustee in a Commercial Context: Does This Separate Commercial Trusts from Trusts?' (2021) 42 *Business Law Review* 262, 267–68. A detailed discussion can also be found in Sin (n 7) 170–73.

liable in equity for breach of duty of care?[20] It is debatable that the tension between the demand for efficient decision-making, allowing for the effective management of the trust, and the power-sharing outcome arising from the contractual arrangement (a trust deed made between the trustee and the manager) creates a distorted incentive scheme.[21] After the Second World War, the exigency to diversify investments (the key to the success of unit trusts) spurred legislative change in several European countries.[22] Rudden conceptualises this new dimension of trust law by discerning between the legal regimes applicable to things considered as investments and that applicable to things considered as portions of the physical world.[23]

ii. Investment Trusts

The investment trust, despite its adoption of the name 'trust', is now considered to be a company, and more precisely, an investment trust company.[24] They operated initially as common law trusts for the aggregation of capital invested in non-land assets, for example, bonds and stocks. But when the first Companies Act was passed in the 1860s, doubts about the legality of their status led investment trusts to restructure to become public limited companies.[25] In contrast to a real trust, such as a unit trust, investors in the investment trust company are corporate shareholders and have no direct interest in the underlying investment fund. These investors cannot redeem their investment at will pursuant to the capital maintenance rule of the company.[26]

Similar to the unit trust, the investment trust company is also primarily used as a collective investment scheme that pools money of investors and spreads it across a diversified portfolio of shares and stocks. Professional investment managers, who act independently of the company directors, select and manage the portfolio. In many cases, it is possible to buy investment trusts and unit trusts with almost identical portfolios that are managed by the same people.[27] Both the unit

[20] A leading case is *Nocton v Lord Ashburton* [1914] AC 932, 957. It found that the client succeeded on the footing that there was a breach of a duty arising from a fiduciary relationship. Further support of the existence of a fiduciary duty of care can be found in *Woods v Martins Bank Ltd* [1959] 1 QB 55.

[21] M Graziadei, U Mattei and L Smith, 'Commercial Trusts in European Private Law: The Interest and Scope of the Enquiry' in M Graziadei, U Mattei and L Smith (eds), *Commercial Trusts in European Private Law* (Cambridge, Cambridge University Press, 2005) 40.

[22] For example, in France, Germany and Italy.

[23] See B Rudden, 'Things as Thing and Things as Wealth' (1944) 14 *OJLS* 81.

[24] Investment Trust (Approved Company) (Tax) Regulations 2011, SI 2011/2999.

[25] See C Swirski and others, 'Investment Trusts: Tax' (2016) *Practice Law* 2: investment trusts were defined as 'associations of more than 20 persons for the acquisition of gain', unless registered under the Companies Act 1862 and the Joint Stock Companies Act 1856. The test case of *Sykes v Beadon* (1879) 11 Ch D 170 deemed the investment trusts to be illegal, and they were therefore hastily restructured as investment trust companies to avoid being wound up. Although *Sykes v Beadon* was reversed by *Smith v Anderson* (1880) 15 Ch D 247, investment trusts continued to be established as companies from that point forward.

[26] See Companies Act 2006, pt 18; *Trevor v Whitworth* (1887) 12 App Cas 409.

[27] Graziadei, Mattei and Smith (n 4) 459.

trust and investment trust company allow investments to be diversified in different portfolios (ie investors can put their eggs in divergent baskets), allowing investors to reduce their investment risk. And they both enable small investors to invest on a larger scale by placing their money into a pool.[28]

B. Trusts Underpinning Commercial Loan Arrangements

In addition to investment uses, trusts in commerce can also be found to facilitate commercial loan arrangements. Due to its comparative contractual advantages, a trust is adopted to assure that loan lenders are protected from borrower's bankruptcy or insolvency. Typical examples of this form of trust are Quistclose and security trusts.

i. Quistclose Trusts

A Quistclose trust refers to the type of trust that commonly arises where a loan is made on terms ensuring that if money or other property cannot be used for the purpose for which it is advanced, it will be returned to the lender. In essence, its arrangement shows some of the features of a resulting trust.[29]

The term 'Quistclose trust' derives from the case *Barclays Bank Ltd v Quistclose Investments Ltd*.[30] Quistclose (an investment company) advanced £209,000 to Rolls Razor for the purpose of allowing the latter to pay a dividend that it had already declared. The sum was paid into a special account with Barclays Bank, with which Rolls Razor had an existing overdraft. Before using the money to pay the dividend intended, in which case Quistclose would have been an ordinary creditor, Rolls Razor went into liquidation and Barclays sought to count the money in the special account against Rolls Razor's overdraft. The House of Lords opposed this action. It held that Rolls Razor held the money for a specific purpose of paying the dividend and that, upon its failure to do so, the money was held in trust for Quistclose. Lord Wilberforce took the position that a primary trust existed in favour of the shareholders. Then, on the failure of the primary trust, a secondary trust arose in favour of the original lender, Quistclose.[31] That is, where

[28] R Zhang, 'Principal Forms of Commercial Trusts in the UK and the Rethinking of Traditional Approaches' (2022) 28(8) *Trusts & Trustees* 787, 791–92.

[29] See *Twinsectra Ltd v Yardley* [2002] UKHL 12, [2002] 2 AC 164 [92]. Referring to and endorsing Dr Chamber's model of resulting trusts, Lord Millett characterised the Quistclose trust as a resulting trust that 'responds to the absence of an intention on the part of the transferor to pass the entire beneficial interest, not to a positive intention to retain it. Insofar as the transfer does not exhaust the entire beneficial interest, the resulting trust is a default trust which fills the gap and leaves no room for any part to be in suspense'.

[30] *Barclays Bank Ltd v Quistclose Investments Ltd* [1970] AC 567 (HL).

[31] ibid 582. Lord Wilberforce stated: 'In the present case the intention to create a secondary trust for the benefit of the lender, to arise if the primary trust, to pay the divided, could not be carried out, is clear and I can find no reason why the law should not give effect to it'.

the stipulated purpose for which money is advanced fails to be undertaken, the lender of the money can recover their property through a secondary trust that arises from the failure of the primary purpose.

The leading authority now, however, claims that there will normally be only one trust throughout; the characterisation of the so-called 'primary trust' is a power, rather than a trust in the strict sense. In standard cases, the beneficiary interest remains with the lender during the lifetime of the so-called 'primary trust', with the lenders, accordingly, having the sole right to enforce that interest.[32] The effect of the Quistclose trust is not to provide security for the repayment of the loan[33] but to reserve, in the lenders, the beneficiary interests in the money or property until it is used for the designated purpose. In this way, the lenders are provided with proprietary security regardless of whether their borrowers are solvent.[34]

The money or property furnished for a specific purpose under a Quistclose trust must be separated from the borrower's other assets, thereby strengthening the inference that the borrower does not have the property on loan at their free disposal and that they are not simply contract debtors.[35] In *Quistclose* and *Carreras Rothmans v Freeman Matthews*,[36] for example, special bank accounts were set up to receive the money. In absence of such separation, no trust is created, simply a contract; a trust only emerges when it concerns a specific fund.[37] According to *R v Common Professional Examination Board, Ex Parte Mealing-McLeod*[38] there is no intention to create a trust when the money on loan has not been segregated, even if the contract of loan includes a provision stating: 'You must using the cash loan for any purpose specified overleaf … You will hold that loan, or an part of it, on trust for us until you have used it for that purpose'. In other words, despite any specific provisions in the loan contract, it is still advisable to look at how the money has been advanced. A resulting trust may only be necessary in cases where it is unclear whether a lender expressly intended to create a trust but it is clear that they did not plan for the borrower to have the free disposal of the money.[39]

Moreover, although a Quistclose trust arises as a result of a loan for a specified purpose, it does not necessarily occur merely because money is paid out for a particular purpose.[40] In addition, it does not occur merely because the lender

[32] See *Twinsectra Ltd v Yardley* [2002] UKHL 12, [2002] 2 AC 164, per Lord Millet.

[33] ibid [72].

[34] ibid [13] and [100].

[35] *Re Farepak Food and Gifts Ltd* [2006] EWHC 3272 (Ch), [2008] BCC 22.

[36] *Carreras Rothmans v Freeman Matthews* [1985] Ch 207, [1985] 1 All ER 155, [1984] 3 WLR 1016.

[37] Although there are cases that seem to advise that a separate account is not an absolute requirement for a Quistclose trust (or even that it is not necessary to segregate funds) at the very least the money must be earmarked for the particular purpose and no other. However, payment into a special dedicated account is the clearest way of evidencing this segregation. See especially *Re EVTR* [1987] BCLC 646; *Re Farepak Food and Gifts Ltd*; *Cooper v PRG Powerhouse Ltd* [2008] EWHC 498 (Ch); *Maundy v Brown* [2011] EWHC 377 (Ch).

[38] *R v Common Professional Examination Board, Ex Parte Mealing-McLeod* [2000] EWCA Civ 138.

[39] J McGhee and others (eds), *Snell's Equity*, 34th edn (London, Sweet & Maxwell, 2022) para 25-036.

[40] *Twinsectra Ltd v Yardley* [2002] UKHL 12, [2002] 2 AC 164 [73]. This was applied in *Shalson v Russo* [2005] Ch 281 [128]–[30].

has a particular purpose or motive prompting their advancement of money to the borrower. To determine whether a Quistclose trust arises, it is necessary to consider whether the parties intended to place the money at the borrower's disposal while requiring that it should not be applied for any purpose other than that stipulated.[41] Lord Millet provides the best explanation of scenarios where loans will be treated as giving rise to Quistclose trusts.[42] For example, if an arrangement can be interpreted as one in which the borrower, essentially, is spending the lender's money to achieve a purpose that the lender cannot achieve by spending their own money directly, a Quistclose trust arises.[43]

The specific rules of the Quistclose trust convey an example of how trust law has developed in a way that operates differently to that concerning private or familial arraignments, and that legal reform is necessary given the desire to use trusts in business dealings.

The Quistclose trust can be considered as a complex version of the traditional trust, in the sense that it essentially engages a trust combined with a loan, and that the trust only exists either before the property is used for the purpose specified in the loan or when the property is used beyond that purpose.[44] Should the borrower trustee spend the money on a purpose beyond the agreed loan purpose, a breach of the trust duty will occur. In addition, should the borrower become insolvent before spending the money for the stipulated purpose, the lender retains the equitable beneficial interest in the money under the trust, and so is safe from the borrower's insolvency.[45]

Due to the above features, Quistclose trusts are often involved in insolvency cases.[46] When the borrower trustee fulfils the terms of the trust (ie uses the trust property for the specific purpose of the loan) the Quistclose trust turns into a pure loan (with the borrower liable to pay back the lender the money at whatever interest rate has been agreed), because no money or property is now held on trust. In other words, the Quistclose trust will end once the designated purpose agreed between the lender and borrower is achieved, whereupon the relationship between these two parties will turn into a normal relationship between a creditor and debtor of the loan.

[41] ibid [73]–[76].

[42] ibid.

[43] ibid.

[44] Zhang (n 28) 796.

[45] L Tucker, N Le Poidevin and J Brightwell, *Lewin on Trusts*, 20th edn (London, Sweet & Maxwell, 2020) para 8-54.

[46] Cases seeking to invoke Quistclose trusts are typically insolvency cases or cases where it is unclear who the beneficial owner of the funds is post a poor investment or fraud. This is because if the borrower of the funds were to become insolvent before using the funds for the particular purpose, the funds cannot then be used to satisfy the borrower's creditors. Because the transferor retains property in the funds, the funds have to be returned to them if the exclusive purpose is frustrated or if the power is not valid. If the funds are applied in accordance with the terms of the trust, the Quistclose trust ends and the transferor becomes an unsecured creditor. Therefore, the Quistclose trust does not function as a security interest; instead, it protects the transferor from the misapplication of their funds.

In this way, Quistclose trusts also represent a departure from regular loans and add a layer of protection for lenders over that provided by regular loans. Regular loans are the default position when money is lent in a commercial context. Normally, if A lends money to B, B immediately becomes the legal owner of the money and A is simply an ordinary creditor who has no beneficial interests in the money. If B spends the money other than in the way that has been agreed to, B just commits a breach of contract, which does not result in the money returning to A.[47] In comparison, under a Quistclose trust, in cases where either the purpose fails or a court determines that a given application as not valid, the money is to be returned to A.

The Quistclose trust seems to be the best option for the lender: the lender is able to receive the value of the loan relying on the trust when the borrower becomes insolvent before using the money, or demand full payment based on the loan when the borrower has spent the money for the purpose agreed (and thus the trust terminates).[48] So a person who might be most interested in adopting the Quistclose trust is a creditor (lender) in response to imminent financial distress. The Quistclose trust protects creditors from bankruptcy or insolvency that cannot be achieved by taking security, either because their loan is not of a sufficient size or because the borrower simply has no property left to levy.[49] Occasionally, however, financial distress trusts may also arise from the insistence of the debtor themselves.[50]

ii. Security Trusts

Another example of a trust used to buttress commercial loan arrangements is the security trust. It is created to hold security over debtors' assets for the benefit of their lenders who are the beneficiaries of the trust. The trustee of security trust is under a range of responsibilities to ensure the fulfilment of payments.[51] Security trusts are primarily used to hold corporate assets for debenture holders, possess real estate for syndicated mortgage lenders, or involve project finance with a multi-layered debt structure.[52] The advantages of security trusts are seen where there is a large group or diverse groups of lenders or when the trust beneficiaries are ever-changing, simply because amendments of security documents are

[47] JE Penner, *The Law of Trusts*, 12th edn (Oxford, Oxford University Press, 2022) 272.

[48] ibid 250.

[49] S Wilson, *Todd & Wilson's Textbook on Trusts & Equity*, 12th edn (Oxford, Oxford University Press, 2015) 453.

[50] See *Re Kayford Ltd* [1975] 1 All ER 604: debtors do not seeking the creation of a trust to protect themselves, but instead to protect their creditors against the consequences of them losing their property upon bankruptcy or insolvency, ie to protect specific creditors against the general consequences that arise upon insolvency. See also *Re Chelsea Cloisters Ltd* (1980) 41 P & CR 98; *Re Multi Guarantee Co Ltd* [1987] BCLC 257 (failed attempt).

[51] In cases of syndicated loans, one of the lenders is often selected to act as the trustee.

[52] See especially DJ Hayton, SCJJ Kortmann and HLE Verhagen (eds), *Principles of European Trust Law* (The Hague, Kluwer Law International, 1999) 6; Thomas and Hudson (n 4) part I, 51 and 52.

not required when changes occur to the security trust (eg selling a loan). Security trusts recall and replace the old pattern of bank-intermediated financing, but is more advanced than conventional financing because the trust is bankruptcy remote. In other words, in a security trust, the investor is no longer a simple lender but the owner of a beneficial interest in a separate pool of trust assets, and should the debtor become insolvent, the trust would not be impinged upon.[53]

What makes a security trust notably different from a traditional family trust is that the beneficiaries under the security trust can regulate or agree upon the terms under which the security will be enforced; the trustee may then simply enforce the security or release assets following instructions from the (majority of the) beneficiaries.[54]

C. Trusts Protecting Assets in Insolvency

A trust is very often used as a shield to protect assets against the claims of people such as the settlor's or trustee's creditors in the event of insolvency or death. This function is largely reinforced by the foundational principle that trust assets are distinguished from the property of trustees, settlors or other persons.[55] Trust law requires that the trust property be earmarked appropriately (such as by being put into a separate account) to prevent the trustee from commingling the trust property with their own property. This makes the trust, as an investment vehicle, popular in family contexts and for commercial uses.

The third principal role that the trust plays in commercial contexts can be categorised as protecting assets in insolvency; that is, trusts are adopted to organise assets and affairs in advance, so as to safeguard these assets against potential losses resulting from a future calamity.[56] In the UK, various types of trusts may be adopted to protect assets in insolvency, including pension trusts, employee benefit trusts, and client and customer money trusts.

i. Pension Trusts

Trusts have also played a significant role in a pension context; this can be ascribed to the current spotlight on the need to make financial provision for retirement. Pension provision is one of the biggest socioeconomic projects of recent years and the attractiveness of a trust arrangement, in terms of its ability to preserve assets over a long retirement period, was crucially recognised by the Report of

[53] See Langbein (n 1) 172.

[54] See 'Security trusts in finance transactions: overview' available at https://uk.practicallaw.thomsonreuters.com/7-519-6017; 'Security trust deeds: overview' available at https://uk.practicallaw.thomsonreuters.com/6-521-4583.

[55] DJ Hayton (ed), *The International Trust*, 3rd edn (Bristol, Jordan Publishing, 2011) 345.

[56] See Wilson (n 49) 37. The trust that arises in insolvency cases might be both similar to and different from that which arises in instances of personal bankruptcy.

the Pension Law Review Committee[57] and the Pension Act 1995.[58] Section 252 of the Pensions Act 2004[59] requires an occupational pension scheme that has its main administration in the UK to be established under irrevocable trusts before the trustees or managers accept any funding payment.[60]

A pension trust, arising from a contract of employment, establishes a scheme by which deferred compensation can be paid out to beneficiaries in their retirement.[61] The employer, acting as the trust settlor, creates and makes consistent contributions to a separate trust, which protects the contributed assets from the claims of the employer's general creditors in the employer's insolvency.[62] These assets are available to pay members' pensions, regardless of whether the employer stays in business, because present and future employee-beneficiaries look to the trust, not to the bankrupt employer, for payment of their pensions.[63] Thus, the employees are guaranteed an income, although deferred until retirement, under the pension trust.[64]

In addition to employees (members of the pension scheme), their spouses and dependents are also usually express beneficiaries under the terms of the pension scheme, because they will be contingent beneficiaries if the scheme provides for benefits to be paid to them following the death of the members. They can be given directly enforceable rights in equity against the trustee.[65]

The trustee (usually a corporate trustee[66]) holds assets under the pension scheme and is responsible for managing and administering the scheme and its investments.[67] For example, in this age of deficits rather than surpluses, they have key powers to set the ongoing contribution rate from the employers,[68] veto changes proposed by the employers,[69] and to wind up the pension scheme,[70]

[57] *The Report of the Pension Law Review Committee* (Cm 2342).

[58] Pensions Act 1995.

[59] Pensions Act 2004.

[60] ibid s 252.

[61] The pension trust is a specialised and complex subject closely connected with pension schemes and pension law. There is detailed literature on pension trusts, including scholarly output and specialised practitioner work. Information and references can also be found on the websites of the Pensions Regulator (www.thepensionsregulator.gov.uk) and the Pension Protection Fund (www.ppf.co.uk). This book will only examine the fundamental rules of pension trusts from an overview perspective.

[62] See especially *Re Kayford Ltd* [1975] 1 All ER 604; *Heritable Reversionary Co Ltd v Millar* (1892) 19 R (HL) 43, [1892] AC 598.

[63] Langbein (n 1) 180.

[64] Zhang (n 28) 792–93.

[65] See D Pollard, *The Law of Pension Trusts* (Oxford, Oxford University Press, 2013) para 2.6, paras 8.9–20 and para 9.18.

[66] The trustees of pension trusts are usually corporate trustees, such as pension companies, trust companies or commercial banks. They are required to inform the pension authority if they notice anything wrong with the trust or parties involved.

[67] Pensions Act 1995, ss 34–35.

[68] Pensions Act 2004, pt 3.

[69] This depends on the amendment power in the trust instrument.

[70] This depends on the terms of the scheme, but the Pensions Regulator has a statutory power to wind up the scheme under the Pensions Act 1995, s 11.

which usually generates an immediate funding obligation on the employers.[71] The trustees must exercise their powers and discretions complying with their fiduciary duties and in the best interests of the scheme members.[72] While the trustees can delegate tasks to various specialists, such as fund managers, the responsibility for those tasks remains with the trustees.

The pension trust is the most recognisable commercial trust from the viewpoint of the traditional personal trust. It is the only type of commercial trust that has been assimilated into conventional trust law. For example, like a traditional family trust, it usually allows for a gratuitous transfer.

The pension trust has similarities with traditional trusts but also has patent differences. One of the key tenets of the Pension Act 1995 was its accommodation of the reality that beneficiaries under a pension scheme differ from those under a standard trust arrangement. In a traditional trust, the beneficiaries are granted trust interests with no pre-obligation to provide a service or contribute to the trust. By contrast, the employee-beneficiaries of a pension trust have paid for their interests by contributing to the trust and working for the employer.[73] Another major deviation of pension trusts from private family trusts is that employers (settlors) in pension trusts are entitled to more powers and discretion. It is common in pension trusts for the trust deed to include an express provision for the employer to have various critical powers, including the ability to appoint and remove the trustees.[74] There has also been disagreement over whether the trustee should consider the employer's interests when managing the pension trust. Some cases suggest a broader view, arguing that it would be legitimate for trustees to regard the employer's interests in the appropriate circumstance.[75] Nevertheless, the Pension Regulator seems to side with the narrow view that only the members' interests will be considered. Its guidance and public pronouncements indicate that trustees of defined benefit schemes with a deficit should treat themselves as creditors of the employers in the same way as banks.[76] Also, the pension trust's tax environment is separate from private family trusts. A pension trust has no adverse tax effect if its settlor retains some form of control or interest, while in many private trusts undesirable tax implications would be imposed if the settlor retains an interest in the trust.[77] Although fundamental trust principles govern pension trusts,

[71] Pollard (n 65) para 9.13.

[72] See, eg, *Cowan v Scargill* [1985] Ch 270.

[73] This is recognised in a series of cases, eg *Mettoy Pension Trustees Ltd v Evans* [1990] 1 WLR 1587; *Imperial Group Pension Trust Ltd v Imperial Tobacco Ltd* [1991] 1 WLR 589; *Stannard v Fisons Pension Trust Ltd* [1992] IRLR 27; *Wilson v Law Debenture Trust Corporation* [1995] 2 All ER 337; *Sieff v Fox* [2005] EWHC 1312 (Ch); *Betafence Ltd v Veys* [2006] EWHC 999 (Ch); *Smithson v Hamilton* [2007] EWHC 2900 (Ch). See also the Pensions Regulator (www.thepensionsregulator.gov.uk); the Pension Protection Fund (www.ppf.co.uk).

[74] Pensions Act 2004, s 241–43.

[75] See especially *Edge v Pensions Ombudsman* [1999] EWCA Civ 2013; *Stevens v Bell* [2002] PLR 247.

[76] See the Pensions Regulator (www.thepensionsregulator.gov.uk).

[77] Pollard (n 65) paras 2.31–33.

many provisions of the trust legislation are not applied,[78] such as the rule against perpetuities.[79] And it is uncertain whether existing case law for private trusts can always be taken as a realistic guide for pension trusts.[80]

ii. Employee Benefit Trusts

Another type of trust established by a company to benefit current or former employees is the employee benefit trust; this trust, in turn, assists the company to attract and retain high-quality employees. The employee benefit trust is created by a company through a trust deed in order to hold and transfer its shares to employees in certain events or via a share scheme.[81] Examples of the uses of employee benefit trust include cash-funded employee benefit trusts (where payment of a bonus is to be deferred until certain future events occur); share plan trusts (which hold a company's shares until they are transferred to employees); and medical benefit trusts (which are an alternative to conventional health insurance).

Under an employee benefit trust, the settlor company makes recommendations pertaining to the use of the trust property that are usually followed by the trustee. However, the trustee holds the trust property independent of the settlor company and under its own legal ownership, and it has considerable discretion regarding the distribution of the trust fund. The trust is maintained when the settlor company becomes liquidated or wound up or changes ownership, and any creditors of the company have no claim over the trust property. Former and current employees of the company and their subsidiaries, families or dependants are the beneficiaries of the trust. Benefits received by the beneficiaries come in different forms; these might be shares in the company, options to purchase shares at a discounted price, or income from the shares that is paid as dividends.[82]

The employee benefit trust is acknowledged as creating an internal share market wherein employees can acquire and sell shares; this prevents shareholder dilution as the trust provides an opportunity to acquire and sell existing shares instead of issuing new ones. Nevertheless, there are potential disadvantages to consider when creating an employee benefit trust; for instance, if the shares are acquired and designated (ie earmarked) for a particular purpose before they are distributed to the beneficiaries, this may be subject to pay-as-you-earn (PAYE) taxation. Additionally, should the shares increase in value, the trustee may be subject to a taxable gain.[83]

[78] ibid paras 2.17–34 and ch 3.

[79] Perpetuities and Accumulations Act 2009, s 2(4).

[80] Pollard (n 65) para 2.30.

[81] The company's board of directors must approve the trust in a formal minute and lay out reasons for its creation. Acquisition of shares by the employee benefit trust is usually funded by the company through a loan, outright contribution or a guarantee of a bank loan. Company funding must comply with rules on financial assistance regarding acquisition of its own or its parent company's shares.

[82] Zhang (n 28) 794.

[83] ibid.

iii. Client and Customer Money Trusts

The value of the trust in providing asset protection in solvency also promotes the formation of a client and customer money trust; this protects the client or customer's assets from their manager's insolvency by dividing the customer's assets from those belonging to the manager in their personal capacity.[84] In many areas, the client and customer trust is implied by law.

Client and customer money trusts appeared in the mid-Victorian English case law. The primary issue in those cases was whether the solicitor or broker held the funds in a fiduciary or quasi-trustee capacity so as to entitle the claimant to equitable proprietary relief.[85] The Financial Conduct Authority requires that, unless otherwise permitted, client money must be kept separate from a firm's own money, and a firm's creditors are not entitled to the client money should the firm become insolvent.[86] For example, a law firm should open a client account for client money held on trust that is separate from its office (or private) account, so that its clients' money will be shielded if the law firm becomes insolvent. Similarly, in insurance, when a customer pays a premium to a broker, that money is protected from the broker's potential insolvency in the period before the money is passed to the insurance provider.

A client and customer trust may also be set up when a company is experiencing financial difficulties and may be heading for insolvency. That company could potentially continue to trade as long as new money taken from customers is held on trust, so that it can be returned to the customers if the company becomes unable to complete their orders.

D. Trusts Relating to Shareholdings

Shares are a tremendously popular type of trust property and there have been many instances where attempts have been made to create trusts of shares.[87] A typical example, which will be briefly discussed here, is voting trusts.

A voting trust is an arrangement that combines the company shares of different (mainly minority) shareholders. In a voting trust, the abovementioned shareholders (being both the settlors and the beneficiaries of the trust) collectively transfer their voting rights to a trustee for a period of time. The trustee holding their voting rights is then able to vote on company matters on behalf of the beneficiary shareholders, who are treated as one unit. The trustee exercises the voting rights subject to the trust instrument and its fiduciary duty and transfers

[84] N Moloney, *EC Securities Regulation* (Oxford, Oxford University Press, 2008) 469–70.

[85] See especially *Re Hallett's Estate* (1880) 13 Ch D 696; *Thomson v Clydesdale Bank* [1893] AC 282.

[86] *Financial Conduct Authority Handbook* (*FCA Handbook*), CASS 5.5 and 7.13.

[87] Wilson (n 49) 36.

the voting rights back to the shareholders once the designated period comes to an end.[88]

A voting trust can be used by shareholders to achieve various objectives and benefits. First, unified vote can improve shareholders' capacity to protect and preserve their control in the company; this is especially true when the group is made up of minority shareholders whose position would be weaker and more precarious if they were to be taken individually.[89] By pulling their voting rights together, the shareholders create a vehicle that can enable them to pass or reject a decision made by the company through an ordinary or special resolution.[90] Granting voting rights to a trustee also allows shareholders to play a more passive role in the company, which they might prefer if they are involved in other business activities.[91]

II. A Brief Introduction to Commercial Trusts in Other Common Law Jurisdictions

Commercial trusts are not only a UK matter; global competition to attract investment and business on an international basis has incentivised other common law countries to develop and expand their use of trusts. Two key examples of such jurisdictions are Australia and the US.

The modern Australian commercial trust is comprised of two main types of trusts: public unit trusts and trading trusts. Regulated as a managed investment scheme,[92] a public unit trust is typically used to raise funds from the public, although the regulatory regime of managed investment schemes does allow for public unit trusts to include private arrangements if they satisfy the definitional criteria in the Corporations Act.[93] By contrast, a trading trust, which may be in the form of either a unit trust or a discretionary trust, is used exclusively for private arrangements and not for raising public funds. A trading trust may be a managed

[88] See especially HA Cushing, *Voting Trusts: A Chapter in Recent Corporate History* (Charleston, BiblioBazaar, 2018); JA Leavitt, *The Voting Trust: A Device for Corporate Control* (New York, Columbia University Press, 2020).

[89] Minority shareholders may obtain more protection from the voting trust than through shareholders agreement because they are not subject to the defences available under normal contract law.

[90] See Companies Act 2006, pt 13 ch 1.

[91] See JJ Woloszyn, 'A Practical Guide to Voting Trusts' (1975) 4(2) *University of Baltimore Law Review* 245.

[92] According to the Australian Securities & Investments Commission (ASIC), managed investment schemes are also known as 'managed funds', 'pooled investments' or 'collective investments'. Generally in a managed investment scheme: (1) people are brought together to contribute money to get an interest in the scheme ('interests' in a scheme are a type of 'financial product' and are regulated by the Corporations Act 2001); (2) money is pooled together with other investors (often many hundreds or thousands of investors) or used in a common enterprise; and (3) a 'responsible entity' operates the scheme. Investors do not have day-to-day control over the operation of the scheme (asic.gov.au/for-finance-professionals/managed-investment-scheme-operators/starting-a-managed-investments-scheme/what-is-a-managed-investment-scheme/).

[93] Corporations Act 2001 (Australia).

investment scheme.[94] Trading trusts are also in use in New Zealand, and the concept has been cited with approval by the Canadian authorities and in Canadian literature on the subject.[95] A similar concept, that of a statutory business trust, has also been adopted in Singapore.[96]

The American market is even more developed. In the US, a trust is best known as a device for planning an individual's personal estate, and it is increasingly used as a tool for facilitating commercial transitions. Examples of commercial transactions in which the use of trusts is prevalent, if not predominant, include mutual funds for pooling investment assets, pension funds and trusts to secure repayments of corporate debts.[97] Asset securitisation has become one of the most important commercial uses of a trust in the US. A large fraction of all mortgage, credit card, automobile and student loan debt is financed or more accurately, refinanced, through asset securitisation trusts.[98] Investment trusts exist in a variety of forms, such as general mutual funds, real estate investment trusts (REITs) and oil and gas royalty trusts. A mutual fund offers expertise, economies of scale and a level of diversification far superior to that obtainable by the typical investor constructing an individual portfolio. A REIT is a mutual fund that invests in real property, mortgages on real property or both. An oil and gas royalty trust is another asset-specific form of investment trust found in oil-producing states. The creation and success of these entities are derived in part from the tax advantages that they accrue. As Langbein explains:

> In a typical transaction, a corporation that has developed an oil field (or some other extractive asset) will transfer ownership to a trust, distributing beneficial interests in the trust to the corporation's shareholders. As owner of the royalty-bearing asset, the trust distributes directly to the beneficiaries of the trust the royalty income that the trust asset generates. The beneficiaries then escape corporate-level taxation.[99]

Not only are trust interests marketable but a number of larger royalty trusts are traded on the stock exchange.

III. Commercial Trusts: A Different Setting for a Different Context

From the different forms and uses of trusts discussed above, it can be seen that trusts and their associated obligations have been found to be exceedingly useful

[94] See N D'Angelo, *Commercial Trusts* (Chatswood, LexisNexis Butterworths, 2014) 70. The author focuses on the commercial trusts engaging in risk-taking entrepreneurial endeavours, such as nominee trusts, custodian trusts and bare trusts.

[95] ibid 31.

[96] See Business Trusts Act 2004 (Chapter 31A) (Singapore).

[97] D English, 'The Fiduciary Duties and Powers of a Trustee under the Uniform Trust Code' (2014) 20 *Trusts & Trustees* 52, 54.

[98] Langbein (n 1) 170–73.

[99] ibid 171.

in commercial contexts. Commercial uses appear to be providing a new paradigm for trust law in the twenty-first century as they become applied across different social and economic spheres, and it might even become more significant still.[100] The sophistication and complexity of the commercial uses of trusts suggests a law that keeps abreast of dynamism and innovation in this area.

Commercial trusts depart widely from the traditional view of trusts. 'Once economic life became more, complex, there were more demands on trustees' ability to manage trust assets. This might be difficult for trustees who did not possess either the ability or the time to look after affairs of their friends.'[101] For this reason, the role of a commercial trustee (especially those involved in business transactions) is normally played by a limited liability company – a 'corporate trustee' or 'trustee company'[102] – which has brought a differentiation in trustees' functions.[103] A corporate trustee is granted the fullest possible powers; this is crucial to the commercial use of trusts as it enables the effective management of the business.[104] The new awareness of the current role played by the trust outside the traditional context corresponds with the impressive growth of fiduciary law.[105] It has been assumed that the trustee bears no personal liability beyond the value of the trust property and has the right to exhaust the trust fund, if need be, in order to satisfy creditors' claims.[106] A creditor will not receive payment out of the assets of the commercial trust if the transaction was ultra vires the trust.[107]

The distinction between commercial and traditional trusts has been received by judicial interpretations in higher courts. For example, taken as a long-standing judicial acknowledgement, Lady Hale stated in *Stack v Dowden* that 'context is everything' in the law: 'the domestic context is very different from the commercial world'.[108] In the House of Lords case *Target Holdings v Redferns*,[109] Lord Browne-Wilkinson said:

> It is important, if the trust is not to be rendered commercially useless, to distinguish between the basic principles of trust law and those specialist rules developed in relation to traditional trusts which are applicable only to such trusts and the rationale of which has no application to trusts of quite a different kind.[110]

[100] Wilson (n 49) 469–71.

[101] Sin (n 7) 187.

[102] The corporate trustee can be one of two types: a corporate trustee for just one set of assets with one trust deed as one single business venture, or a trustee company that is responsible for several trusts. In general, the trustee company itself has few or no assets of its own, aside from its right to indemnity out of the trust assets.

[103] G Keeton, *Modern Developments in the Law of Trusts* (Belfast, Northern Ireland Legal Quarterly, 1971) 16.

[104] Hayton (n 55) 525.

[105] Zhang (n 28) 798–99.

[106] See *Octavo Investments Pty v Knight* [1979] HCA 61; *RWG Management Ltd v Commissioner for Corporate Affairs* [1985] VR 385 (however, the trustee may not have such a right, in which event the trustee will be personally liable up to the relevant limit without any right of reimbursement).

[107] *Re Johnson* (1880) 15 Ch D 548, 552.

[108] *Stack v Dowden* [2007] UKHL 17, [2007] 2 AC 432.

[109] *Target Holdings Ltd v Redferns* [1996] AC 421.

[110] ibid 435.

And in the Supreme Court case *AIB Group (UK) plc v Mark Redler & Co Solicitors*,[111] Lord Toulson emphasised that it is important, in making court decisions, to consider the element of the engagement of underlying contract in a trust (a difference of commercial trusts from traditional ones). That is, the fact that the trust is part of the machinery affecting the performance of a contract is relevant to the loss the bank suffered due to the breach of trust. This is because it would be artificial and unreal to analyse the trust in isolation from the obligations that were originally why it was brought into being.[112]

The procedures and requirements that derive from the particular familial uses of trust apply uniquely to that type of trust and should be abandoned or modified to suit a commercial trust. Although still of the essence of trust, and the fundamental principles of trust that make the trust an advantageous legal scheme remain, commercial trusts arise from a different context from traditional family trusts and form in various types for distinct uses. Therefore, a redeveloped trust law regime is required and specific rules should be established that coincide with different types of trusts and respond to the evolved role of the trust and the trust participants, including trustees, beneficiaries and trust creditors.

IV. Conclusion

This chapter offers a systematic understanding of in what forms, and to what extent, trusts have evolved in commercial uses, compared to traditional approaches, and answers the question as to whether trust law needs to be developed to meet the new use of trusts in a commercial context.

[111] *AIB Group (UK) plc v Mark Redler & Co Solicitors* [2014] UKSC 58.
[112] ibid 71.

3

A Comparative Study of Commercial Trusts in Civil Law Jurisdictions*

In contrast to the traditional common law use of trusts as a scheme of intergenerational wealth management, civil law jurisdictions instead introduced the trust as a legal device for commercial use. This chapter first analyses the essence of a trust as the theoretical basis for research on the legal transplant of trusts into civil jurisdictions and then examines the introduction of trusts into such jurisdictions, including a general introduction to the legal transplant of trusts into both mixed systems and pure civil law systems and a more detailed discussion on two specific cases: Scottish trust law and Chinese trust law. These jurisdictions are interesting for comparative studies of commercial trusts because their trust legislation can be considered to be a product of the development of international investment, which is the main incentive for the introduction of trusts in modern times.

I. The Essence of Trusts

To provide a good understanding of the legal transplant of trusts into civil law, the first question that needs to be answered is which aspects of trust law relating to property and obligations are essential to a trust. This book argues that the common law concept of dual ownership, which finds no place in civil law property systems, is not the essence of a trust, and it does not prevent the introduction of trusts in civil law or the worldwide development of trusts for commercial purposes. The essence of trusts lies in the split between the management and the enjoyment of trust properties, which actually gives life to the commercial uses of a trust.

The spirit of the common law trust is not in the separation of legal titles (a trustee's legal ownership of trust assets and a beneficiary's equitable title to those same assets), but is 'a split between management/administration and benefit/enjoyment'.[1]

* This chapter draws on previously published work in R Zhang, 'A Comparative Study of the Introduction of Trusts into Civil Law and its Ownership of Trust Property' (2015) 21 (8) *Trusts & Trustees* 902; and R Zhang, 'Trust Law of China and Its Uncertainties: Examination of the Rights and Obligations of Trust and Ownership of Trust Property' (2015) 10(1) *National Taiwan University Law Review* 45.

[1] T Honoré, 'Trusts: The Inessentials' in J Getzler (ed), *Rationalizing Property, Equity and Trusts: Essays in Honour of Edward Burn* (Oxford, Oxford University Press, 2003) 1, 11.

The essence of the trust lies in the imposition of an equitable obligation on a trustee that requires the trustee to act in good faith and in the best interests of the beneficiary. A beneficiary's rights mirror the obligations of the trustee owed to them in respect of the trust property. Because the beneficiary has no direct control over the trust property, the realisation of their rights depends on trustee performance. The focus of the trust is on property. There will be no equitable proprietary remedy available where the property at issue is unidentified or where that property has been damaged leaving no traceable substitute.[2] In a sense the whole point of the trust is to separate the benefit of trust property from the right to exercise the powers that go with having legal title.[3]

The idea of a separation between administration and enjoyment is not confined to common law systems. It has also been admitted by other legal systems. Indeed, 'there is a much greater acceptance of the idea in modern civil law that the owner of an asset may hold it for the benefit of others rather than for his own'.[4] Therefore, the argument, which is based on the misunderstanding of the essence of trusts, that a civil law trust or commercial trust is not a 'real' trust is a mistake.

In fact, not only is the common law concept of dual ownership not the essence of a trust but the definitions of ownership in common law and civil law are different, thus causing a misapprehension of the legal transplant. As Hohfeld put it, the language used to discuss the law of trusts in both the civil and common law system is so disparate as to be misleading.[5] Additionally, Maitland states that some of the basic terminology of trust law, such as ownership, almost carries unexpected meaning, which tends to deviate from its strict definition.[6] Clarification of the different terminologies of ownership is important in providing a theoretical basis for comparative studies or legal transplants because disparate meanings of ownership lead to differences in the rights and obligations of trust parties. The true meaning of the terminology should be interpreted based on a review of its context and function.

In civil law, ownership is both perpetual and exclusive. According to article 544 of the French Civil Code (1804),[7] which is considered the most well-known model for a civil law system this day, ownership includes a complete power of three types of rights over the thing: *usus* – the right to use the thing; *fructus* – the right to take its fruits; and *abusus* – the right to destroy or alienate it. All these rights

[2] *Westdeutsche Landesbank Girozentrale v Islington London Borough Council* [1996] AC 669. The only exception to this rule is the constructive trust imposing personal liability to account for dishonest assistance in a breach of trust.

[3] R Zhang, 'A Developed Understanding of the Beneficiary's Interest in Commercial Trusts through a Comparative Study of Chinese Law' (2020) 27(3) *Maastricht Journal of European and Comparative Law* 343, 347.

[4] P Matthews, 'The Compatibility of the Trust with the Civil Law Notion of Property' in L Smith (ed), *The Worlds of the Trust* (Cambridge, Cambridge University Press, 2013) 313, 338.

[5] WN Hohfeld, 'Fundamental Legal Conceptions as Applied in Judicial Reasoning' (1917) 26 *Yale Law Journal* 710, 718.

[6] FW Maitland, *Equity: A Course of Lectures*, 2nd edn (Cambridge, Cambridge University Press, 1936) 23.

[7] Code Napoléon (1804) (France).

should belong to a single person or group of persons in relation to any particular thing. Ownership in Chinese law, following the same tradition as French theory, comprises four kinds of rights: rights of possession, use, beneficial enjoyment, and disposal of property. Article 240 of the Civil Code of the People's Republic of China[8] (Civil Code of China) stipulates that '[t]he owner of a realty or chattel is entitled to possess, utilise, seek profits from and dispose of the realty or chattel in accordance with law'.[9] As opposed to the civil law model of ownership, however, '[t]he old common law never thought in terms of absolute ownership',[10] and people do not own things (a physical approach), they own rights in things (a metaphysical approach). Ownership tends to be a practical assembly of uses and entitlements over the property under common law.

From a purely theoretical perspective, identical characteristics of ownership are not required in legal transplant. The language, ie the concept of dual ownership or equitable remedies, does not matter. It is generally accepted that as long as its effects are relatively similar in practice to those of the common law trust, a civil law jurisdiction's designation of a particular institution as a trust does not necessarily mean that this institution is identical or similar to the common law trust.[11] For instance, 'the duties ascribed to trustees in Anglo-American and civilian systems are in fact remarkably similar … [Thus], there is no need to postulate a special remedy confined to breaches of "equitable duties"'.[12] The concept of separating funds is not only seen in common law; it has also been found in civil law systems, for example, the *peculium* granted under the law of the Roman Empire, the *Sondervermögen* of German law, and the *patrimoine d'affectation* of French law.[13]

The notion of special patrimony has been widely used to accommodate common law dual ownership in civil law property systems. It was applied to the trust by the French comparatist Pierre Lepaulle in his *Traité Théorique et Practique des Trusts* in 1932, who stated that although patrimony was unknown to the common law, the trust could nonetheless be explained as a special patrimony, which he called a *patrimoine d'affectation*.[14] Besides France, Lepaulle's concept of special patrimony has also been interpreted into different versions and used to describe the trust in other civil law jurisdictions – for example, patrimony by appropriation in Quebec law and multiple patrimonies in Scots law.

[8] Civil Code of the People's Republic of China (Order No 45 of the President of the People's Republic of China). It was adopted at the Third Session of the Thirteenth National People's Congress on 28 May 2020, and came into force on 1 January 2021).

[9] ibid art 240.

[10] D Waters, L Smith and M Gillen, *Waters' Law of Trusts in Canada*, 5th edn (Toronto, Carswell, 2021) 10.

[11] G Fortin, 'How the Province of Quebec Absorbs the Concept of the Trust' (1999) 18 *Estates, Trusts & Pensions Journal* 285, 286.

[12] Honoré (n 1) 17.

[13] T Honoré, 'Obstacles to the Reception of Trust Law? The Example of South Africa and Scotland' in AM Rabello (ed), *Aequitas and Equity: Equity in Civil Law and Mixed Jurisdictions* (Jerusalem, The Hebrew University of Jerusalem, 1997) 793, 812.

[14] GL Gretton, 'Trusts Without Equity' (2000) 49 *ICLQ* 599, 610, fn 61.

The Scottish notion of special patrimony indicates that a trustee may have segregated patrimonies of assets and liabilities: the trustee's own general or private patrimony and a special patrimony dedicated to a special purpose of trust at the same time. Likewise, one patrimony may belong to more than one person: these are called joint trustees. The private patrimony is the collection of the trustee's personal assets, legal rights and liabilities. All the property there is prima facie vulnerable to the claims of the trustee's personal creditors upon the insolvency of the trustee. A trust patrimony, in contrast, contains the trust property held by the trustee or joint trustees as a whole and any obligations the trustee or joint trustees incurred in the administration of the trust. Although owned by the same person, the civil law tradition acknowledges that the assets and liabilities of a special patrimony, which is viewed as the trust, are separated from a general/private patrimony. 'The two patrimonies are distinct in law, and should also be kept distinct in practice, by proper labelling and accounting.'[15]

The special patrimony theory has particular importance in relation to the rights of creditors and the rights of heirs. 'When civil lawyers are trying to understand why it is that the beneficiaries can make claims against third parties for the return of trust assets, or that personal creditors of the trustee cannot seize trust assets in satisfaction of their claims, they often see an analogy with the patrimony idea.'[16] In other words, the special patrimony design explains why the trust property is immune from the claims of the trustee's personal creditors. That is because a trustee, who is the holder and manager of the trust property, has two separated patrimonies – the trustee's private patrimony and the trust patrimony – and each patrimony has its own creditors. As explained by Reid:

> A private creditor must claim from the private patrimony and a trust creditor from the trust patrimony. If that patrimony is empty, he must go without, for the other patrimony is not available.[17]

Trust beneficiaries' rights are against trustees concerning the special or trust patrimony, whereas private creditor's rights are enforceable against the trustee's personal capacity. This is why the beneficiary's right appears to prevail over the claims of the trustee's personal creditors. It is not because the beneficiaries were the real owners of the trust property, but simply because these two claims fall into different patrimonies and the trustee's personal creditors cannot claim against the trust patrimony.[18]

The dual patrimony theory also helps to explain why value received by the trustee automatically becomes part of the trust fund if the trust property is transferred in breach of the trust. This is because 'when the trust property is transferred,

[15] KGC Reid, 'Patrimony Not Equity: The Trust in Scotland' (2000) 8 *European Review of Private Law* 427, 432.

[16] Matthews (n 4) 324.

[17] Reid (n 15) 432.

[18] R Zhang, *A Better Understanding of Common Law Ownership of Trust Property and its Introduction in China Through Comparative Studies* (Guangzhou, World Publishing Corporation, 2019) 45.

the trustee is deemed to receive any proceeds into his trust – as opposed to private patrimony. This is also the case in respect of any profits that a trustee makes in breach of the principle that he must not act as *auctor in rem suam*.'[19] For the same reason, any sales or exchanges of the trust property are allocated to the trust patrimony, without affecting the trustee's personal assets, and vice versa. This underpins the reason why a trust can continue when all trustees are dead or become insolvent. On the grounds of the separate trust fund, the bankruptcy of a trustee's private patrimony cannot cause the end of the trust.

Therefore, without adopting the common law concept of dual ownership, the special patrimony theory can provide a convincing explanation of the nature of the trust and a theoretical basis for the rules of trust law. It shows that, from a theoretical perspective, it is possible for civil law countries to introduce the trust into their legal systems by adopting a legal instrument playing the same role as dual ownership, in spite of differences in concepts.

II. A General Comparative Study of the Introduction of Trusts in Civil Law Jurisdictions

Introducing trusts into civil law is not only possible in theory but also in practice. Dating back to the seventeenth century, the oldest mixed jurisdiction that adopted the term 'trust' was Scotland.[20] In the nineteenth century, trusts gradually appeared in other mixed jurisdictions, such as South Africa, Quebec and Sri Lanka. Louisiana followed the introduction of trusts in the 1920s and 1930s.[21] At that time, the trust was also incorporated in several civil law countries, starting with Latin American countries; for instance, Columbia (1923), Panama (1925), Chile (1925), Mexico (1926), Bolivia (1928), Peru (1931), Costa Rica (1936), Venezuela (1940), Nicaragua (1940), Guatemala (1946), Ecuador (1948) and Honduras (1950).[22] In Asia, modern trusts were also introduced for commercial and investment purposes. The trust was first transplanted into Japan in 1922, in South Korea in 1961, and much later, in mainland China in 2001.[23] Trusts no

[19] *Discussion Paper on the Nature and the Constitution of Trusts* (Scot Law Com DP No 133, 2006), para 2.19.

[20] GL Gretton, 'Trusts' in KGC Reid and R Zimmermann (eds), *A History of Private Law in Scotland* (Oxford, Oxford University Press, 2000) 480, 482. It is noted that the term 'trust' first appears in the seventeenth century but this does not mean that trusts first appeared in the seventeenth century. They might have existed earlier, without the name.

[21] KGC Reid, 'Conceptualising the Chinese Trust: Some Thoughts from Europe' in L Chen and CH van Rhee (eds), *Towards a Chinese Civil Code: Historical and Comparative Perspectives* (Leiden, Martinus Nijhoff Publishers, 2012) 209, 216.

[22] ibid 210, fn 4: For details, see R Batiza, 'The Evolution of the Fideicomiso (Trust) Concept under Mexican Law' (1957) 11 *Miami Law Quarterly* 478, 479. See also N Malumian, *Trusts in Latin America* (Oxford, Oxford University Press, 2009).

[23] L Ho, 'The Reception of Trust in Asia: Emerging Asian Principles of Trust?' (2004) *Singapore Journal of Legal Studies* 287, 287.

longer exist only in common law countries.[24] Regional and international bodies, such as the United Nations[25] and the Hague Conference on Private International Law (HCCH),[26] have made efforts to facilitate the introduction of trusts into civil law, and respond to the evolution of trusts for commercial uses.[27]

A. Introduction of Trusts in Pure Civil Law Jurisdictions

This section takes continental European countries and Latin American countries as examples to analyse how the trust has been incorporated into pure civil law jurisdictions for commercial purposes.

Civil law jurisdictions in continental Europe have begun to remove impediments and promote commercial trusts over the past century. Frequent contact between their banking and financial communities and the Anglophone world has rendered the use of a trust to segregate assets familiar to money managers throughout Europe.[28] That said, the design of a trust is suitable in European civil law countries, and the trusts that best draw the interest of European citizens are those that occur in the context of business relations.

The presumed need to diversify investments spurred legislative change in several European countries. Liechtenstein became the first jurisdiction in continental Europe to invite the concept of the trust. As Meier and Schmidt explain,

> [t]he motivation to introduce the trust into Liechtenstein law was, on the one hand, to make available as many legally operative forms as possible for the investment, administration and commercial utilisation of assets, and on the other hand, to deal explicitly and specifically with the fiduciary transactions already in existence in civil law.[29]

In 1926, articles 897–932 of the Law of Persons and Associations first provided the term '*Treuhanderschaft*', which was modelled precisely upon the common

[24] P Panico, *International Trust Laws*, 2nd edn (Oxford, Oxford University Press, 2017) 1.

[25] See Unidroit – International Institute for the Unification of Private Law, UPL 1957, Paper XL, Trust – Document 1, 'Report on Possible Uses of Certain Principles of the Trust in Civil Law Countries'; Unidroit – International Institute for the Unification of Private Law, UPL 1958, Paper XL, Trust – Document 2, 'Memorandum Concerning the Introduction of Some Principles of Trust into the "Civil Law Legislations"'.

[26] In 1984, the delegates of some 26 member countries of the Hague Conference met in their fifteenth session and discussed the fashioning of a Convention to recognise the trust. As a product of that conference, the Hague Convention on the Law Applicable to Trusts and on their Recognition (concluded 1 July 1985, entered into force 1 January 1992) was published.

[27] R Zhang, 'A Comparative Study of the Introduction of Trusts into Civil Law and its Ownership of Trust Property' (2015) 21(8) *Trusts & Trustees* 902, 908.

[28] See M Graziadei, U Mattei and L Smith, 'Commercial Trusts in European Private Law: The Interest and Scope of the Enquiry' in M Graziadei, U Mattei and L Smith (eds), *Commercial Trusts in European Private Law* (Cambridge, Cambridge University Press, 2005) 3, 25, fn 63: H Coing, *Treuhand kraft privaten Rechtsgeschäfts* (Munich, Beck, 1973) 62: early experiments with the idea of replicating the mode originated from the necessity to set up a vehicle to hold German investments on the New York Stock Exchange in the late nineteenth century.

[29] G Meier and O Schmidt, 'Liechtenstein' in A Kaplan (ed), *Trusts in Prime Jurisdictions*, 3rd edn (London, Globe Law and Business, 2010) 275, 275.

law trust. It defined the nature of trust relationship as 'the transfer of assets from the settlor to the trustee on the strength of a trust agreement, so that the trustee may hold, manage and apply these assets in his own name, in accordance with the agreement and in favour of the beneficiaries'.[30] And then in 1928, article 932(a) was added to the Law of Persons and Associations introducing the concept of *Treuunternehmen*, which is strictly translated as a 'trust enterprise' – a form of incorporation that was modelled upon the Massachusetts business trust.[31]

In order to make the concept of trust compatible with the civil law environment, the Law of Persons and Associations avoided any reference to legal and equitable interests. It did not explain the nature of a trustee's ownership but excluded the right of enjoyment from the trustee's ownership. Article 897 stipulated that the trustee is a person, firm or corporate entity to whom or to which assets of any kind have been transferred with the obligation to administer or use that trust property that is vested in the trustee's own name as independent owner but for the benefit of another.[32] The law also regulated the assignments of rights and obligations between the trustee, settlor and beneficiary. It said that '[t]he trustee is responsible to the settlor or, failing the settlor, to the beneficiaries to the full extent of his assets for any loss he causes as a result of a breach of trust'.[33] The trustee, as owner of the trust fund, is empowered to take any action in regard to it, as far as third parties are concerned. Internally, however, the trustee must observe the provisions of the deed of settlement and the general law. The trustee must take appropriate measures to safeguard and manage the trust fund and insure the assets against foreseeable risks, with the care expected of a prudent businessman.[34]

The Liechtenstein's model of *Treuunternehmen* was also taken up in other jurisdictions. Germany, for example, in 1957 adopted the *Gesetz uber die Kapitalanlagesellschaften*,[35] which introduced a similar legal form as well as a *Treuhand*-based solution, while France passed the first legislation on *fonds commun de placement*[36] in the same year. Spain followed suit in 1964, and Italy put *fondi comuni di investimento* on its statute book in 1977.[37]

The success of commercial trusts was not limited solely to civil law jurisdictions in Europe. Latin American countries also implemented a legislative movement in 1921 to introduce the trust, which was promoted by the US as lying in their trading and financial interests. A significant number of Central and South American countries have adopted the *fideicomiso*, the most familiar

[30] The Law of Persons and Associations (Liechtenstein), art 897.

[31] DWM Waters, 'The Institution of the Trust in Civil and Common Law' (1995) 252 *Recueil de Cours* 113, 379.

[32] The Law of Persons and Associations (Liechtenstein), art 897.

[33] ibid.

[34] D Loretz, 'Liechtenstein Trusts and Foundations: Creation and Operation' in A Kaplan (ed), *Trusts in Prime Jurisdictions*, 4th edn (Surrey, Globe Law and Business, 2016) 287, 292.

[35] Germany Federal Law Gazette (BGBl) 1957 I, 378.

[36] Décret 57-1342 of 28 December 1957 (France).

[37] Graziadei, Mattei and Smith (n 28) 25.

investment fund, by introducing the trust.[38] The *fideicomiso* in Latin America is seen almost exclusively as a trusteeship on the part of a bank or financial institution which is holding funds as private investment. It grants loans at interest, holds land as security and manages mortgage repayment, or manages developed real estate, though in this last instance seldom holding title to the real estate.[39]

The concept of *fideicomiso* was first adopted by Colombia in 1923, followed by Panama, which swiftly enacted a law on the *fideicomiso* in 1925. In Mexico and Venezuela, *fideicomisos* can be created for familial, charitable and business purposes; whereas, only banks can act as trustees, and a trustee cannot be a beneficiary.[40] That is, the trust is primarily used as a scheme of financial investment in theses jurisdictions, as well as in Bolivian and Guatemalan. Despite this, natural persons are accepted as trustees in some Latin American countries such as Panama, Costa Rica, El Salvador and Venezuela.[41]

In those Latin American jurisdictions, the trustee is the owner of the trust property and 'the creditors of the trustee shall succeed only if they are creditors in the administration of the trust'.[42] For the beneficiaries, they have the right to follow the trust property when the trustee improperly transfers the property and when required they have the right to trace the property in the hands of a third party, unless the third party was a bona fide purchaser for consideration without notice. The trustee's and creditors' positions are widely accepted, but the status of the beneficiary in pursuing *in rem* actions is less clear. For example, in Panama and Puerto Rico, doubts arise as to whether a beneficiary can bring an *in rem* action against a transferee on the trustee's behalf. Evidence of the settlor's right to intervene in the administration of the *fideicomiso* is not infrequently found in Latin American countries.[43]

B. Introduction of Trusts in Mixed Jurisdictions

Not only has the trust been accommodated in pure civil law jurisdictions, but also in a number of mixed jurisdictions. For instance, the legal system of Louisiana in the US and South Africa, which will be introduced as the two examples in this section.

Louisiana's experience of the introduction of trusts is one of the most interesting cases for comparative studies. This State was governed by a civil code that was closely connected to the Napoleonic code. It is a mixed jurisdiction, with private

[38] M Lupoi, *Trusts: A Comparative Study* (Cambridge, Cambridge University Press, 2000) 269.
[39] Waters (n 31) 382.
[40] See especially Lupoi (n 38) 269; Waters (n 31) 382.
[41] Zhang (n 27) 910.
[42] Waters (n 31) 383.
[43] ibid.

law drawn from civil law conventions and public law derived from the common law tradition.[44]

Louisiana codified a special law covering all aspects of trusts in the Trust Code of 1964, which remains in force.[45] The 1964 Code solved numerous fundamental problems. It granted the title to the trust property to the trustee, in consideration of the tax difficulties that would result if Louisiana adopted a different rule from the system in the rest of the US (where the trustee takes legal title). As stated in section 1781, '[a] trustee is a person to whom title to the trust property is transferred to be administered by him as a fiduciary'.[46] In order to localise this anomaly in civil law terms, the Code carefully defines a trust as a 'relationship resulting from the transfer of title to property to a person to be administered by him as a fiduciary for the benefit of another'.[47]

With regards to the question of the nature of the beneficiary's right, ie whether it is a real right or personal right, Louisiana chose to leave open the conceptual side of how the beneficiary might enforce his right, and instead delineate the remedies available to the beneficiary. As Waters explains,

> Part VIII of the Trust Code retains the personal right of action against the trustee which had been a part of the 1938 Law, and otherwise follows the American Law Institute *Restatement (Second) of Trusts* in permitting the beneficiary to enforce a right of the trust estate against a trustee who acts improperly with trust property and any third party who receives with knowledge of the breach or gratuitously.[48]

The 1964 Trust Code follows the conceptual structure of the common law trust as it is set out in the American Restatement,[49] and concerns itself with translating that Code into a doctrinal expression that is considered compatible with Louisiana's civil law.

In contrast to Louisiana, which is a civil law jurisdiction in a common law country, the South African legal system is characterised by its mixed nature

[44] M McAuley, 'Truth and Reconciliation: Notions of Property in Louisiana's Civil and Trust Codes' in L Smith (ed), *Re-imagining the Trust: Trusts in Civil Law* (Cambridge, Cambridge University Press, 2012) 119, 119.

[45] Since 1882, Louisiana has recognised the trust for particular purposes by statute; and in 1938 it, for the first time, introduced a generalised statute permitting the trust for any purpose. The 1938 Act defined the trust in largely the same terms as the First Restatement. It stated that the trust 'refers to an express private trust, and means a fiduciary relationship with respect to property, subjecting the person by whom the property is held, to deal with the property for the benefit of another person, which arises as a result of a manifestation of an intention to create it'. See Louisiana Trust Estates Act (US), Act 81 of 1938; La RS 1950, Title 9, as amended, 9:1792(16). Nevertheless the 1938 Act created both practical and conceptual problems and it did not integrate the trust into the civil law of Louisiana. As a result, it was ultimately replaced by the 1964 Code.

[46] Louisiana Trust Code (US), Act 338 of 1964, La RS 9:1721-2252 (Supp 1964), s 1781.

[47] ibid s 1731.

[48] Waters (n 31) 373–74.

[49] In addition to the Restatement First and Restatement Second, the Restatement Third indicates the current understanding of the trust device in the Anglo-American world, although it is not a direct source for the Trust Code.

occasioned by the coalescence of Roman-Dutch law with English law. That makes it of great interest for comparative studies.

In South Africa, the trust is used intensively for investment purposes and plays an active estate-planning role outside pure common law jurisdictions.[50] The concept of a trust as seen in English law was introduced deliberately during the British conquest of the Dutch settlers.[51] However, the common law notion of dual ownership is foreign to South African law's adherence in a typically civil law tradition to single or unitary ownership in the form of a dominium,[52] and as a result, very little of the rules of English trust law have been imported into South Africa. Nevertheless, it cannot be denied that English law remains an important source of comparative jurisprudence for the development of South African trust law, especially when courts and scholars in South African address novel trust problems. The English law was set up for business as part of African law.[53]

The most recent legislation on trust in South Africa is the Trust Property Control Act 57 of 1988.[54] The Act recognises two forms of the so-called trust: first, an arrangement where the trustee is vested with the ownership of trust property and, secondly, where the ownership of trust property vests in the trust beneficiaries with the trustee as mere administrator.[55] The former type of trust is generally known as an 'ownership trust', which is the most common type of trust; while the latter is known as the *bewind* trust in South African and corresponds with the institution of *bewind* in modern Dutch law and that of *bewindhebber* in Roman-Dutch law.[56]

In the ownership trust, the trustee is the owner of the trust property, but devoid of any beneficial interest in such ownership. The trustee's ownership is therefore considered as bare because the trust property forms no part of the assets of the trustee.[57] In *Land and Agricultural Bank of South Africa v Parker*,[58] the

[50] Waters (n 31) 356.

[51] See especially MM Corbett, 'Trust Law in the 90's: Challenges and Change' (1993) 56(2) *Journal of Contemporary Roman-Dutch Law* 262, 267; Waters (n 31) 353.

[52] See *Braun v Blann and Botha NNO* [1984] 2 All SA 197 (D), 859 E–F; F du Toit, 'Jurisprudential Milestones in the Development of Trust Law in South Africa's Mixed Legal System' in L Smith (ed), *The Worlds of the Trust* (Cambridge, Cambridge University Press, 2013) 257, 258.

[53] Zhang (n 18) 56–57.

[54] Trust Property Control Act (SA), No 57 of 1988.

[55] See ibid s 1: '[T]he arrangement through which the ownership of property of one person is by virtue of a trust instrument made over or bequeathed (a) to another person, the trustee, in whole or in part, to be administered or disposed of according to the provisions of the trust instrument for the benefit of the person or class of persons designated in the trust instrument or for the achievement of the object stated in the trust instrument, or (b) to the beneficiaries designated in the trust instrument, which property is placed under the control of another person, the trustee, to be administered or disposed of according to the provisions of the trust instrument for the benefit of the person or class of persons designated in the trust instrument or for the achievement of the object stated in the trust instrument.'

[56] du Toit (n 52) 269.

[57] ibid 271, fn 57: WD Geach and J Yeats, *Trusts: Law and Practice* (Wetton, Juta, 2007) 2. Section 12 of the Trust Property Control Act prescribes that trust property does not form part of the personal estate of a trustee except insofar as such trustee is entitled to such property as a beneficiary under the trust.

[58] *Land and Agricultural Bank of South Africa v Parker* 2005 (2) SA 77 (SCA), para 19.

court noted the essence of the trust in South African law: the functional separation between a trustee's ownership or control of trust property and the enjoyment deprived by the beneficiaries from the trustee's exercise of such ownership or control. It is described by Honoré as a doctrinal hybrid – a *jus tripertitum* of Roman-Dutch, English and indigenous South African rules, but in its end-product a *jus civiles*.[59]

The successful introduction of the trust in South Africa is depicted by Beinart:

> The recipe for absorption of a useful institution such as the trust into a Civilian system appears to be avoidance of excessive conceptualism and of too great an insistence on legal purity or rigidity or historical precedents, and calling on a judicious adaptation of conceptual categories to the demands of practice.[60]

III. A Specific Case Study of Commercial Trusts in Scotland

The basic statute regulating trusts in Scotland is the Trusts (Scotland) Act 1921,[61] which is now quite outdated in both style and substance.[62] Nowadays, the trust is used more for the purposes of tax and estate planning, to regulate a family's business interests, or for commercial purposes.[63] These changes are not reflected in the Trusts (Scotland) Act 1921. Therefore, a few regulations have been passed subsequently that amend the 1921 Act and provide further free-standing provisions. The main statutory provisions are the Trustee Investments Act 1961,[64] the Trusts (Scotland) Act 1961,[65] the Law Reform (Miscellaneous Provisions) (Scotland) Act 1966[66] and the Charities and Trustee Investment Act 2005.[67]

The introduction of the trust in Scots law is a very interesting case. English law, the place of origin of the trust, plays a significant role in the development of the Scottish trust, and some Scottish regulations are even derived from English common law.[68] Nevertheless, property law in Scotland is particularly civilian.[69]

[59] See E Cameron and others, *Honoré's South African Law of Trusts*, 6th edn (Cape Town, Juta and Company Pty Ltd, 2018) 21–30.

[60] B Beinart, 'Trusts in Roman and Roman-Dutch Law' (1980) 1(1) *Journal of Legal History* 6, 44.

[61] Trusts (Scotland) Act 1921.

[62] Much of the Act deals with old trusts that were used to hold landed estates or, through the marriage contract trust, to manage weaknesses in the law regarding the property of married women.

[63] *Discussion Paper on the Nature and the Constitution of Trusts* (Scot Law Com DP No 133, 2006), para 1.5.

[64] Trustee Investments Act 1961.

[65] Trusts (Scotland) Act 1961.

[66] Law Reform (Miscellaneous Provisions) (Scotland) Act 1966.

[67] Charities and Trustee Investment (Scotland) Act 2005.

[68] This is particularly the case since the end of the eighteenth century, as England and Scotland have shared the House of Lords as a common final appellate court since 1707.

[69] Scholars believe that the Scottish trust originated from the Roman *fideicommissum*. See WA Wilson and AGM Duncan, *Trusts, Trustees and Executors*, 2nd edn (Edinburgh, Green for the Scottish Universities Law Institute, 1995) 3.

Scots law has never known, and does not know today, the distinction between the legal and the equitable estate.[70] Therefore, as in other civil law jurisdictions, how to accommodate the common law notion of dual ownership in its own system where there is an absence of legal and equitable estates becomes the key question.

A. Different Theories of Ownership Developed in Scotland

In response to this question, different theories with respect to the ownership of trust property have been raised in Scotland.

One theory is the legal person theory, whereby the trust is considered as a legal person and itself the owner of the trust property.[71] However, this theory has been strongly rejected by the Scottish Commission. On 1 March 2005, the Scottish Law Commission hosted a seminar and discussed the concept of legal personality for trusts; namely, whether the trust should be recognised as an artificial legal entity with its own juristic personality and therefore become the owner of the trust property. The feasibility of recognising a legal personality for trusts was noted in the seminar; however, the participants[72] felt that the operational disadvantages of conferring legal personality on trusts far outweighed any presentational advantages.[73] Their concerns are mainly related to two aspects.

First, the legal person theory would cut Scotland off from future developments in trust law elsewhere because the concept of a legal device wherein a property is owned by one person on behalf of another was being developed at European[74] and international levels.[75] Second, this method would complicate issues. The value of a trust is its simplicity and, therefore, its adaptability for use in new economic and social environments. If the trust is a legal person,

> [it] would have to exercise its active legal capacity through agents, presumably the trustees. Apart from issues of *vires*, the agency rules which would govern the relationships between the trust, the trustees and third parties would not be simple. It was accepted that even if a trust had separate juristic personality, trustees would continue to owe fiduciary obligations to the beneficiaries as well as the trust: difficult conflicts of interest could be envisaged.[76]

[70] Waters (n 31) 349.

[71] L Smith, 'Trust and Patrimony' (2009) 28 *Estates, Trusts & Pensions Journal* 332, 354, fn 93: P Lepaulle, 'La notion de « trust » et ses applications dans les divers systèmes juridiques' in Institut International Pour l'Unification du Droit Privé, *Actes du Congrès international de droit privé tenu à Rome en juillet 1950*, vol 2 (Rome, L'unification du droit, 1951) 207. Lepaulle states: 'I do not deny that this is an easy way out: instead of struggling with delicate concepts and bold creations, it settles for taking an old idea from our familiar armoury' [translated by L Smith].

[72] Twenty-four participants consisting of a mix of both academics and practitioners.

[73] *Discussion Paper on the Nature and the Constitution of Trusts* (Scot Law Com DP No 133, 2006), paras 1.3–1.4.

[74] See for example the Hague Trust Convention and the work of the Coordinating Group on Trust Law.

[75] *Discussion Paper on the Nature and the Constitution of Trusts* (Scot Law Com DP No 133, 2006), para 2.43.

[76] ibid para 2.41.

Furthermore, not only is it unnecessary, but it is also wrong to characterise the trust as a legal person. Smith criticised the theory of legal person and stated that 'it would be a mistake for any legal system to conceptualize the trust as a legal person, since the result will only be to eliminate the trust as a fundamental legal institution'.[77] In order to be a fundamental institution, the trust cannot be another institution such as a sub-category of legal persons or contracts.[78] As a result, the legal person theory was also denied by Scots law because it requires statutory intervention and cannot explain the trust as it currently exists.[79]

Another theory that has been discussed often to explain the ownership of the trust property is the beneficiary's ownership. For example, in the late nineteenth century, Lord McLaren stated that both the trustee and beneficiary are simultaneously the owners of the property and coined the phrase 'personal right of property' to explain the beneficiary's right.[80] A few years later, Lord Watson said that 'the [beneficiary], to whom the whole beneficial interest belongs, is the true owner'.[81] This theory has also now been rejected.

Scots law rejected the theory of a beneficiary's ownership because it would result in uncertainty or a legal limbo of the ownership of trust property in some circumstances (eg when a trust was created for unborn person) because a beneficiary in a Scottish trust can be undetermined or non-existent. Moreover, if the beneficiary, but not the trustee, were the owner of the trust property, it would be hard to explain why the trustee can transfer good title to a third party.[82] It violates the principle of *nemo plus juris ad alium transferre potest quam ipse haberet* (no one can give what they do not have), which prevents the non-owner trustee from transferring title to the trust property. Although an agent can dispose assets on behalf of a principal, a trustee is different from an agent and their rights are distinct in nature. 'The trustee simply does not have the relationship with a *beneficiary* which agency would require.'[83]

B. Fiduciary Ownership in the Mixed Scottish Legal System

Negating the legal person theory and theory of a beneficiary's ownership, Scots law adopts the theory of fiduciary ownership. It recognises the absolute title of trust property in the trustee.

[77] Smith (n 72) 334.
[78] ibid 349.
[79] J Chalmers, 'Ownership of Trust Property in Scotland and Louisiana' in VV Palmer and EC Reid (eds), *Mixed Jurisdictions Compared: Private Law in Louisiana and Scotland* (Edinburgh, Edinburgh University Press, 2009) 132, 133, fn 5.
[80] *Hay's Trs v Hay* (1890) 17 R 961, 964.
[81] *Heritable Reversionary Co Ltd v Millar* (1892) 19 R (HL) 43, [1892] AC 598, 46–47.
[82] In order for a trust to function, a trustee is the person who should be granted exclusive powers of management over the trust assets. So, if the settlor or beneficiaries are considered the owners of the trust property, the right of management will be taken away from them and conferred on trustees.
[83] Chalmers (n 80) 143.

The notion of fiduciary ownership – an ownership that receives a specific alignment towards a purpose – provides the possibility of introducing the trust into civil law.

The purpose of the *fiducie*, which is set up by the settlor, imposes a restriction on the trustee's administration and discretion, demanding the trustee to act in the interests of the beneficiary. A third party in good faith should take unchallengeable title in any *fiducie* assets that they require through dealing with the fiduciary in the administration of the *fiducie*.[84] Therefore, fiduciary ownership is seen as only the presence of legal powers but not a subjective right of ownership.[85] This conveys a similarity with dual ownership of the common law. Nevertheless, it does not deny the potential presence of attributes of the traditional absolute ownership. The traditional attributes, 'namely *usus*, *fructus* and *abusus*, can be found within fiduciary ownership, since the trustee has in principle all the powers over the property which is held in *fiducie*'.[86]

Because of its similarity with dual ownership and its potential presence of absolute ownership, fiduciary ownership is a possible device to introduce the trust into civil law jurisdictions. The *fiducie* plays a similar role and achieves objectives akin to those of the trust.[87]

In Scots law, fiduciary ownership arises when the owner of a property is under a duty to use it for the benefit of another and not for themselves. This is evident from the classic statement of Scots trust made by Lord Normand in *Camille and Henry Dreyfus Foundation Incorporated v Commissioners of Inland Revenue*.[88] That is,

> [a] fund is held as their property in trust by persons who are directed to hold it, subject to purpose which operate as a qualification of their rights and constitute a burden on the property preferable to all claims by or through them, and subject also to a reversionary right remaining with the truster, his heirs and assignees, so far as the estate is not exhausted by the purpose.[89]

In the law of trusts, the fiduciary owner of the trust property is the trustee. The beneficiary is the person for whose benefit the trustee must administer the property under a fiduciary obligation. The trust itself is simply a legal device that creates rights and obligations among settlors, trustees and beneficiaries.[90]

The notion of fiduciary ownership addresses the idea that the trustee is the owner of trust property. This idea has been advised by Reid on the grounds of convenience.

[84] Waters (n 31) 394.

[85] Y Emerich, 'The Civil Law Trust: A Modality of Ownership or An Interlude in Ownership?' in L Smith (ed), *The Worlds of the Trust* (Cambridge, Cambridge University Press, 2013) 21, 24.

[86] ibid.

[87] Zhang (n 18) 65–66 and 68.

[88] *Camille and Henry Dreyfus Foundation Incorporated v Commissioners of Inland Revenue* [1956] AC 39.

[89] ibid 48.

[90] *Discussion Paper on the Nature and the Constitution of Trusts* (Scot Law Com DP No 133, 2006), para 2.1.

He believes that attributing the ownership to the trustee will remove the burden of proof from the trustee in showing a third party that the trustee has the power to manage the trust property even without ownership. Moreover, this method is relatively effective to avoid a limbo of ownership; for instance if there are no current beneficiaries or too many; when there is a dispute as to whether a person is a beneficiary; and when the settlor or beneficiary is dead or dissolved. Although with regards to the last example the trustee may also die, it is easier to appoint new trustees than new beneficiaries or settlors.[91]

Another idea that is reflected in the notion of fiduciary ownership is that the nature of the beneficiary's right is classified as a personal claim. In *Commissioner of Inland Revenue v Clarke's Trustee*,[92] Lord President Normand described the beneficiary's right as nothing more than a personal right to sue the trustees and to compel them to administer the property in accordance with the directions which the trust instrument contains. This opinion is nevertheless not agreed with by all Scottish authors because the beneficiary's right seems to lie somewhere in between. According to Gretton,

> The right of a trust beneficiary is, in our law, not a real right which in some ways is like a personal right, but a personal right which in some ways is like a real right … It is this quality that takes the trust wholly out of the law of obligations.[93]

The beneficiary's rights do not behave like ordinary personal rights.[94]

The reason why a beneficiary's personal claim is different from the unsecured rights of a trustee's personal creditors over which it appears to prevail, is not because the beneficiary's right is a real right, but because the trust property is not available to a trustee's ordinary personal creditors.[95] Looking back at the notion of multiple patrimonies in Scotland,[96] when a person becomes a trustee, that person, in fact, owns two separate patrimonies: the private patrimony as before and a new patrimony – a trust patrimony. A beneficiary is claiming against the trustee's special/trust patrimony. As noted, this type of claim is different from the trustee's private patrimony claim against their personal creditors. Therefore, 'the insolvency effect operates in all trusts regardless of whether the rights of the beneficiaries are "real" or not'.[97] Under Scots law, the relationship between the trustee and beneficiary is essentially a claim but not a real right.[98]

[91] Reid (n 21) 216.
[92] *Commissioner of Inland Revenue v Clarke's Trustee* [1939] SC 11 at 22, [1939] SLT 2.
[93] GL Gretton, 'Constructive Trusts' (1997) 1 *Edinburgh Law Review* 281, 287.
[94] GL Gretton, 'Trust and Patrimony' in H MacQueen (ed), *Scots Law into the 21st Century: Essays in Honour of W A Wilson* (Edinburgh, W Green/Sweet & Maxwell, 1996) 182, 184.
[95] *Discussion Paper on the Nature and the Constitution of Trusts* (Scot Law Com DP No 133, 2006), para 2.13.
[96] See section I above.
[97] Gretton (n 14) 606–07.
[98] KGC Reid, 'National Report for Scotland [G]' in DJ Hayton, SCJJ Kortmann and HLE Verhagen (eds), *Principles of European Trust Law* (The Hague, Kluwer Law International, 1999) 67, 70.

Instead of asking which category, *in personam* right or *in rem* right, the beneficiary's right falls into, the real question might be what kind of interest is granted to the beneficiary. The general view is that the beneficiary can sue for the recovery of trust property when the trustee misappropriated the property by transferring it to a third party who was not acting in in good faith (ie had knowledge of the breach of trust or received the property without paying any consideration).[99]

Under Scots law, there seems to be no difficulty in recognising the beneficiary's rights, either to take in succession to a previous chargee or to make proprietary claims against third parties who have received trust property wrongfully transferred by the trustee. Thanks to the notion of fiduciary ownership, Scots law has successfully introduced the trust into its mixed legal system. It rationalises the trustee's ownership in the notion of fiduciary ownership and justifies the interest of the beneficiary in terms of a burden or charge upon absolute ownership.[100]

IV. A Specific Case Study of Commercial Trusts in China

As one of the centres of world trade and one of the first socialist and civil law jurisdictions to introduce a domestic law of trusts, China's legislation and practice also have important research significance. This section examines how trusts are used and how they have evolved in China in the form of commercial trusts and analyses the Chinese legal regime of commercial trusts, highlighting the legal resources, regulatory authorities and special requirements of different types of trust institutions. These institutions include trust companies, investment funds and enterprise annuity funds as well as the use of trusts in insurance products.[101]

A. Evolution of Chinese Commercial Trusts

Seeing the advantages of trusts in investment, banking, financing and property management, China took the bold step of promulgating a domestic trust law, Trust Law of People's Republic of China,[102] in 2001.[103] That is, a Chinese trust is mainly in the form of an evolved commercial trust. Traditional trusts never found

[99] Zhang (n 18) 71–72.

[100] Waters (n 31) 351.

[101] This is not an exhaustive list of Chinese commercial trusts but only the key types of trusts that play a significant role in financial markets.

[102] Trust Law of the People's Republic of China (Order No 50 of the President of the People's Republic of China). It was adopted at the Twenty-first Session of the Ninth National People's Congress on 28 April 2001, and came into force on 1 October 2001.

[103] D Qi and L Yan, 'The Study of Modern Trust Function' (2005) 4 *Journal of Shaoyang University Social Science* 44, 44 [translated by author].

any kind of root or equivalent in dynastic China (pre-1911). Inheritance was predominantly regulated by customary law, and there was little room for testamentary disposition by individuals. Therefore, a traditional trust was not needed for property owners to entrust the management of their property to others.[104]

The commercial use of trusts in China went through an evolution from a macroeconomic tool to a private-sector vehicle for investment schemes, which took place in four main stages. First, starting from 1911, when dynastic rule ended and the Chinese Nationalist Party took over control of the country, the so-called trust business emerged and was operated by trust institutions. These trust institutions were divided into three main types. The first type was trust institutions set up inside banks in the form of a specialised trust department. For instance, in 1919, the Shanghai branch of Ju Xing Cheng Bank established the department of trust to manage its trust business. Second, and in addition to the trust institutions within banks, several governmental trust institutions were also enacted, such as the Central Trust Bureau and Shanghai Xing Ye Trust. Finally, a third type of trust institution, the trust company, was broadly adopted at that time, and still exists as a major form of trust used in China. In August 1921, the first trust company, Tong Shang Trust Company of China was established in Shanghai; and within the next month, 12 similar trust companies had sprung up in China.[105] This was the first stage of the evolution of Chinese trust, from 1911 to 1949.

The second stage was delayed until after the promulgation of the open-door policy. After the Communist takeover in 1949, trust companies came to a halt. Only in 1979, when China adopted an open-door policy for foreign trade and investment, did trust companies obtain a new lease of life.[106] The first trust and investment company of the People's Republic of China was the China International Trust and Investment Corporation. This was established with the approval of State Council in Beijing in 1979.[107] With the growth of private wealth in China, from 1979 to 1988, a number of provinces, cities and financial institutions set up their own trust companies, and the number of trust companies rose to more than 1000.[108] This period is considered to be the second stage of the evolution of the Chinese trust. In this stage, the primary business of the trust company was to act as agents for the government in raising funds or extending credit in order to circumvent the rigid central budget. In other words, the trust company, as a player in the Chinese economy, was designed to serve explicitly macroeconomic

[104] L Ho, 'Trust Laws in China: History, Ambiguity and Beneficiary's Rights' in L Smith (ed), *Re-imagining the Trust: Trusts in Civil Law* (Cambridge, Cambridge University Press, 2012) 183, 186–87.

[105] The 12 trust companies are Zhong Yi, Zhong Guo, Shang Ye, Tong Yi, Da Zhong Hua, Zhong Yang, Shanghai, Tong Shang, Shen Zhou, Zhong Wai, Hua Sheng and Shanghai Yun Shi.

[106] Y Huo, *Discussions of Trust Law* (Beijing, China University of Political Science and Law Press, 2003) 27–28 [translated by author].

[107] J Guan, *Trust Law and Practice in China* (Beijing, China Law Press, 2008) 25 [translated by author].

[108] J Tang and R Chao, *Financial Trust and Financial Market* (Tianjin, Tianjin Science and Technic Press, 1990) 29 [translated by author].

ends. This period also saw the introduction of a new form of commercial trust, the collective capital trust, only operable by trust companies.[109]

Nevertheless, due to the absence of a systematic law of trusts, the Chinese trust developed in an unusual way in the years following 1979. It operated an excessively broad scope of business, including some traditional banking activities, which were not real trust business.[110] To correct the inappropriate promotion of trust companies and to regulate trust business, the Chinese government implemented a series of 'rectifications' between 1988 and 1998 in which trust institutions were separated from banks and the number of trust companies was reduced to 239.[111] This period was the third stage of the evolution of the Chinese trust. In contrast to the macroeconomic goal of the previous stage, the trust was adopted as a means of establishing a modern system for the fiduciary management of assets as a result of the development of international trade and the growth of private wealth in China after its economic reforms. This period ended in 1998 when the Guangdong International Trust and Investment Corporation was acquired by the People's Bank of China[112] and forced into liquidation.

This event can be considered as marking the start of the fourth stage of the evolution of Chinese trusts. A further culling of companies with payment difficulties, insufficient assets or poor management reduced the number of trust and investment companies to 58.[113] Despite crackdowns on specific companies in this stage, with an overall growth in the number of trust companies alongside the booming Chinese economy, the role of trust companies as commercial institutions continued to grow in the Chinese economy. The rapid growth of private wealth in China at that time spurred demand for a greater variety of investment vehicles beyond merely banking deposits or private investments in the stock market or in real estate. In response to this demand, trust companies have reformed to become private-sector vehicles for investment schemes.

[109] L Ho, R Lee and J Jin, 'Trust Law in China: A Critical Evaluation of its Conceptual Foundation' in L Ho and R Lee (eds), *Trust Law in Asian Civil Law Jurisdictions: A Comparative Analysis* (Cambridge, Cambridge University Press, 2013) 80, 80.

[110] See R Zhang, 'Trust Law of China and Its Uncertainties: Examination of the Rights and Obligations of Trust and Ownership of Trust Property' (2015) 10:1 *National Taiwan University Law Review* 45, 49: '[T]rust and investment companies operated an excessively broad scope of business, including traditional banking activities such as the management of retail and corporate loans and deposits. More specifically, the trust companies engaged in trust loans, trust investments and trust deposits, activities which were effectively deposit-taking activities authorized by the lack of legal requirements for the segregation of investor and trustee funds. Whatever profits or losses accrued went to the trust and investment companies rather than to the customers.'

[111] D Su, 'Trusts and Taxes' (2006) 11 *Times Finance* 7, 7 [translated by author].

[112] The People's Bank of China was established on 1 December 1948 based on the consolidation of the Hua Bei Bank, the Bei Hai Bank and the Xi Bei Farmer Bank. In September 1983, the State Council decided that the People's Bank of China would function as a central bank. This was legally confirmed by Law of the People's Republic of China on The People's Bank of China. The official website of the People's Bank of China is www.pbc.gov.cn.

[113] Guan (n 108) 11–12 [translated by author].

The experience of those rectifications became one of the primary reasons for drafting the Trust Law of the People's Republic of China,[114] which attracted much attention both in China and overseas.[115]

B. Regulation of Chinese Commercial Trusts

China went down a tortuous road upon the introduction of trusts until it eventually promulgated the Trust Law of China in 2001.

The drafting of the Trust Law of China initiated in 1993 aimed to regulate trust business.[116] After three years of effort, the working group proposed a draft on 29 November 1996. Out of a total of six chapters, one focused on trust companies.[117] However, when the Trust Law of China was ultimately promulgated in 2001, the Law Committee of National People's Congress revised the legislative objective of the Trust Law to regulate the relationship between trust parties and thus removed the provisions of trust companies from the draft.[118] The Committee noted that the supervision of the trust business should be governed by public law thereby separating the law of trust from the laws surrounding trust institutions.[119] As a result, although commercial use was the impetus for introducing trusts in China and all the drafts of the Trust Law of China until April 2000 consisted of a separate chapter governing the organisation and administration of trust companies, the final promulgated Trust Law of China in 2001 did not have, and still does not have, any express regulation of trust companies.[120]

This is not to say that the Trust Law of China ignores the private sector. In article 4, it delegates the State Council to formulate specific measures for the organisation and administration of trust institutions.[121] Since then, China has passed various

[114] Trust Law of the People's Republic of China (Order No 50 of the President of the People's Republic of China).

[115] See L Ho, *Trust Law in China* (Hong Kong, Sweet & Maxwell Asia, 2003) 2: 'First, there is much hope in China that the Law will put in place an important legal instrument for the professional management of assets and, ultimately, for modernising China's financial infrastructure. Second, the Chinese experiment might be useful to civil law jurisdictions generally as an illustration of how thorny issues regarding the reception of the common law trust can be tackled'.

[116] X Zhou, *Trust Legislation: Theories and Practice* (Beijing, China Legal Publishing House, 2012) 24 [translated by author].

[117] Six chapters of the first draft of Trust Law of China were: general provisions; the relationship between trust parties; special provisions of charitable trust; trust companies; legal liabilities of trust; and supplementary provisions.

[118] Zhou (n 117) 25 and 27 [translated by author].

[119] See H Wu, X Jia and S Cheng, *Trust Law: Legal Regulations of the Development of China Trust Market* (Shanghai, Lixin Accounting Press, 2003) 41 [translated by author]. This fact is recognised in other civil law jurisdictions such as Japan, South Korea and Taiwan.

[120] In the ultimately promulgated Trust Law of China, there are seven chapters containing 74 articles: general provisions (arts 1–5); the creation of the trust (arts 6–13); trust property (arts 14–18); regulations concerning the trust parties: settlor, trustee and beneficiary (arts 19–49); modification to and termination of a trust (arts 50–58); charitable trust (arts 59–73); and supplementary provisions (art 74).

[121] Trust Law of China, art 4.

laws and regulations to provide for the use of trusts in commercial arrangements, focusing in particular on trust companies, investment funds, enterprise annuity funds, and management of insurance assets.

i. Trust Company

The trust company[122] is the most significant type of commercial trustee in China. Because its activities are largely engaged in the financial and banking sectors, the China Banking and Insurance Regulatory Commission (CBIRC) is the regulatory authority[123] that supervises and regulates trust companies and their related activities through a series of regulations: Measures for the Administration of Trust Companies,[124] Measures for the Administration of Net Capital of Trust Companies,[125] and Measures for the Administration of Trust Companies' Trust Plans of Assembled Funds (Amended).[126]

The Measures for the Administration of Trust Companies was published in 2007 and has since acted as the main legal resource regulating trust companies. It stipulates that a trust company is either a limited liability or a share-holding company,[127] and sets out seven basic components that must be constituted in order to establish a trust company: articles of association; eligible shareholders; registered capital of a minimum of 300 million yuan or the equivalent; an eligible board of directors; an organisational structure and a risk control system; and finally, business premises approved by the regulatory authority.[128] Resembling the two key features of common law trust, independence of trust property and segregation of trust management and profits, the Measures for the Administration of Trust Companies provides specific instructions on how to realise those two objectives. As stated in article 29, '[a] trust company shall clearly separate its own assets from trust property and manage them in different accounts, and manage trust property

[122] Trust companies were originally called trust and investment companies in China. Ine 2007 the China Banking Regulatory Commission (CBRC) changed the name to trust companies.

[123] The China Banking and Insurance Regulatory Commission (CBIRC) was established in 2018, by a merger of the China Banking Regulatory Commission (CBRC) and China Insurance Regulatory Commission (CIRC). The official website of the CBIRC is www.cbirc.gov.cn.

[124] Measures for the Administration of Trust Companies (Order No 2 of the China Banking Regulatory Commission). It was adopted at the Fifty-fifth Chairman's Meeting of the China Banking Regulatory Commission on 28 December 2006, and came into force on 1 March 2007.

[125] Measures for the Administration of Net Capital of Trust Companies (Order No 5 of the China Banking Regulatory Commission). It was adopted at the Ninety-ninth Chairman's Meeting of the China Banking Regulatory Commission on 12 July 2010, and came into force on 24 August 2010.

[126] Measures for the Administration of Trust Companies' Trust Plans of Assembled Funds (Amended) (Order No 3 of China Banking Regulatory Commission). It was adopted at the Fifty-fifth Chairman's Meeting of the China Banking Regulatory Commission on 28 December 2006, and came into force on 1 March 2007. This regulation was amended by the Decisions of the China Banking Regulatory Commission on Amending the Measures for the Administration of Trust Companies' Trust Plans of Assembled Funds (2009) (China) in 2009 re art 5(3) and art 27(2).

[127] Measures for the Administration of Trust Companies (China), art 6.

[128] ibid arts 8 and 10.

of different clients in different accounts'.[129] In liquidation, the trust property must be separated from the liquidated assets and will be transferred to a new trustee upon the current trustee's bankruptcy.[130] The trust company must act honestly and in a way that is credible, prudent, efficient and which will maximise the benefits of the trust's beneficiaries.[131] The trust company cannot seek illegitimate gain by taking advantage of its trustee status, provide guarantees with trust property, or use the trust property other than for trust purposes.[132] It must not benefit from its position or provide financial assistance to the connected persons, such as guarantees or transferring assets.[133] The trust company must bear in mind potential conflicts of interests[134] and the principle of confidentiality.[135]

In 2010 the China Banking Regulatory Commission (CBRC) promulgated Measures for the Administration of Net Capital of Trust Companies for the purpose of risk control. It provides that the net capital of a trust company must be no less than 200 million yuan,[136] and the trust company is required to continually comply with the following two risk control indicators: the net capital must not be lower than 100 per cent of the sum of all risk capital; and the net capital must not be lower than 40 per cent of the net assets.[137] If a trust company's net capital and other relevant risk control indicators change by more than 30 per cent compared with the previous quarter or do not meet the prescribed standards, the company is required to report to the regulatory authority in writing within five working days from the date of the occurrence of the situation.[138] Furthermore, the trust company is required to report to the CBRC and disclose the information of its capital calculation and risk control indicator. The trust company is required, within 18 working days from the end of each quarter, to submit to the regulatory authority a quarterly net capital calculation table, risk capital calculation table and risk control indicator supervision statement.[139] It must also disclose in its annual report the relevant information on net capital, risk capital, risk control indicators, etc.[140]

Apart from those regulations, the CBRC also lays down a facilitative framework for trust companies operating trust plans of assembled funds. A special administrative regulation, Measures for the Administration of Trust Companies' Trust Plans of Assembled Funds, was promulgated in 2007 and amended in 2009. It provides that under a trust plan of assembled funds, the trust companies act

[129] ibid art 29.
[130] ibid art 15.
[131] ibid art 24.
[132] ibid art 34.
[133] ibid art 33.
[134] ibid art 25.
[135] ibid art 27.
[136] Measures for the Administration of Net Capital of Trust Companies (China), art 15.
[137] ibid art 16.
[138] ibid art 25.
[139] ibid art 21.
[140] ibid art 24.

as trustees and conduct centralised management, operation or disposal of the funds entrusted by two or more settlors in accordance with the will of the settlors and for the interests of the beneficiaries.[141] The settlors participating in the trust plan are required to be qualified investors and are the sole beneficiaries of the trust plan.[142] Trust companies are required to fulfil fiduciary duties in order to protect the beneficiary's interests. These obligations include a requirement that the trust company must scrupulously perform its duties, fulfil the obligations of honesty, good faith, prudence and diligence, and serve the best interests of the beneficiaries.[143] When using trust capital for securities investment, a trust company is obliged to adopt the mode of portfolio, formulate investment proportions and investment strategies in advance and take effective measures to prevent risks to the funds forming a part of the trust.[144] Moreover,

> [it] may not provide guarantee for any other person; (2) the loans it provides to any other person may not exceed 30 per cent of the paid-in balance of all the trust plans under its management; (3) it may not directly or indirectly use the trust capital for its shareholders or their affiliated parties, except for the circumstance wherein all the trust capital comes from the shareholders or their affiliated parties; (4) it may not conduct any transaction between its inherent properties and its trust properties; (5) it may not conduct any transaction between different trust properties; and (6) it may not invest the trust properties of different trust plans under the management of the same company in a same project.[145]

The Measures for the Management of Trust Companies' Trust Plans of Assembled Funds (Amended) also requires the trust companies to separate trust property

[141] Measures for the Administration of Trust Companies' Trust Plans of Assembled Funds (Amended) (China), art 2. It is worth noting that, according to art 19, the safekeeping system applies to the capital of trust plans. As for non-cash trust properties, the parties concerned to the trust may agree to have them kept by a third party, a custodian. During the period of continued existence of a trust plan, the trust company is required to choose a commercial bank with sound and stable operation performance to act as the custodian. The safekeeping account and special account of the trust properties must be the same.

[142] ibid art 5. Requirements for establishing a trust plan of assembled funds: (1) the settlor shall be a qualified investor; (2) the settlor participating in the trust plan shall be the sole beneficiary; (3) the number of the natural persons involved in a single trust plan may not exceed 50, while the number of natural-person investors with a single entrustment amount of more than 3 million yuan (added by the CBRC Decision on Amending the Measures) and the number of qualified institutional investors is not restricted; (4) the trust period shall be one year or more; (5) there is a clear investment orientation and investment strategies for the trust capital, which shall also be in line with the industrial policy of the state and other relevant provisions; (6) the trust beneficiary right shall be divided into trust units of equivalent units; (7) the trust contract shall stipulate the remuneration for the trustee, and except for fair remunerations, the trust company may not seek profits for itself or anyone else either directly or indirectly by using the trust properties under any name; and (8) other requirements as prescribed by CBRC.

[143] ibid art 4.

[144] ibid art 25.

[145] ibid art 27. Paragraph (2) has been amended following the Decision on Amending the Measures of the China Banking Regulatory Commission, which states that 'the loans it provides to any other person may not exceed 30 per cent of the paid-in balance of all the trust plans under its management, unless the CBRC has specified otherwise'.

from their own assets so that their personal creditors cannot claim against the trust property.

> No trust company may incorporate the properties of trust plans into its inherent properties. The properties and profits obtained by a trust company from the management, operation of the properties of trust plans or any other circumstance shall be incorporated into the properties of trust plans of the company; in case a trust company goes through the procedures for account settlement for such reasons as being wound up according to law, being cancelled according to law, being declared bankrupt according to law or any other reason, the properties of trust plans shall not be treated as liquidation properties.[146]

Trust companies are forbidden from pooling trust assets: not only must they establish separate accounting accounts and conduct separate business accounting systems for each trust, but they must have separate management for different trust plans.[147]

ii. Investment Fund

The investment fund is a more recent development of commercial trusts in China. It is mainly in the form of industry investment funds, futures investment funds, warrants investment funds, and the most broadly used securities investment funds.[148] All levels of the government of the People's Bank of China hope to enhance the investment fund industry to attract investors, particularly foreign institutional investors, so as to help stabilise China's volatile stock markets.[149]

Establishing a robust legal framework for the burgeoning investment fund market – in particular, for the market of securities-based investment funds – is an ongoing challenge.[150] The Chinese government has sought to regulate investment funds through the Securities Investment Fund Law of the People's Republic of China (2015 Amendment)[151] and administrative regulations of the Chinese

[146] ibid art 3.

[147] ibid art 24.

[148] Huo, *Discussions of Trust Law* (n 107) 185 [translated by author]. According to its form of organisation, investment funds can be divided into contractual investment funds and corporation investment funds. China only allows investment funds to be structured as corporations, as US mutual funds are. Investment funds can also be categorised as open-end funds and closed-end funds according to whether the investment fund share can be increased or redeemed. An open-end fund is a fund in which the participants have a right to redeem or sell their interest in the fund at a price related to the net value of the assets held by the fund. The transaction is between investors and fund managers. Open-end funds are quite flexible; it is the fund manager's choice whether to give dividends to the investors. A closed-end fund is a collective investment model based on issuing a fixed number of shares which are not redeemable from the fund. Unlike open-end funds, new shares in a closed-end fund are not created by managers to meet demand from investors.

[149] South China Morning Post, 19 October 2000.

[150] Ho (n 116) 10.

[151] Securities Investment Fund Law of the People's Republic of China (2015 Amendment) (Order No 23 of the President of the People's Republic of China). It was amended and adopted at the Fourteenth Session of the Standing Committee of the Twelfth National People's Congress of the People's Republic of China on 24 April 2015, and came into force on 24 April 2015.

Securities Regulatory Commission (CSRC).[152] The CSRC is the principal regulatory authority that governs investment funds. Its most important and current effective regulation has been the Measures for the Administration of Securities Investment Fund Management Companies (2012 Amendment).[153] In other words, the two main legal resources regulating investment funds in China are the Securities Investment Fund Law (2015 Amendment), which governs the private law regulations to which investment funds must conform, and the Measures for the Administration of Securities Investment Fund Management Companies (2012 Amendment), which states the public law standards to which investment funds must meet.

The 2012 Measures requires that, to establish an investment fund management company in China, registered capital of no less than 100 million yuan must be paid up by shareholders with monetary capital.[154]

Where the net assets of a fund management company is less than 40 million yuan, or its disposable current assets such as cash, bank deposit and national debt is less than 20 million yuan and less than the company's business revenue in the previous accounting year, the CSRC may suspend the acceptance and examination of the company's application for collecting a fund product or any other business application, and require the company to improve financial liquidity within a prescribed time limit. If the financial status of the company continues to deteriorate, the CSRC will order it to cease business operations for rectification.[155]

Where a shareholder holds the highest shareholding in the fund management company, which must not be less than 25 per cent, it is the majority shareholder of the company. As a majority shareholder, the shareholder's registered capital must be no less than 300 million yuan.[156] Foreign shareholders of a Sino–foreign joint venture fund management company are required to pay a capital amount of no less than the convertible currency equal to 300 million yuan. These requirements are also applied to investment institutions based in the Hong Kong Special Administrative Region, the Macao Special Administrative Region, and the Taiwan Region.[157]

The 2012 Measures also defines the fiduciary duty under trusts, albeit in a general sense. It stipulates that senior managers and other staff members of a

[152] The Chinese Securities Regulatory Commission (CSRC) is a ministerial-level public institution directly under the State Council, which performs a unified regulatory function, according to the relevant laws and regulations, and with authority given by the State Council, over the securities and futures market of China, maintains an orderly securities and futures market order, and ensures a legal operation of the capital market. CSRC has 18 functional departments, one inspection division and three centres. See the official website of the CSRC (www.csrc.gov.cn).

[153] Measures for the Administration of Securities Investment Fund Management Companies (2012 Amendment) (Order No 84 of the China Securities Regulatory Commission). It was amended and adopted at the Nineteenth Chairman's Executive Meeting of the China Securities Regulatory Commission on 19 June 2012, and came into force on 1 November 2012.

[154] ibid art 6(3). Foreign shareholders are obliged to contribute capital in convertible currencies.

[155] ibid art 76.

[156] ibid art 8.

[157] ibid art 9.

fund management company must perform duties faithfully and diligently, and must not seek illegal benefits.[158] Corporate governance, notwithstanding internal documentation to the contrary, is required to give priority to the interests of fund shareholders, and not management.[159] A fund management company must insist on the concept of sound business operations; match the scale of assets under management with its staff reserves, investment research and client service ability, tolerance of information technology systems, risk management and internal control level; and effectively protect the long-term interests of fund shareholders.[160]

More specific regulations regarding different parties' rights and obligations as well as the key features of a trust (independence of the trust property and segregation of trust management and benefits enjoyment) are established in the 2015 Securities Investment Fund Law as the fundamental legislation. According to this, securities investment funds involve a triangular structure whereby fund shareholders enjoy fund income, fund assets are kept by a custodian, and the overall arrangement is managed by a management institution.[161] A fund management institution must be a company or a legally formed and registered partnership[162] whose registered capital is no less than 100 million yuan.[163] The fund management institution, or a fund service institution authorised by it, manages the subscription, redemption and registration of the fund share of an open-end fund.[164] In a publicly offered fund, the fund management institution is obliged to use fund assets for securities investment akin to a standard wealth portfolio.[165] Where a fund is not publicly offered, it must be under the custody of a fund custodian, except as otherwise agreed upon in the fund contract.[166]

A fund custodian, on the other hand, must be a registered commercial bank or other financial institution.[167] The fund custodian and the fund management institution may not be the same institution, and must not make capital contribution to each other's businesses or hold shares in each other.[168] The fund custodian is believed to be the trustee of the fund. It performs the functions of safekeeping fund assets, handing clearing and settlement matters in a timely manner according to the investment orders of the fund management institution as agreed

[158] ibid art 46.

[159] ibid art 37. In order to protect investors' interests, art 6(4) stipulates that the number of a fund management company's proposed senior managers and research, investment, valuation, marketing and other business personnel who qualify for the fund business must be no less than 15.

[160] ibid art 48.

[161] Securities Investment Fund Law of the People's Republic of China (2015 Amendment), art 3.

[162] ibid art 12.

[163] ibid art 13(2).

[164] ibid art 65.

[165] ibid art 71. Except as otherwise required by the securities regulatory authority of the State Council.

[166] ibid art 88.

[167] ibid art 32.

[168] ibid art 35.

upon in the fund contract, and overseeing the investment operations of the fund management institution.[169] On top of this, the fund custodian plays a supervisory role over that of the management institution. By law, should a fund custodian discover that any investment order of a fund management institution, including orders already executed under otherwise valid trading procedures, violate any law, administrative regulation or other relevant provision of the fund contract, it is obliged to refuse to execute the order, immediately notify the fund management institution, and report to the securities regulatory authority of the State Council in a timely manner.[170]

Finally, fund shareholders[171] are the beneficiaries of securities investment funds, and they enjoy the rights of sharing income from fund assets and participating in the distribution of residual fund assets upon liquidation. They also reserve the right to institute an action against the fund management institution, fund custodian or fund service institution[172] for any conduct that infringes upon the lawful rights and interests of the fund shareholder.[173] Moreover, the fund management

[169] ibid art 36. A fund custodian shall perform the following functions: (1) The safekeeping of fund assets. (2) Opening the capital accounts and securities accounts for fund assets according to the relevant provisions. (3) Maintaining separate accounts for the assets of different funds under custody and ensuring the integrity and independence of fund assets. (4) Preserving records, account books, statements and other relevant materials regarding the fund custody business. (5) Handling clearing and settlement matters in a timely manner according to the investment orders of the fund management institution as agreed upon in the fund contract. (6) Handling information disclosure matters related to the fund custody business. (7) Offering opinions on the fund's financial accounting reports and semi-annual and annual reports. (8) Reviewing and examining the net asset value of the fund and the subscription and redemption prices for fund shares as calculated by the fund management institution. (9) Convening the fund shareholders' meeting according to the relevant provisions. (10) Overseeing the investment operations of the fund management institution according to the relevant provisions. (11) Other functions prescribed by the securities regulatory authority of the State Council.

[170] ibid art 37.

[171] When an investment fund is listed, there must be no less than 1000 fund shareholders, and the capital raised of the fund must not be less than 200 million yuan (Securities Investment Fund Law of the People's Republic of China (2015 Amendment), art 62). But if the fund is not publicly offered, the number of the qualified investors to whom it is offered must not exceed 200 cumulatively (Securities Investment Fund Law of the People's Republic of China (2015 Amendment), art 87).

[172] Securities Investment Fund Law of the People's Republic of China (2015 Amendment), art 97. Fund service providers are entities which provide the sale, trading payment, share registration, valuation, investment advice, rating, information technology system and other fund services for publicly offered funds and they undergo registration or recording formalities in accordance with the provisions of the securities regulatory authority of the State Council.

[173] ibid art 46. The fund shareholders shall enjoy the following rights: (1) Sharing income from fund assets. (2) Participating in the distribution of the residual fund assets upon liquidation. (3) Transferring or requesting redemption of the fund shares respectively held by them in accordance with law. (4) Requiring that the fund shareholders' meeting be convened or convening the fund shareholders' meeting according to the relevant provisions. (5) Exercising their voting rights regarding matters deliberated at the fund shareholders' meeting. (6) Instituting an action against the fund management institution, fund custodian or fund service institution for its conduct that infringes upon their lawful rights and interests. (7) Other rights as agreed upon in the fund contract. The fund shareholders of a publicly offered fund shall have the right to consult or copy the publicly disclosed information and data regarding the fund; and the fund shareholders of a non-publicly offered fund shall have the right to consult the financial accounting books and other financial data of the fund where their personal interests are involved.

institution and fund custodian must, as agreed upon in the fund contract, provide fund information to the fund shareholders.[174] The fund shareholders' meeting, composed of all fund shareholders, can exercise the powers of replacing the fund management institution or fund custodian.[175]

From the specific provisions stipulating the rights and obligations of different parties, it can be seen that under an investment fund, the fund shareholders are the beneficiaries who enjoy fund benefits, and fund assets are kept by a custodian and managed by a management institution. This is in line with the essence of trusts; that is, to split property management and beneficial enjoyments between trustees and beneficiaries. In addition to these essential elements, the 2015 Securities Investment Fund Law also summarises the trustees' fiduciary duties: to perform obligations in good faith and with prudence and diligence and to prevent and control risks in investment effectively,[176] emphasising the independence of the trust property:

> Fund assets shall be independent from a fund management institution's or a fund custodian's own assets. The fund management institution or fund custodian shall not incorporate any fund assets into its own assets. All property and income obtained by the fund management institution or fund custodian from managing, utilising or otherwise disposing of fund assets shall be incorporated into fund assets. Where the fund management institution or fund custodian is liquidated for being dissolved, administratively dissolved or declared bankrupt in accordance with law or any other reason, fund assets are not liquidating property.[177]

As a result, '[t]he claims enjoyed by fund assets shall not be used to offset the debts incurred by a fund management institution's or a fund custodian's own assets; and the claims enjoyed and debts incurred by the assets of different funds shall not be offset mutually'.[178] No enforcement may be conducted against fund assets, except for the debts incurred by fund assets.[179] Not only the fund management institution or the fund custodian, but also directors, supervisors, senior executives and other employees of the fund management institution are prohibited by the statute from mixing their own assets or the assets of the institution with fund assets to engage in securities investment.[180]

[174] ibid art 95.
[175] ibid art 47.
[176] ibid art 9. Fund management institutions and fund custodians in managing and utilising fund assets and fund service institutions in conducting fund service activities shall devote themselves to their duties and perform their obligations of good faith, prudence and diligence. Fund management institutions shall, when investing fund assets in securities, comply with the rules on prudential business operations and develop methodical and rational investment strategies and risk management rules to effectively prevent and control risks. Fund employees shall be qualified for engaging in the fund business and comply with laws, administrative regulations, professional ethics, and the code of conduct.
[177] ibid art 5.
[178] ibid art 6.
[179] ibid art 7.
[180] ibid art 20.

iii. Enterprise Annuity Fund and Insurance Product

In addition to trust business run by trust companies and investment funds, the trust has also been adopted for other commercial uses in China, specifically in managing enterprise annuity and issuance products.

Trusts have become the first choice for annuity investment in China.[181] Many occupational pension schemes are established in the form of trusts because the trust mechanism benefits the interests of both the employee-beneficiaries and the trustees (pension companies, trust companies or commercial banks). The regulation of trustees' duties is less rigorous in enterprise annuity funds than public interest requires. Although this lowers the correlative rights of the employee-beneficiaries, the employee-beneficiaries remain protected in the event of their employer's insolvency insofar as the trust fund is separated from the employer's assets. The enterprise annuity funds are supervised by its regulatory authority, the Ministry of Human Resources and Social Security of the People's Republic of China (MOHRSS),[182] and are mainly regulated by two administrative regulations of the MOHRSS: Measures for the Management of Enterprise Annuity Funds (2011 Amendment)[183] and Interim Measures for the Qualification Accreditation of Enterprise Annuity Fund Management Institutions (Amended).[184]

Those regulations stipulate that, under an enterprise annuity fund, contracts of trust management must be signed between the trustee and the account manager (the enterprise annuity fund account management institution), the trust custodian (the enterprise annuity fund trust institution), and the investment manager (the enterprise annuity fund investment management institution).[185] The trustee, account manager, custodian and investment manager, as well as other natural

[181] S Ni, 'Commercial Trusts and Companies as Business Organisations: Through Comparative Studies' (2012) 6 *Securities Law* 410, 411 [translated by author].

[182] The Ministry of Human Resources and Social Security of the People's Republic of China (MOHRSS) was created in 2008 by merging the Ministry of Personnel and Ministry of Labour and Social Security, following a decision announced at the National People's Congress. It is a ministry under the State Council which is responsible for national labour policy standards, regulations and managing the national social security system. The official website of the MOHRSS is www.mohrss.gov.cn.

[183] Measures for the Management of Enterprise Annuity Funds (2011 Amendment) (Order No 11 of the Ministry of Human Resources and Social Security, China Banking Regulatory Commission, China Securities Regulatory Commission and China Insurance Regulatory Commission). It was amended and adopted at the Fifty-eighth Executive Meeting of the Ministry of Human Resources and Social Security on 11 January 2011, and came into force on 1 May 2011.

[184] Interim Measures for the Qualification Accreditation of Enterprise Annuity Fund Management Institutions (Amended) (Order No 24 of the Ministry of Labour and Social Security). It was adopted at the Ninth Executive Meeting of the Ministry of Labour and Social Security on 24 December 2004, and came into force on 1 March 2005.

[185] Measures for the Management of Enterprise Annuity Funds (2011 Amendment), art 3. There shall be only one trustee, one account manager and one custodian in any one enterprise annuity fund. An appropriate number of investment managers may be selected based on the size of the asset (art 5). The trustee, under enterprise annuity funds, is the pension management company or other trusted legal person, institution or enterprise annuities council (art 14); the beneficiaries are the employees of an enterprise who have participated in the enterprise annuity fund and are entitled to the beneficial rights (art 24).

persons, legal persons or other organisations that provide services for management of enterprise annuity funds, must carefully perform their duties and fulfil their obligations of honesty, good faith, prudence and due diligence.[186] The trustee is required to establish a risk control system to ensure the independence of different business managements and apply unified standards to all investment managers, thereby reflecting the principles of openness, fairness and impartiality.[187] Properties under enterprise annuity funds should be held separate from the existing properties of, and other properties managed by, the settlor, trustee, account manager, custodian, investment manager and other persons (natural or legal), as well as from the properties managed by organisations that provide services for the management of enterprise annuity funds.[188] Enterprise annuity properties will not fall into the scope of liquidation should any of those members' assets be liquidated for the purpose of termination due to lawful dissolution, cancellation or bankruptcy.[189] Consequently, the creditor's rights over an enterprise annuity fund may not be offset against the debts of the above-named settlor, trustee, account manager, custodian, investment manager or other persons or organisations.[190]

Trusts in China are also employed as a means of managing insurance products.[191] This type of business is supervised by the regulatory authority of the CBIRC[192] and must comply with trust and insurance laws and regulations, principally the Insurance Law of the People's Republic of China (2009 Amendment)[193] and the Provisions on the Administration of Insurance Asset Management Companies.[194]

The Contract Law of the People's Republic of China[195] is often referred to when addressing trust issues. Some scholars, in fact, seek to equate the role of

[186] ibid art 12. The specific qualifications required of the trustee, account manager, custodian, and investment manager of enterprise annuity funds can be found in arts 5, 6, 7 and 8 of the Interim Measures for the Qualification Accreditation.

[187] ibid art 7.

[188] ibid art 8.

[189] ibid art 9.

[190] ibid art 10.

[191] A trust used to manage insurance products is a specialised and complex subject closely connected with insurance schemes and insurance law. There is detailed literature on this subject, and thus this book only touches on the key authorities and rules.

[192] Insurance industry was regulated by the China Insurance Regulatory Commission (CIRC) before the CIRC was replaced by the CBIRC in 2018.

[193] Insurance Law of the People's Republic of China (2009 Amendment) (Order No 11 of the President of the People's Republic of China). It was amended and adopted at the Seventh Session of the Standing Committee of the Eleventh National People's Congress of the People's Republic of China on 28 February 2009, and came into force on 1 October 2009.

[194] Provisions on the Administration of Insurance Asset Management Companies (Order No 2 of the Chairman of China Insurance Regulatory Commission). It was reviewed and approved at the China Insurance Regulatory Committee Chairman Meeting on 8 December 2003, and came into force on 1 June 2004.

[195] Contract Law of the People's Republic of China (Order No 15 of the President of the People's Republic of China). It was adopted at the Second Session of the Ninth National People's Congress on 15 March 1999, and came into force on 1 October 1999.

the contract in Chinese trust law to that of the trust deed in common law.[196] This argument is valid, to some extent, because contracts in China constitute the basic structure of commercial trusts. The Trust Law of China requires a trust to be set up by contracts, testaments or other documents authorised by laws or administrative regulations.[197] Not only that, but (as Chinese trusts mainly take the form of trust companies) the nature of the relationship between the trust companies and their clients is frequently, if not exclusively, contractual.[198] Given the overwhelming predominance of commercial trusts over that of testamentary trusts, trust contracts have been the most common form of trusts in China, with contract law serving as an important tool in the resolution of trust-related disputes.

The above argument is tenuous, however, as it cannot explain the beneficiary's right to trace trust property, to supervise trust management, or to receive trust benefits, given that the beneficiary is not a party to the contract between the settlor and the trustee. That being said, where Chinese trust law and other relevant regulations are silent on salient factors, China's courts have not hesitated to invoke Chinese contract law to fill any normative gaps that remain.[199] Unfortunately, China's supporting legal infrastructure of trusts remains underdeveloped due in part to a scarce jurisprudential basis and subsequently weak doctrinal basis. Instead, practitioners and jurists rely on a mixture of statutes and regulatory practices to address issues as they arise.

V. Conclusion

This comparative study of trusts in civil law showed that the commercial use of trusts not only promoted the evolution of the trust in common law but also spurred the introduction of trusts into civil law jurisdictions to attract international investment and facilitate cross-border transactions, although the traditional use of a trust did not take root in most civil law jurisdictions. The laws of trusts have been gradually liberalised over time to allow for a wider and more commercial use of a trust.

[196] Ho, Lee and Jin (n 110) 83.

[197] Trust Law of China, art 8.

[198] L Gao, *The Misunderstood Trust: Principles on Trust Law* (Shanghai, Fudan University Press, 2010) 258 [translated by author].

[199] See *Yan Xin Co Ltd v Hua Bao Trust and Investment Co Ltd*, Shanghai Intermediate People's Court Case No 226 of 2004 (16 March 2005); on appeal from *Yan Xin Co Ltd v Hua Bao Trust and Investment Co Ltd*, Case No 201 of 2004 (25 November 2004).

4

A Developed Understanding of the Beneficiary's Interest in Commercial Trusts*

After the fundamental inspection of the evolved role of trusts for commercial uses and the introduction of trusts into civilian jurisdictions as a result of the evolution, this book goes on to examine the changes and challenges the newly developed commercial trusts have brought to the specific trust parties of beneficiaries and trustees. This chapter provides a developed understanding of the beneficiary's interest to adjust the traditional trust notions to meet the demands of commercial practices. It first introduces the beneficiary's rights that originated in England, and then it proposes a more comprehensive understanding of the nature of the beneficiary's interest – a special personal claim – that responds to the newly evolved role of trusts for commercial uses and to the consequence of the accommodation of trusts into civil law.

I. A Beneficiary's Rights as Originated in England

There has been controversy over the nature of the beneficiary's rights.[1] It has often been said that legal ownership is a right *in rem* whilst equitable ownership is a right *in personam* because it is given only against persons and not things. The beneficiary's right is a personal claim, a right *in personam*, against the trustee in the event that the trustee should commit a breach of the trust.[2] In such a circumstance, the trustee is obliged to effect a specific restitution of the property from the trust or to pay equitable compensation to the beneficiaries. Similarly, any third party who knowingly receives the property in breach of the trust[3] or who acts as

* This chapter draws on previously published work in R Zhang, 'A Developed Understanding of the Beneficiary's Interest in Commercial Trusts through a Comparative Study of Chinese Law' (2020) 27(3) *Maastricht Journal of European and Comparative Law* 343.

[1] The majority opinion was held by Sir Frederick Maitland, an English legal historian of the late nineteenth century, who argued that the right of the trust beneficiary is merely a personal right with *in rem* connections. Opposite this, Austin Scott proposed that the beneficiaries have a direct proprietary interest in the trust property.

[2] AH Oosterhoff, R Chambers and M Mclnnes, *Oosterhoff on Trusts*, 9th edn (Toronto, Carswell, 2019) 37.

[3] See *Re Montagu's Settlement Trusts* [1987] Ch 264.

a dishonest assistant to the breach of the trust[4] will bear personal obligations to account to the beneficiaries for any loss suffered by the trust.[5] The beneficiary's interest never binds third parties except those whose rights derive from the rights of the trustee. As stated by Smith, this shows that the beneficiary's interest binds the trustee's rights in the trust property, not the trust property itself.[6] Unlike legal rights that prevail against persons generally, equitable rights only prevail against a limited group of persons.[7]

Moreover, the beneficiary's right is considered a personal claim because its realisation relies on another person's performance, ie the trustees' management of trust assets. The beneficiary's right is 'an indirect interest in the nature of an encumbrance on the trustee's rights in the trust property'.[8] Where a third party owns a common law obligation in relation to the trust property, it is the trustee who enforces it as a legal owner. The beneficiaries 'do not bind the bona fide purchaser for value of the legal estate without notice'.[9] Therefore, a beneficiary has no full proprietary interest until the trustee's discretion is exercised in their favour. The beneficiary only has an expectation that the trustees will perform their duty to manage the assets and distribute income in favour of the beneficiary.

Although the execution of the beneficiary's rights is based on the trustee's administration and disposal over the trust property, the beneficiary does not act simply like a personal creditor of the trustee. That is because, first, the fate of beneficiary's rights is tied up with the fate of the trust property. A beneficiary's rights will only be effective as long as the trust property exists. As Penner says:

> If the trust property is stolen or lost and cannot be recovered, or is destroyed, then the trust essentially evaporates, because there is no property to which the beneficiary's rights under a trust can attach … Thus, if the property disappears, then so does the trust, and so does the beneficiary's right.[10]

In this respect, the beneficiary's rights are different from those of a creditor. Second, the beneficiary's rights are capable of binding certain third parties except for 'equity's darling' – the bona fide purchaser for value of the trust property without actual or constructive notice of the equity. In other words, the

[4] See *Royal Brunei Airlines Sdn Bhd v Tan* [1995] UKPC 4, [1995] 2 AC 378; *Twinsectra Ltd v Yardley* [2002] UKHL 12, [2002] 2 AC 164; *Dubai Aluminium Co Ltd v Salaam* [2002] UKHL 48.

[5] G Thomas and A Hudson, *The Law of Trusts*, 2nd edn (Oxford, Oxford University Press, 2010) 26.

[6] L Smith, 'Scottish Trusts in the Common Law' (2013) 17 *Edinburgh Law Review* 283, 288.

[7] In England, this limited group of persons originally comprised persons who were not bona fide and now includes those who were not able to take advantage of special protective provisions in the Law of Property Act 1925. Exceptionally, if the equitable interest is owned by an actual occupier or registered land it can rank as an overriding interest so as to bind other persons generally: Land Registration Act 2002, sch 3, para 2. See P Matthews and others, *Underhill and Hayton Law of Trusts and Trustees*, 20th edn (London, LexisNexis Butterworths, 2022) 82.

[8] Smith (n 6) 293.

[9] G Watt and P Todd, *Cases & Materials on Equity & Trusts*, 10th edn (Oxford, Oxford University Press, 2016) 10.

[10] JE Penner, *The Law of Trusts*, 12th edn (Oxford, Oxford University Press, 2022) 33.

beneficiary can exercise equitable proprietary remedies against certain third parties as the transferees of the trust property and trace the property so as to have the property or its product restored as an accrual to the trust fund.[11] As Lord Collins SCJ observed in *Roberts v Gill & Co Solicitors and others*,[12] when the trustee unreasonably refuses to, or fails to, sue the third party, the beneficiary can proceed to trace the property and recover it from the third parties who are not equity's darling.[13] A beneficiary's trace may have the recovered property added back to the trust fund but not to the beneficiary's personal assets. In short, the nature of the beneficiary's interest can be concluded as a personal claim against the trustee but involves an indirect interest in the trust property while concerning the external relationship against certain third parties. The case of equity's darling is treated as a justifiable exception to the general *nemo dat* rule[14] that protects security of title.[15]

The major specific rights of the beneficiary that are granted by equitable title are the rights to compel due administration; to bring a derivative action on behalf of a trust when the trust is not properly administered; and to terminate a trust.

First, when a trust is inappropriately administered, the beneficiary can take steps to compel its proper administration.[16] As part of the right to compel due administration, a beneficiary is entitled to enforce claims, ie to apply to the court if the trustee fails to take any action necessary to preserve the trust assets.[17] The beneficiary can either issue an application to the court for the determination of a specific question or questions[18] or issue proceedings for the general administration of the trust.[19] If the improper administration is caused by a third person, the

[11] Matthews and others, *Underhill and Hayton* (n 7) 83–84.

[12] *Roberts v Gill & Co Solicitors and others* [2010] UKSC 22.

[13] ibid para 62.

[14] The Latin phrase *nemo dat quod non habet* means 'no one can give what they do not have'. This principle is commonly referred to as the *nemo dat* rule – a person who does not have adequate ownership of goods or property cannot transfer the ownership of those goods or that property to someone else.

[15] See Penner (n 10) 35–36 and 46–48.

[16] In general, a beneficiary has no right to interfere in the administration of a trust, but has to wait passively to receive benefits to which he is entitled when the trusts are properly administered.

[17] *Fletcher v Fletcher* (1844) 4 Hare 67.

[18] A beneficiary may employ the first method in the following circumstances: applying to a court to approve a specific transaction that is for the interests of the beneficiaries as a whole but in the absence of general law and trust instrument (*Boardman v Phipps* [1967] 2 AC 46); applying to a court to direct the trustees to do a particular act which they ought to do or to refrain from doing a particular act that they ought not to do; applying to a court to construe the provisions of the trust instrument or to ascertain the classes of beneficiaries (*Syffolk v Lawrence* (1884) 32 WR 899 [14]–[122]); applying to a court to direct payment of money in the hands of the trustees to the court (Trustee Act 1925, s 63); and applying to a court to determine any other specific question which arises in the course of the administration of a trust.

[19] The second method is usually only necessary in three situations: where there have been constant disputes between the trustees; where the circumstances of the trust give rise to recurring difficulties that would require frequent single applications to the court; and where clear prima facie doubts exist as to the bona fides of the trustees. See AJ Oakley, *Parker and Mellows: The Modern Law of Trusts*, 9th edn (London, Sweet & Maxwell, 2015) 817–18.

court may either direct the trustees to enforce that claim or allow the beneficiary to sue the third party directly for the benefit of the trust in the name of the trustees, or to sue the trustees directly.[20]

Derived from the right to compel due administration, the beneficiary also has the right to bring a derivative action on behalf of the trust.[21] Where the trust is a bare trust,[22] the beneficiary has the right, upon giving a proper indemnity, to require the trustee to lend the trustee's name to the action to vindicate the legal right.[23] The beneficiary can also bring an action for the benefit of the trust under complex trusts and bare trusts where compelling the trustee to lend the trustee's name would have proved useless, for instance, when the trustee is disabled from suing or it is either difficult or inconvenient for the trustee to sue. Since they sue to enforce duties owed to the trustee, ie derived from the trustee, the beneficiary cannot be in a better position than the trustee.[24]

Last but not least, beneficiaries have the right to terminate the trust. A sole beneficiary who is *sui juris* (of the age of majority, and with full capacity) or beneficiaries who are all *sui juris* and all in agreement, can terminate trusts without reference to the wishes of the trustees or the settlor. This is known as the Rule in *Saunders v Vautier*.[25] Although doubts arose that beneficiaries' interests were defeasible when the trust property remained subject to a special power of appointment vested in trustees,[26] Lord Walker stated in *Schmidt*[27] that a mere power of appointment had the negative ability to block the application of the Rule in *Saunders v Vautier*. Nevertheless, it is noted that the beneficiaries cannot terminate the trust as of right when there are legacies contingently charged on the trust fund.[28] Moreover, the trust cannot be terminated when the trustee has outstanding obligations under a contract which is held as a trustee and has no power to transfer the trust asset to the beneficiary or to the beneficiary's order.[29]

With respect to the application of the right to terminate trusts, a question arises as to whether it is necessary to have an ascertained group of beneficiaries as a collective to terminate the trust. This would be true if the identity of all of the beneficiaries can be determined, ie if the *Broadway Cottages*[30] test applies, which requires the trustees to formulate a complete list of all the beneficiaries. However,

[20] See Matthews and others, *Underhill and Hayton* (n 7) 998; Oakley, *Parker and Mellows* (n 19) 818.

[21] According to the general rule, a beneficiary can only sue the beneficiary's trustee or a person who is constructively treated as a trustee, but has no cause of action against a third party who commits a wrongful act in respect of trust property or assists the trustee in breach of the trust. It is the trustee who has a cause of action and can bring proceedings on behalf of the trust against such a third party.

[22] A bare trust, also called a simple trust, means a trust in which the settlor gives no active duties to the trustee; the trustee's duty is merely to follow the instructions of the beneficiary.

[23] *Foley v Burnell* (1783) 1 Bro CC 274.

[24] *Hayim v Citibank NA* [1987] AC 730.

[25] *Saunders v Vautier* [1841] EWHC J82, (1841) 4 Beav 115, (1841) Cr & Ph 240, 41 ER 482 (Ch Div).

[26] Matthews and others, *Underhill and Hayton* (n 7) 989.

[27] *Schmidt v Rosewood Trust Ltd* [2003] UKPC 26, [2003] 2 AC 709.

[28] *Weatherall v Thornburgh* (1878) 8 Ch D 261 (CA).

[29] *Don King Productions Inc v Warren* [2000] Ch 291, 321 (Lightman J).

[30] *Commissioners of Inland Revenue v Broadway Cottages Trust* [1995] Ch 20.

there are circumstances where the identity of all the beneficiaries cannot be ascertained. As the House of Lords held in *McPhail v Doulton*,[31] the *Broadway Cottages* test was not appropriate, at least for discretionary trusts. 'Instead, the majority affirmed that for discretionary trusts it was sufficient if the beneficial class was conceptually certain in the sense that it was possible for the trustees to say for any given individual that he or she either was or was not a member of the class.'[32] It is difficult or impossible to list all the beneficiaries under a discretionary trust. This is because such a trust might be created for a huge class of beneficiaries (for example, for the employees and ex-employees of a large multi-national corporation). Similarly, it is not possible to assert that every one of a trust's beneficiaries has agreed to terminate that trust. Therefore, discretionary trusts do not require the identity of all the beneficiaries to be provided, which allows the existing trustees to terminate the trust.[33]

II. A Developed Understanding of the Beneficiary's Rights

To utilise the full advantages of a trust, especially its commercial uses, it is this author's opinion that a better understanding of the trust is as a binary system of real rights and personal claims, where the trustee is granted a prima facie ownership that is limited to the right to control and administer the trust property (although settlors may retain the ownership),[34] and the beneficiary holds a right in the nature of 'a special personal claim'. Unlike typical personal claims, the beneficiaries' rights are special because their rights go beyond enforcing the trustee's duties to distribute benefits to them under the trust. They have rights to enforce due performance of the trust in a broader sense, which involves holding the trustee to the trustee's administrative and dispositive duties.

[31] *McPhail v Doulton, Re Baden's Deed Trusts (No 1)* [1971] AC 424.

[32] TG Watkin, 'Changing Concepts of Ownership in English Law During the Nineteenth and Twentieth Centuries: The Changing Idea of Beneficial Ownership under the English Trust' in M Dixon and GLLH Griffiths (eds), *Contemporary Perspectives on Property, Equity and Trusts Law* (Oxford, Oxford University Press, 2007) 139, 153.

[33] R Zhang, *A Better Understanding of Common Law Ownership of Trust Property and its Introduction in China Through Comparative Studies* (Guangzhou, World Publishing Corporation, 2019) 35–36.

[34] See R Zhang, 'A Developed Understanding of the Beneficiary's Interest in Commercial Trusts through a Comparative Study of Chinese Law' (2020) 27(3) *Maastricht Journal of European and Comparative Law* 343, 349. The trustee's ownership is a prima facie ownership because the trustees cannot obtain benefits arising from trust assets or arbitrarily dispose of trust property. Unlike a real owner, the trustees cannot freely abandon trust property but have duties to safeguard the trust property and exercise reasonable care over it; they have no right to put up trust property as collateral on their own personal obligation; and they are not liable for any accidental losses of the trust property, or for costs awarded to a third party in an action against the trustees as legal owners of the trust property. Those differences between a trustee's ownership and real ownership are due to the fact that the real purpose of the trust is not to give the trust property to the trustees as a gift, but simply to authorise them to manage and administer the trust property for the benefit of the beneficiaries or a specified purpose. See especially *Benett v Wyndham* (1862) 4 De GF & J 259; *Re Raybould* [1900] 1 Ch 199.

The 'special personal claim' is adapted to the evolution of trust for commercial uses as well as being equally applicable to traditional family trusts. Compared with the traditional common law argument of equitable rights, which may be both personal and proprietary, the 'special personal claim' provides a more developed and unified understanding of the beneficiary's interest.

In the following section, to support the position of a 'special personal claim', this chapter first criticises the beneficiary's real rights and other theories before analysing the personal claim theory, and then explains why it is a more unified and broad understanding of the beneficiary's interest, particularly in the commercial context.

A. Denial of Real Right Theory and Other Academic Theories

There are various academic theories about the beneficiary's rights. Taking China[35] as an example, in 1987, He Xiaoyuan suggested that the ownership of trust property be transferred to a trustee, while a beneficiary has the right to revoke the trustee's disposition of trust property in breach of trust purpose and a right to follow the trust property.[36] Wen Shiyang proposed a different explanation in 2005. He stated that a beneficiary's equitable right is a genuine ownership whereas trustees' ownership is only a right of administration.[37] In addition, Zhou Xiaoming in 1996[38] and Li Qunxing in 2000[39] raised the argument that there is a new type of right or right combination.

The argument that a beneficiary's right is a new type of right or an in-between right that is neither a completely real right nor a personal claim takes a bold step in the theoretical ideas of the nature of the beneficiary's right. This effort, however, is not fully successful. Its weakness is that a type of right belonging to both real rights and personal claims has never been recognised in civil law systems.

The beneficiary's real right theory also has a number of weaknesses. In Scots law the real right theory is refused because, if the beneficiary, but not the trustee, were the owner of the trust property, it would be hard to explain why the trustee can transfer a good title to a third party because it violates the *nemo dat* principle (ie no one can give what they do not have) that precludes the non-owner trustee

[35] There is no explicit provision in the Trust Law of China that stipulates the nature of the beneficiary's interests, although specific rights of the beneficiary are regulated in various provisions (arts 43–49).

[36] X He, 'Studies of Trust Law' (1987) 1 *Chung Hsing Law Review* 1, 6 [translated by author]. The right to revoke the trustees' disposal of trust property and the right to follow the trust property are two aspects of the same kind of right.

[37] S Wen and X Feng, 'Ownership of Trust Property: On the Improvement of China's Legislation' (2005) 2 *Wuhan University Journal* 203, 206 [translated by author].

[38] X Zhou, *Comparative Studies of Trust Law* (Beijing, China Law Press, 1996) 210 [translated by author].

[39] Q Li, 'The Legal Nature and Basic Principles of Trust' (2000) 3 *Chinese Journal of Law* 118, 121 [translated by author].

from transferring the title to the trust property.[40] Furthermore, in the absence of ownership, the trustee's administration of trust property is less convenient and less efficient. The trustee needs to request and wait for the property owner's permission and co-operation in the trust management, such as a permission to enter into a transaction. Additionally, if the beneficiary's real right theory were to prevail, the ownership of trust property would be in legal limbo for a certain period in some cases, such a charitable trust, private purpose trust or discretionary trust, where there are no certain beneficiaries. For example, in the civil law case *Tucker v Royal Trust Co*,[41] primary beneficiaries did not exist when the deed of donation and the trust were made; consequently, for a certain period of time ownership of the property in the trust would have been vested in no one. Last but not least, secrecy is deemed to be one advantage of the trust system. If the beneficiary's right was considered as a real right, it should be registered and in that case the beneficiary's identity would have to be revealed.

In China, the beneficiary's real right theory faces a number of challenges. First, the beneficiary's right does not meet the definition of a real right in the Civil Code of China. Article 114 of the Civil Code states that real rights are the right to directly and exclusively control a specific thing in accordance with the law. These rights are made up of ownership, usufructuary rights and security rights.[42] However, the Trust Law of China grants the beneficiary no exclusive right to manage or control the trust property. Beneficiary's rights cannot be viewed as usufructuary rights; this is because the right to usufruct requires that the rightsholder possess the property in question.[43] As noted, because in trusts it is the trustee rather than the beneficiary who holds the possession of trust property,[44] this right would appear to be immediately precluded. Neither can beneficiary's rights be viewed as security rights; this is because security rights give secured creditors precedence over unsecured creditors in regard to having their claim paid with the trust property.[45] Nevertheless, the beneficiary has no priority against other trust creditors except for the personal creditors of a trustee due to the independence of trust assets.[46]

Moreover, the beneficiary's right cannot be attributed to any specific type of real rights. Pursuant to article 116 of the Civil Code of China, '[t]he varieties and contents of real rights shall be prescribed by law'.[47] However, the beneficiary's right is not expressly or implicitly regulated as a type of real right by the Trust Law of

[40] Although an agent can dispose of property on behalf of a principal, a trustee is distinct from an agent and their rights are different in nature.

[41] *Tucker v Royal Trust Co* [1982] 1 SCR 250, 264–65.

[42] Civil Code of China, art 114.

[43] X Sun, *Property Law* (Beijing, China Law Press, 2008) 79 [translated by author].

[44] A trustee is the person who should be granted exclusive powers of management over the trust assets in order for a trust to function.

[45] Z Wang, *Principles of Personal Claims*, 4th edn (Beijing, Beijing University Press, 2021) 13 [translated by author].

[46] D Chen, *Trust Law and the Innovation of Trust System in China* (Shanghai, Lixin Accounting Publishing House, 2003) 113 [translated by author].

[47] Civil Code of China, art 116.

China or other legislation. In order to avoid recognising the beneficiary's right as a right directly enforceable against trust property, the Trust Law of China stipulates that the legal bases of the enforcement of the beneficiary's rights are the trust documents but not the legislation itself.[48] Although article 116 of the Civil Code does not prevent legislation from creating new types of real rights, it is still difficult to classify the beneficiary's rights as real rights because of the inherent instability of (typically fungible) trust property. A real right requires stability in the property; however, the particular assets that constitute a trust fund are liable to change from time to time, depending on the management of the trust. For example, a trust fund could readily be converted from cash to securities as a result of management decisions.

Therefore, the beneficiary's right cannot be defined as a real right, at least not until the trust is terminated and the ownership is transferred to the beneficiary.

B. Proposal of Special Personal Claim Theory

Based on a case study of Chinese law, the author proposes that the nature of the beneficiary's interest is a special personal claim. It is special because, unlike a typical personal claim that binds two parties in a creditor–debtor relationship,[49] the beneficiary's right can affect a third party's right to the trust property – for example, by annulling a trustee's transfer of the property to a third party. Moreover, the beneficiary has the right to supervise trust affairs, which is beyond the scope of a typical personal claim. Nevertheless, the beneficiary's right is still a personal claim as opposed to a real right. Although only real rights are exigible against third parties in general, secondary personal claims can arise against third parties who are guilty of interference in the performance of the trustee's performance of their primary duties to the beneficiary. In the author's view, the beneficiary's right to supervise trust affairs and annul a trustee's wrongful disposal of the trust property, both of which are beyond the narrow scope of personal claims, should be deemed the appurtenance and the preservation of the personal claims, respectively.

First, jurists have interpreted the beneficiary's right to supervise trust affairs as appurtenant or incidental to their personal claim to enforce the trustee's duties to distribute assets pursuant to the trust terms. Although the right of supervision directly falls into neither personal claims nor real rights, it is in essence derived from the beneficiary's personal claim to ensure that the trustee performs the trust terms.[50] This concept is well-founded, because the right of supervision must be

[48] Trust Law of China, art 9: The following items shall be stated clearly in the written documents required for the creation of a trust: … (5) the form and means through which the beneficiary gains benefits from the trust.

[49] Wang (n 45) 15 [translated by author].

[50] See, eg, H Yu, 'China's Reception of the Dual Ownership of Anglo-American Trust' (2010) 3 *Modern Law Science* 159, 164 [translated by author]; H Yu, *How to Localise the British and American Law on Trust Property in China* (Beijing, China University of Political Science and Law Press, 2011) 111 [translated by author].

transferred along with the transfer of the beneficiary's personal claims. In the same fashion, once the beneficiaries waive their personal claims, the right of supervision must also be waived. From the perspective of its function and status, therefore, the right of supervision is in a subordinate position, to support and realise the beneficiary's personal claims. Thus, the right of supervision is essentially an auxiliary and derivative right to make personal claims (ie the beneficiary's core right).

Second, regarding the beneficiary's right to annul the trustee's disposal of trust property against the trust purpose, the position advanced here is that this right also exists as a means of preserving the beneficiary's personal claim. This right comes from the nature of a creditor's right to revoke, rather than a right of recovery based on real rights.

Taking Chinese law as an example, the beneficiary's right of revocation is regulated in article 22, paragraph 1 of the Trust Law of China:

> Where the trustee disposes of the trust property in breach of the purposes of the trust, or causes losses to the trust property due to his departure from his administrative duties or improper handling of trust business, the settlor shall have the right to apply to the People's Court for annulling such disposition and the right to ask the trustee to restore the property to its former state or make compensation. Where a transferee of the said trust property accepts the property while knowing the violation of the purposes of the trust, he shall return the property or make compensation.[51]

These stipulations appear to present similarities between the right of revocation in trusts and the right of recovery under the real rights regime; that is, '[w]here an immovable or movable property is possessed by a person not entitled to do so, the rightsholder may request restitution'.[52] However, this conceptualisation ignores the fact that the right of recovery under the real rights regime is not the only analogue of the beneficiary's right of revocation and that real rights are not the only basis for the right of revocation. In actual fact, the right to annul the trustee's wrongful disposal can also be based on personal claims. Similarly, pursuant to the right of revocation in personal claims, a creditor may also request that the court annul a debtor's disposal of property or rights when it would jeopardise the realisation of personal claims. As prescribed in article 74 of the Contract Law of China:

> Where the obligor waives its creditor's right against a third party that is due or assigns its property without reward, thereby harming the obligee's interests, the obligee may petition the People's Court for cancellation of the obligor's act. Where the obligor assigns its property at a low price which is manifestly unreasonable, thereby harming the obligee's interests, and the assignee is aware of the situation, the obligee may also petition the People's Court for cancellation of the obligor's act.[53]

It can be seen therefore that the right of revocation is not solely based on real rights but can also be exercised by creditors with personal claims when debtors damage their interests.

[51] Trust Law of China, art 22.
[52] Civil Code of China, art 235.
[53] Contract Law of China, art 74.

The author's argument is that the beneficiary's right of revocation is in the nature of a creditor's revocation right but not a recovery of real rights. That is because, in contrary to the recovery of real rights for which the purpose is to resume the control of property,[54] the right of revocation in the trust aims primarily at preserving the trust property instead of controlling them. Even when the trust property is returned to the trust as a result of the beneficiary's right of revocation, it reverts back to the control of the trustee while the beneficiary still has no power over the trust property. In addition, some of the beneficiary's rights to annul the trustee's act can only be a creditor's rights to annul. For instance, when the trustee releases the debts that are held as trust property, the beneficiary's right to annul this disposal cannot be a recovery of real rights because an application of real rights recovery requires the trustee to dispose of the trust property.[55] Nevertheless, a creditor's right to annul can apply to preserve the trust property.[56] Consequently, it is more reasonable to characterise the beneficiary's right to annul trustee's disposal as a creditor's right of revocation, rather than a right of recovery associated with real rights.[57]

In sum, therefore, this chapter interprets the beneficiary's rights as a special personal claim that constitutes of three parts: the main claim (personal claims); appurtenant rights (right of supervision); and security rights (right of revocation). This aligns with the basic rule of trusts, which states that the independence of trust property requires the separation of trust assets from trustees' personal wealth, in that the beneficiary's interest is secured in the event of the trustees' bankruptcy or death.

C. Special Personal Claim Theory: A Developed Understanding of the Beneficiary's Interest

The theory of special personal claim provides a more unified and developed understanding of the beneficiary's interest. On the one hand, it better suits civil law systems compared with the common law theory of rights against rights. The special personal claim theory causes no fundamental change to either the basic rule of trusts or the civil law framework. On the other hand, it provides a simple, unified restatement of the beneficiary's interests that is applicable in both family and commercial and to both fixed and discretionary contexts, while the traditional common law argument of equitable rights is limited to fixed trusts.

[54] L Wang, *Property Law Research*, 4th edn (Beijing, China Renmin University Press, 2016) 201.

[55] ibid 204.

[56] Wang (n 45) 190 [translated by author].

[57] A similar point is also made in Scots law. See, for example, GL Gretton, 'Trusts Without Equity' (2000) 49 *ICLQ* 599, 606–08. The reason why the beneficiary's rights seem to prevail over those of unsecured rights of trustee's personal creditors is not because the beneficiary's rights are real rights. Instead, it is because the beneficiary is claiming against the trustee's special patrimony. This type of claim is different from the trustee's personal patrimony claim against the trustee's personal creditors.

The recent argument of common law scholars claims that equitable property rights are best understood as rights against rights, but not as property rights (rights against things) or as personal rights (rights against persons).[58] The notion of rights against rights – a type of right belonging to neither real rights nor personal claims – finds no place in civilian legal frameworks. By contrast, the special personal claim theory, which does not prevent the beneficiary's right from being characterised to a personal claim, is more suitable in civil law jurisdictions. As Smith argues,

> [t]his idea is not alien to the civil law, which also recognizes that while a personal obligation does not create a real right but only a claim against a particular debtor, nonetheless it is possible that there might be claims in delict against third parties who wrongfully interfere in the performance of an obligation.[59]

As opposed to the 'rights against rights' argument, the theory of a beneficiary's special personal claim fits well into the civil law property system, where ownership is absolute. A long-standing historical debate on the nature of beneficiaries' rights is particularly concerned with the application of the common law concept of ownership (rights *in rem* and rights *in personam* under the English law of property) where it is ill-fitting.[60] The theory of a beneficiary's special personal claim overcomes this difficulty, and provides a developed understanding of the beneficiary's interests that not only provides a response to the evolution of trust for commercial uses, but also broadly applies in a worldwide context, where the concept of equitable ownership does not universally apply.

Under common law, a widely accepted theory of the nature of a beneficiary's right holds that a beneficiary has a variety of equitable rights arising from the trust, which may be both personal and proprietary. That is, a beneficiary's rights can be predicated both on the beneficiary's personal rights against the trustees and on any proprietary interests in an external relationship with a third party.[61] By this reading, a beneficiary may bring proceedings *in personam* against trustees for a breach of trust; however, such a claim may be subject to time limits imposed by a limitation statute.[62] The beneficiary might also execute a proprietary right against the trustees to recover (ie trace) the trust property.[63] As Smith notes,

> [t]he rights of beneficiaries in the common law trust are neither purely personal rights against the trustee, nor are they real rights in the trust property, but rather they are

[58] See B McFarlane and R Stevens, 'The Nature of Equitable Property' (2010) 4 *The Journal of Equity* 44.

[59] L Smith, 'Trust and Patrimony' (2009) 28 *Estates, Trusts & Pensions Journal* 332, 343.

[60] Penner (n 10) 41.

[61] PS Davies and G Virgo, *Equity & Trusts: Text, Cases, and Materials*, 3rd edn (Oxford, Oxford University Press, 2019) 485.

[62] For example, see Limitation Act 1980, s 21 Time limit for actions in respect of trust property, para (3): 'an action by a beneficiary to recover trust property or in respect of any breach of trust, not being an action for which a period of limitation is prescribed by any other provision of this Act, shall not be brought after the expiration of six years from the date on which the right of action accrued'.

[63] M Ramjoin, *Text, Cases and Materials on Equity and Trusts*, 4th edn (Oxon, Routledge Cavendish, 2008) 539.

> rights over the rights which the trustee holds as trust property; they have a proprietary character since they persist against many third party transferees of the trust property.[64]

Lord Browne-Wilkinson recognised a beneficiary's proprietary rights under common law in *Westdeutsche Landesbank Girozentrale v Islington London Borough Council*,[65] holding that the beneficiary has a proprietary interest in the trust property, which is, in equity, enforceable against any subsequent holder of the property other than a purchaser for value of the legal interest without notice. Noland's classic statement on the nature of a beneficiary's proprietary rights asserts that '[t]he key proprietary features of a beneficiary's interest under a trust are his primary negative right to exclude non-beneficiaries from enjoyment of trust assets and secondary rights to vindicate that primary right if it is infringed'.[66]

While preserving the fundamental rule of common law, the theory of a beneficiary's special personal claim is more developed than the traditional common law argument of equitable rights. This is because the special personal claim theory provides a simple and unified restatement of the beneficiary's interests that applies to different types of trusts, both fixed and discretionary. In contrast, traditional common law analysis perceives the nature of a beneficiary's rights as dependent on the type of trust involved;[67] it recognises proprietary rights in fixed trusts but not in discretionary trusts. In *Gartside v Commissioners of Inland Revenue*,[68] Lord Wilberforce made clear that the object of a discretionary trust, a trust under which the trustee has the discretion to select for distribution amongst members, does not have a proprietary right to trust property.

'One consequence of the beneficiary having a proprietary interest in the trust property is that, if the trustee becomes insolvent, the property will not be available to the trustee's creditors.'[69] This seems to suggest that, according to the common law theory of personal and proprietary rights, a beneficiary in a discretionary trust cannot be protected from the claims of a trustee's personal creditors. This clearly contradicts with the essence of trusts: that trust property is independent from trustees' personal assets. Moreover, the common law proprietary theory advocates that the beneficiary in a discretionary trust is unable to recover trust property when the property is misappropriated by the trustee and transferred to a third party. This also conflicts with the fundamental rule of trust that beneficiaries are able to trace trust property in the hand of a third party who are not in good faith. Therefore, when comparing with the common law theory of personal and proprietary right, the theory of special personal claim provides a more complete protection to beneficiaries, especially in discretional trusts where the proprietary claim imposes disadvantages.[70]

[64] Smith (n 59) 332.
[65] *Westdeutsche Landesbank Girozentrale v Islington London Borough Council* [1996] AC 669, 705.
[66] R Nolan, 'Equitable Property' (2006) 122 *LQR* 232, 236.
[67] Davies and Virgo (n 61) 485.
[68] *Gartside v Commissioners of Inland Revenue* [1968] AC 553, 617.
[69] Davies and Virgo (n 61) 487.
[70] Zhang (n 34) 355.

A universal restatement of the nature of a beneficiary's interests not only resolves any discrepancy incurred when applying the law to different types of trusts but also responds to the recently developed role of trusts within a commercial context. Commercial dealings have significantly influenced the beneficiary's rights,[71] and consequently driven the development of the law.

First, almost all of the recent litigation surrounding the proprietary tracing claim and the 'knowing' stranger personal actions engage parties in a contractual relationship and at least one of them is a commercial actor, such as in *Halifax BS v Thomas*.[72] Even going beyond the context of a contractual relationship, beneficiary's actions still primarily involve those who have been victims of fraud or theft.[73] In other words, personal claims have been used as the main remedy in both cases of a contractual relationship or a tort.[74]

Thus, the theory of a special personal claim provides a consistent understanding of and protection for a beneficiary's rights in different commercial contexts. Key common law advocates have envisaged that commercial cases would both seek to accommodate the proprietary entitlement of owners in law and equity alike and permit the simplicity of the common law approach (notably, the unified set of tracing rules envisioned by Lord Millett). The huge volume of commercial fiduciary litigation generated thus far has encouraged this idea and indicated the need for a universal set of tracing rules.[75] The theory of a special personal claim responds to this need and provides a unified and simplified rule as anticipated.

III. Conclusion

The evolved role of trusts in commercial contexts and their introduction into civil law require a new judicial interpretation of the beneficiary's interest. This chapter addresses this issue and argues that the beneficiary's rights can be explained

[71] Commercial dealings have significantly influenced the beneficiary's rights in relation to both the proprietary tracing action and equity's personal actions for knowing receipt and dishonest assistance. See S Wilson, *Todd & Wilson's Textbook on Trusts & Equity*, 12th edn (Oxford, Oxford University Press, 2015) 450 and 452: 'The so-called commercial swap agreements from the 1990s involving public authorities have been enormously influential in shaping the nature of the proprietary tracing claim for the twenty-first century. A number of cases – famously, *Westdeutsche*, but also *Guinness Mahon & Co v Kensington and Chelsea* [1998] 2 All ER 272 and earlier *Hazell v Hammersmith* [1991] 2 WLR 372 – became the battleground for competing views on proprietary entitlement and restitution.' With respect to the liability for knowing receipt, the significance of the commercial dealings has been crucial in the difficulties experienced in establishing the standard for liability to arise. 'Indeed as a number of cases prior to *BCCI (Overseas) Ltd v Akindele* [2000] 3 WLR 1423 demonstrate, it is the speed of commercial transactions that is seen as being responsible for difficulties in determining what degree of knowledge under *Baden Delvaux* [1983] BCLC 325 was required for liability to arise ….'

[72] *Halifax BS v Thomas* [1996] Ch 217.

[73] Wilson (n 71) 451.

[74] Zhang (n 34) 355–56.

[75] See Wilson (n 71) 452.

as personal claims as opposed to real rights, and they are special because some rights are beyond the traditional scope of personal claims. The special personal claim consists of three parts: the main claim (personal claims); appurtenant rights (rights of supervision); and security rights (rights of revocation). It is hoped that this book will give rise to a reassessment of the traditional theory of the beneficiary's interest.

5

A Developed Understanding of the Trustee's Role in Commercial Trusts*

Along with the evolved commercial uses of trusts, a trustee's rights and obligations have become more expanded and onerous in response to beneficiaries' increasing expectations. This invites scholars to examine the changes and challenges of the trustee's role developing from family trusts to commercial trusts. It also raises the question of whether the changes and challenges that the commercial uses have brought to trusts advocate a separation of commercial trusts from trusts. This chapter addresses those two questions in two separate parts.[1]

I. Changes and Challenges of the Role of a Trustee

This section examines the key differences between the trustee's role in family trusts and their role in commercial trusts, analysing how challenges and changes to these roles have impacted trust law. These changes and challenges can be divided into five types: those affecting the person acting as a trustee; those affecting trust property; those affecting trustees' rights and powers; those affecting trustees' duties and liabilities; and those determining whether a trustee's role is regulated by the law or by the terms of the trust.

A. Changes and Challenges Affecting the Trustee

The first difference between a trustee's role in a traditional family context and their role in a commercial trust is in the trustees themselves. In most cases, the trustee of a traditional family trust is a friend or family member of the settlor or a person of high repute,[2] who is well-known to, and trusted by, the settlor.[3] They are

* This chapter draws on previously published work in R Zhang, 'Changes and Challenges of the Role of a Trustee in a Commercial Context: Does This Separate Commercial Trusts from Trusts?' (2021) 42 *Business Law Review* 262.

[1] Analysis in this chapter mostly focuses on trusts for investment purposes in the UK as an example, but the principles developed could have a wider application to various types of commercial trusts.

[2] Family trusts nowadays also adopt professional trustees, such as lawyers or legal persons.

[3] See especially C Stebbings, *The Private Trustee in Victorian England* (Cambridge, Cambridge University Press, 2002) 129; N D'Angelo, *Commercial Trusts* (Chatswood, LexisNexis Butterworths, 2014);

commonly non-experts who have the sole and simple duty of transferring wealth to the trust beneficiaries in due course.[4] For example, in the earliest cases of trusts, a landowner (the settlor) executed a conveyance known as a 'feoffment', which transferred ownership of their land to a friend or gentleman to act as the trustee. The trustee held the property with the understanding that, at a future date, they would transfer the property to the trust beneficiaries (eg, to the settlor's children, the settlor's spouse, to the trustee themselves, or to others according to instructions from the settlor).[5]

Modern trust practice has evolved and expanded beyond these historical examples. In contrast to traditional family trustees, who are natural persons in most cases, a commercial trustee is normally a corporate trustee: a legal person that remains at arm's length from all the other participants in the trust (such as a depository or equity investors[6]).[7] Unlike trustees in traditional trusts, who jointly exercise the trustee's rights and duties, the functions of commercial trustees are often delegated to professionals, who are expected to provide specific expertise to the role.[8]

Investments in trust funds require a high degree of insight and commercial acumen; for this reason, trustees with specialist skills are needed.[9] In a UK unit trust (see chapter two, section I.A) the functions of a trustee are performed by two parties: a trustee in name, who holds the trust assets; and a trust manager, who selects and runs the investments, makes decisions relating to the value of the trust units, and administers the investment fund.

Both the trustee in name and the manager are corporations and must be separate entities.[10] The trustee in name is usually a well-known bank that legally holds a trust fund on behalf of unitholders (the beneficiaries and settlors of the trust). It is able to obtain the unitholders' trust and invest in it through the immense amount of available capital it holds and its stable financing base.

S Wilson, *Todd & Wilson's Textbook on Trusts & Equity*, 12th edn (Oxford, Oxford University Press, 2015) 29.

[4] See especially *Robinson v Pett* (1734) 3 Peere Williams 249, 251; JH Langbein, 'The Contractarian Basis of the Law of Trusts' (1995) 105 *Yale Law Journal* 625, 632–43.

[5] See JH Langbein, RL Lerner and BP Smith, *History of the Common Law: The Development of Anglo-American Legal Institutions* (New York, Aspen Publishers, 2009) 299–311.

[6] In commercial trusts, particularly trusts for investment purposes, the beneficiaries are usually the same person as the settlors, who invest their property to a trust for their own interests, and are known as equity investors. Investors occupy the position of trust beneficiaries, and thus have a beneficial interest in the underlying investment.

[7] D'Angelo (n 3) 152.

[8] A professional trustee is defined in s 28(5) of the Trustee Act 2000: 'a trustee acts in a professional capacity if he acts in the course of a profession or business which consists of or includes the provision of services in connection with (a) the management or administration of trusts generally or a particular kind of trust, or (b) any particular aspect of the management or administration of trusts generally or a particular kind of trust'.

[9] M Haley, 'Section 61 of the Trustee Act 1925: A Judicious Breach of Trust?' (2017) 76(3) CLJ 537, 541.

[10] Financial Services and Markets Act 2000, ss 242(2) and 243(4)(5).

The manager, with whom the trustee in name will have signed a trust deed, is an investment expert who is able to identify new areas and asset classes that the trustee may not be aware of due to a lack of sufficient knowledge and expertise in the area.[11] Thus, the manager is responsible for the day-to-day running of the unit trust, which role includes investment selection and trust fund administration. The manager sets a value for the trust units according to a formula and is obliged to buy back units when the investors (the unitholders) wish to redeem them.[12]

This reveals that the role of a commercial trustee, in a broad sense, is a complex form of the traditional trustee, and such complexity (eg delegating the trustee's role to professionals) is the result of, and response to, the challenges that elaborate business and diverse commercial use have brought to trusts.[13]

Due to their professional skills and active management of trust funds, commercial trustees (as opposed to traditional trustees) do not act for free nor for a nominal payment. Trusteeship within a commercial context has become a well-paid role in the UK and in other jurisdictions.[14] For example, *Cradock v Piper*,[15] an Australian case in 1850, the court permitted a solicitor-trustee to charge for his professional services in relation to litigation he performed in the absence of a charging clause. At that time, this decision was in apparent violation of the strict and general principle of the law of trusts that stated that trustees had to act without being remunerated for doing so. The Trustee Act 2000 states that '[a]ny payments to which the trustee is entitled in respect of services are to be treated as remuneration for services.'[16] The level of remuneration to which trustees are entitled may be seen as a deterrent to the creation of trusts.[17] As Langbein has contended, the distinction between gratuitous transfer and bargained-for exchange forms the fundamental division between traditional trusts and commercial trusts.[18]

B. Changes and Challenges Affecting Trust Property

Following the development of a trust, the property that trustees hold or manage has expanded from landholdings, to all kinds of property within the family, and

[11] M Wain and M Shenkin, 'Trustee Investment Powers and the Use of Asset Managers' (2009) 15(2) *Trusts & Trustees* 72, 76.

[12] See especially Financial Services and Markets Act 2000, s 243(10); M Graziadei, U Mattei and L Smith, 'Commercial Trusts in European Private Law: The Interest and Scope of the Enquiry' in M Graziadei, U Mattei and L Smith (eds), *Commercial Trusts in European Private Law* (Cambridge, Cambridge University Press, 2005) 459; N Simmonds and M Shah, 'Investment Funds: Overview' (2016) *Practice Law*, uk.practicallaw.thomsonreuters.com/4-203-1837.

[13] R Zhang, 'Changes and Challenges of the Role of a Trustee in a Commercial Context: Does This Separate Commercial Trusts from Trusts?' (2021) 42 *Business Law Review* 262, 263.

[14] WA Lee, 'Trustee Investing: Homes and Hedges' (2001) 1(1) *Queensland University of Technology Law and Justice* 3, 19.

[15] *Cradock v Piper* (1850) 1 Mac & G 664.

[16] Trustee Act 2000, s 28(4).

[17] Lee (n 14) 19.

[18] JH Langbein, 'The Secret Life of the Trust: The Trust as an Instrument of Commerce' (1997) 107 *Yale Law Journal* 165, 184.

then to its significant use today, which is a portfolio of financial assets (ie incorporeal wealth).[19] Also, the scope of investments that commercial trustees can make has extended from a narrower range of the so-called 'safe' investment to any kind of investment that is granted by the general power of investment.

Traditionally, trust law imposed, by default, a set of heavy restrictions on investment. One such restriction was that trustees could invest only in land, followed by government securities, while investments in new commercial vehicles were forbidden.[20] In the early eighteenth century, trustees' investments in England mainly took the form of investments in land, although there were sizeable trust funds in existence, and investment opportunities in new and exciting commercial ventures arose. These new opportunities received a negative reaction, to the extent that investment in commercial enterprises was viewed as speculative and an undesirable means of trust investment.[21] This perception lasted for a significant period, persisting even when investment spread out from land to government securities when the boom years of the nineteenth century engineered a belief in the reliability of government stock.[22]

The extreme popularity of trusts among the industrial and professional middle classes of Victorian England facilitated the inclusion of financial securities, in increasing proportions, into trust assets.[23] In the 1950s, by order of the court, trustees were allowed to invest in fixed interest stocks and equities.[24] A fairly extensive list of investments was authorised in England by the Trustee Act 1925,[25] which was superseded by the Trustee Investment Act 1961.[26] The Trustee Investment Act 1961 restricted investment to a defined scope of so-called 'safe' investments, while a wider range of investments could only be made based on advice.[27] The authorised list of investments permitted by the 1961 Act was determined to be too restrictive and out of touch with modern portfolio theory; it was thought that the written advice requirement was unnecessary, because advisers were already regulated by the standards listed in the Financial Services Act 1986.[28] The Law Reform Committee advocated that the statutory powers of investment in the

[19] PS Davies and G Virgo (eds), *Equity & Trusts: Text, Cases, and Materials*, 3rd edn (Oxford, Oxford University Press, 2019) 25.

[20] MR Chesterman, 'Family Settlements on Trust: Landowners and the Rising Bourgeoisie' in GR Rubin and D Sugarman (eds), *Law, Economy and Society, 1750–1914: Essays in the History of English Law* (Abingdon, Professional Books, 1984) 124, 159–60.

[21] A trustee, as a person of ordinary prudence, was asked to avoid hazardous investments, per Lord Watson in *Learoyd v Whiteley* [1887] UKHL 1, (1887) 12 AC 727, 733.

[22] HL Thompson, 'Impact of the New Law on Trustee's Investment Powers' (1998) 4(8) *Trusts & Trustees* 16, 16.

[23] P Panico, 'Trustee Investment Powers in International Trust Law' (2009) 15(2) *Trusts & Trustees* 96, 96.

[24] B Dale, 'Varying Trustees' Investment Powers' (1988) 5 *The Conveyancer and Property Lawyer* 380, 381.

[25] Trustee Act 1925.

[26] Trustee Investment Act 1961.

[27] ibid sch 1, pts II and III.

[28] Thompson (n 22) 16.

Trustee Investments Act 1961 ought to be revised as they were tiresome, cumbrous and out of date.[29] As a result, the Trustee Act 2000[30] repealed the former Trustee Investment Act 1961 and reformed the law to grant a trustee 'the general power of investment', which enables a trustee to 'make any kind of investment that he could make if he were absolutely entitled to the assets of the trust'.[31] The law governing permitted investments now allows the inclusion of funds that invest in land[32] and in high-risk investments like futures and options.[33]

C. Changes and Challenges Affecting Trustee's Rights and Powers

Traditional trustees are expected to hold trust property in a passive and risk-averse manner. That is, a traditional trustee is often required to simply hold trust property, preserve its value, and transfer it to trust beneficiaries, with no or very few responsibilities regarding managing the trust property.[34] This is because the principle behind the creation of a traditional trust was that, by giving property to a trustee, a landowner could avoid a set of obligations that applied to them. The most famous example of this is the set of death taxes and military obligations that modern historians call the 'feudal incidents'.[35] In other words, the family trust plays the traditional role of providing custodianship over ring-fenced assets,[36] requiring the trustee to engage in no or very little active management over the trust assets.[37] From late medieval times to the early twentieth century, a trustee's main job was simply to hold a family estate[38] and pass it over to the next generation; the fiduciary duties of the trustees prevented them from disobeying a family's wishes by

[29] Dale (n 24) 380–81.

[30] Trustee Act 2000.

[31] ibid s 3(1). The general investment power is 'subject to restriction or exclusion imposed by the trust instrument or by any enactment or any provision of subordinate legislation', per s 6(1)(b).

[32] See Trustee Act 2000, the general power of investment does not permit a trustee to make investments in land other than in loans secured on land, per s 3(3), with exception that a trustee may acquire freehold or leasehold land in the UK as an investment, having all the powers of an absolute owner in relation to the land, per s 8.

[33] See 'High Return Investment' (FCA, 1 June 2020).

[34] See especially *Re Boston's Will Trusts* [1956] 1 Ch 395, 405; *Hallows v Lloyd* (1888) 39 Ch D 686, 691; *Elektrim SA v Vivendi Holdings 1 Corp* [2008] EWCA Civ 1178; Langbein, Lerner and Smith (n 5) 299–311; Davies and Virgo (n 19) 530.

[35] See JMW Bean, *The Decline of English Feudalism, 1215–1540* (Manchester, Manchester University Press, 1968) 5–20.

[36] M Yip, 'The Commercial Context in Trust Law' (2016) 5 *The Conveyancer and Property Lawyer* 347, 358.

[37] Examples of little active power possessed by family trustees can be found in spendthrift trusts, wherein a trustee (usually the settlor's surviving spouse) has freedom to distribute benefits to a different person or decide when to distribute income or capital to the selected beneficiaries in changing circumstances.

[38] Originally consisted exclusively of land but now includes all kinds of family property.

doing anything beyond this,[39] and trust law at that time disabled the trustees' ability to exercise several of their powers.[40] By default, trustees had almost no powers unless a settlor expressly granted powers to them. They could not buy or sell trust property without specific authorisation.[41] Even in a discretionary trust, the trustee's discretion to allocate trust assets among a class of beneficiaries is authorised by the settlor.[42] Trust law grew into this mould through habitual action; that is, it matched what trustees had traditionally always done.[43]

However, this passive and risk-avoiding approach has introduced difficulties and challenges to the use of trusts for commercial purposes. It has hobbled the trustees' endeavours to carry out the complex and varied activities required by commercial trusts.[44] Nowadays, trusts are mostly used as commercial vehicles to raise funds by investors who purchase an equitable interest, and thus acquire beneficiary status, by subscription or transfer in return for a risk premium. Therefore, it is no longer satisfactory that investments or businesses are simply held and preserved by trustees to be safe and sound.[45] The trustees of commercial trusts are expected to generate profits through various business activities, involving risk-taking behaviour.[46] The trustee's role has transitioned from primarily that of custodianship and being passive and risk-avoiding to embracing the active and risk-taking management of a trust fund for a commercial purpose.[47]

Trustees in commercial contexts have greater discretion than that permitted to traditional trustees. This leeway allows them to promptly respond to rapidly changing markets and to increase (rather than merely preserve) the value of the trust property.[48] When the 'authorised investment list' approach was very much in force in England, the decision of *Re Harari's Settlement Trusts*[49] established that a clause permitting trustees to select investments as they saw fit was valid and should be construed according to its widest meaning. Given the large amount of

[39] See especially Langbein (n 4) 640–42; JH Langbein, 'The Rise of the Management Trust' (2004) 143 *Real Property, Trust and Estate Law Journal* 52, 53; JH Langbein, 'Questioning the Trust Law Duty of Loyalty: Sole Interest or Best Interest?' (2005) 114 *Yale Law Journal* 929, 947; J Baker, *An Introduction to English Legal History*, 5th edn (Oxford, Oxford University Press, 2019) 269–70.

[40] Langbein (n 4) 640–42.

[41] Chesterman (n 20) 159–60.

[42] Known as trustee's power of selection under discretionary trusts, a trustee has the discretion to determine the amount and time to dispose of trust property as they think fit. At times, they also have the discretion as to the form in which the disposition is to be made.

[43] J Morley, 'The Common Law Corporation: The Power of the Trust in Anglo-American Business History' (2016) 116(2) *Columbia Law Review* 2145, 2195.

[44] R Harris, *Industrializing English Law: Entrepreneurship and Business Organization, 1720–1844* (Cambridge, Cambridge University Press, 2009) 147–59.

[45] *Alexander v Johnstone* [1899] SLT 453_2.

[46] See especially *Cowan v Scargill* [1985] Ch 270 [8]; D'Angelo (n 3) 7 and 160.

[47] See W Cornish and others, *The Oxford History of the Laws of England: Volume XII: 1820–1914 Private Law* (Oxford, Oxford University Press, 2010) 232–68.

[48] See especially M Kahan, 'Rethinking Corporate Bonds: The Trade-off between Individual and Collective Rights' (2002) 77 *New York University Law Review* 1040; Graziadei, Mattei and Smith (n 12) 38.

[49] *Re Harari's Settlement Trusts* [1949] 1 All ER 430.

social wealth, the modern trends in trustees' discretion are claimed to be towards liberalisation, freedom of choice, and the free participation of trust funds in commercial markets, in accordance with modern portfolio theory and the modern paradigm of prudence.[50]

In practice, however, some cases have gone too far, with courts allowing actions by trustees that seem to abuse their discretion by waiving their core duties in commercial contexts. This should be corrected and avoided when recognising and regulating commercial trustee's rights and duties. For example, in *Citibank NA v MBIA Assurance SA*,[51] Citibank, the security trustee, applied to the court for direction as the trust deed advised that it need not have regard to the interests of the noteholders (the beneficiaries) when acting on MBIA's instructions. MBIA acted as the note guarantor, which had the right to give Citibank mandatory instructions. In the author's view, the issues that arise in this case are twofold: (a) Can a trustee's core duty to act for the interests of beneficiaries be waived by trust terms? Or, more broadly, can the principle of freedom of contract supersede trust law principles?[52] And (b) can a trustee be obliged to act following a third person's direction (the note guarantor MBIA in this case), except for when a settlor retains the ownership of trust property and any of its incidental powers?[53] The answers to both questions are negative; otherwise, it would violate the fundamental rule of trusts: trustees are required to act in the best interests of the beneficiaries, and the trustees are the legal owners of trust property, who have the freedom to manage and administer the trust property.[54]

In this case, and to the author's disappointment, Arden LJ noted that Citibank's powers as a trustee were not so diminished that it ceased to be a trustee because Citibank still owed at all times an obligation of good faith, and there were other provisions in the trust deed that granted Citibank real discretion permitting it exercise independently.[55] This decision, unsurprisingly, was not well accepted by equity lawyers.[56] Acting in good faith does not justify the removal of a trustee's core duty to act in the interests of beneficiaries by the trust's terms. Indeed, the duty to act in the beneficiary's interests is the basis of its derived duty of acting in good faith.[57] '[T]he duties of good faith and that the trustee is required to act for

[50] G Watt and P Todd, *Cases & Materials on Equity and Trusts,* 10th edn (Oxford, Oxford University Press, 2016) 387.

[51] *Citibank NA v MBIA Assurance SA* [2007] EWCA Civ 11.

[52] A Trukhtanov, 'The Irreducible Core of Trust Obligations' (2007) 123 *LQR* 342; cf T Cutts, 'The Nature of Equitable Property: A Functional Analysis' (2012) 6 *Journal of Equity* 44, 48–49.

[53] The settlor's retention of certain investments is not a breach of trust itself. Proof can be found, in particular in the statutes of jurisdictions that adopt the 'prudent investor standard', such as New Zealand (Trustee Act 1956, s 13H), the Bahamas (Trustee Act 1998, s 7), and those still partially sticking to the UK Trustee Act 1925, such as the Cayman Islands (Trusts Law (2007 Revision), s 38).

[54] See especially *Cowan v Scargill* [1985] Ch 270; *Armitage v Nurse* [1998] Ch 241; JE Penner, *The Law of Trusts*, 12th edn (Oxford, Oxford University Press, 2022) 3–8.

[55] *Citibank NA v MBIA Assurance SA* [2007] EWCA Civ 11 [82].

[56] G Virgo, *The Principles of Equity & Trusts*, 5th edn (Oxford, Oxford University Press, 2023) 505.

[57] Zhang (n 13) 265.

the benefit of the beneficiaries relate to the performance of all the trustee's functions, and not merely some of them.'[58]

D. Changes and Challenges Affecting Trustee's Duties and Liabilities

The changes to, and challenges affecting, a trustee's role, which have arisen from the use of trusts in a commercial context, are also reflected in the trustees' liabilities and duties. Traditional trustees are burdened with unlimited personal liability, whereas commercial trustees' liabilities are limited.

Limited liability, as Morley states, was simply not an issue in early trust law. In the prototypical family gift trust of medieval England, a trustee held only land and not active businesses, and for this reason the trustee rarely owned any liabilities that could spill onto beneficiaries or necessitate limitations on their liabilities.[59] In other words, it is not necessary to limit a trustee's liability in traditional family trusts when the trustee's duty is too simple to go beyond holding and distributing trust property. In commercial trusts, the trustee's duty is no longer that straightforward.[60] More participants are involved and they conduct composite business. In these circumstances, where a trustee breaches their duties, limited liability will apply for loss thereby occasioned.[61]

Although limited, the liabilities and duties of the commercial trustees are more rigorous and intricate than those of traditional trustees. Amateur trustees of traditional family trusts are more likely to be relieved of liability for breaches of trust.[62] While the Privy Council fell short of advising that relief should never be extended to a professional trustee, Sir Ford North emphasised that the position of commercial trustees was 'widely different from that of a private person acting as gratuitous trustee'.[63] Relief might be denied to a trustee on the basis that it is a trust company that has received payment for its services, as suggested in *National Trustees Co of Australasia Ltd v General Finance Co of Australasia Ltd*[64] and *Cherney & Ors v Neuman & Ors*.[65] As asserted by the Law Commission, '[v]ery different considerations apply where professional trustees are concerned'.[66] Trustee's fault is not

[58] Yip (n 36) 357.
[59] Morley (n 43) 2175.
[60] Zhang (n 13) 265.
[61] See, eg, *Cox v Hickman* (1860) 8 HLC 268.
[62] Davies and Virgo (n 19) 749–52.
[63] *National Trustees Co of Australasia Ltd v General Finance Co of Australasia Ltd* [1905] AC 373, 381. Sir Ford North also added that 'it is a circumstance to be taken into account, and they [their Lordships] do not find here any fair excuse for the breach of trust, or any reason why the respondents, who have committed no fault, should lose their money to relieve the appellants, who have done a wrong'.
[64] *National Trustees Co of Australasia Ltd v General Finance Co of Australasia Ltd* [1905] AC 373.
[65] *Cherney & Ors v Neuman & Ors* [2011] EWHC 2156 (Ch) [321] (Henderson J).
[66] *Trustee Exemption Clauses* (Law Com CP No 171, 1999) paras 4.12 and 4.29.

required for liabilities.[67] And higher standards of care are imposed on professional trustees who act for reward by both case law and legislation. Harman J stated in *Re Waterman's Will Trust*[68] that 'a paid trustee is expected to exercise a higher standard of diligence and knowledge than an unpaid trustee'.[69] According to *Bartlett v Barclays Bank Trust Co Ltd*,[70] commercial trustees must exercise their special skills and care that they profess to and are being paid to have.[71] Pursuant to the Trustee Act 2000, when a trustee is engaged in a business or profession, it should exercise the duty of care according to its special knowledge or experience that is reasonably expected.[72] The core duty of a trustee (the fiduciary duty) is also developed in the sense that, in addition to the general requirements of exercising power in the best interests of the present and future beneficiaries of the trust, an explicit obligation is imposed to request that the trustee yields the best return for the beneficiaries, where the purpose of a trust is to provide financial benefits.[73]

One of the most important, and probably complex, tasks or challenges that arise for commercial trustees is to identify and reduce the level of risk appropriate to the trust.[74] As a trust fund must not be disposed at undue risk, trustees are required to identify trust-appropriate investment strategies when investment power is authorised.[75] A modern portfolio theory is introduced, which suggests that, when considering investment risks, trustees should proactively account for systemic risk (in the context of a portfolio) of the assets rather than their individual risk (taken in isolation).[76] The key principles established by the modern portfolio theory are that a trustee can invest in any kind of asset; each asset should be considered not in isolation but in the context of an adequately diversified portfolio; and the trustee is required to follow a certain standard of care while exercising their investment powers.[77] Also, there are often provisions regulating

[67] *AIB Group (UK) plc v Mark Redler & Co Solicitors* [2014] UKSC 58 [98] (Pattern LJ). The common law rule of remoteness of damage and causation do not apply. That is, the trustee is required to make good the loss suffered by the beneficiary regardless of whether the immediate cause is dishonesty or failure of a third party. As stated by Browne-Wilkinson in *Target Holdings Ltd v Redferns* [1996] AC 421, 434, 'the fact that the loss would not have occurred but for the breach' is necessary condition for imposing liability.

[68] *Re Waterman's Will Trust* [1952] 2 All ER 1054.

[69] ibid 1055.

[70] *Bartlett v Barclays Bank Trust Co Ltd* [1980] 1 Ch 515.

[71] ibid 533.

[72] Trustee Act 2000, s 1.

[73] *Cowan v Scargill* [1985] Ch 270.

[74] Wain and Shenkin (n 11) 74.

[75] As to power of investment, it is worth noting that a trustee of a commercial bare trust has no investment function or power (see *AIB Group (UK) plc v Mark Redler & Co Solicitors* [2014] UKSC 58), and trustees of a family trust may have investment power but less stringent or complex compared with commercial trustees.

[76] See Trustee Act 2000, s 4(3); Restatement (Third) of the Law of Trusts, § 227 (1992) (US); Trustees Act 1967 (Singapore), s 5(3)(b); Trustee Act 1956 (New Zealand), s 13E(a); and examples of offshore legislation: Trustee Act 1975 (Bermuda), s 55A(5), and Trustee Act 1998 (The Bahamas), s 5(1)(c).

[77] For example, Trustee Act 2000, s 4(3): 'The standard investment criteria, in relation to a trust, are (a) the suitability to the trust of investments of the same kind as any particular investment proposed to

the delegation of a trustee's investment management functions.[78] Furthermore, trustees must obtain and consider proper advice regarding the way in which their power should be performed or varied on the basis of standard investment criteria and in consideration of suitability and diversification.[79] In essence, the modern portfolio theory demonstrates the advantages of diversification, which minimises the risks and administrative costs involved in investment. Risk is minimised because diversification averages profits and losses. At the same time, administrative costs are minimised because, according to the efficient market hypothesis, trustees cannot obtain better-than-average returns through expensive enquiries designed to forecast price movements.[80] The desirability of investment diversification has been affirmed by case law from several jurisdictions – for example, the English case of *Nestle v National Westminster Bank plc*[81] and the New Zealand decision of *Re Mulligan*.[82]

Although a trustee's duty has evolved to fit the requirements of a commercial context, it still meets the fundamental requirements of trustee duty. This outlines the minimum content of a trustee's duties while differentiating the trust from other legal vehicles.[83] As Millett LJ stated in *Armitage v Nurse*:[84] 'The duty of the trustees to perform the trusts honestly and in good faith for the benefit of the beneficiaries is the minimum necessary to give substance to the trusts, but in my opinion it is sufficient.'[85] Fiduciary duty is an essential part of a trustee's responsibilities, and there is an extended willingness to adjust equitable principles in the context of commercial relationships.[86] Thus, the development of a trustee's duty in commercial contexts does not separate commercial trusts from trusts.

E. Changes and Challenges Affecting Regulations on Trustees

A traditional family trust has a crucial regulatory function.[87] Given its simplicity, the traditional trustee's role is relatively unified, because the law defines

be made or retained and of that particular investment as an investment of that kind, and (b) the need for diversification of investments of the trust, in so far as is appropriate to the circumstances of the trust'. The trust instrument may set out certain prohibited investments.

[78] Panico (n 23) 99.

[79] Trustee Act 2000, ss 3, 4 and 5.

[80] Lee (n 14) 10.

[81] *Nestle v National Westminster Bank plc* [1992] EWCA Civ 12, [1993] 1 WLR 1260.

[82] *Re Mulligan* [1998] 1 NZLR 481.

[83] Yip (n 36) 356.

[84] *Armitage v Nurse* [1998] Ch 241.

[85] ibid 253–54.

[86] See especially *Kelly v Cooper* [1992] 3 WLR 936, 942 (Lord Browne-Wilkinson); *Clark Boyce v Mouat* [1994] 1 A 428, 437 (Lord Jauncey); *Westdeutsche Landesbank Girozentrale v Islington London Borough Council* [1996] AC 669, 704 (Lord Browne-Wilkinson). See also E McKendrick (ed), *Commercial Aspects of Trust and Fiduciary Obligations* (Oxford, Oxford University Press, 1993).

[87] Yip (n 36) 347.

and regulates it. In contrast, due to the complexity and diversity of commercial trust business, the roles of commercial trustees can be disparate and thus will be predominantly determined by the specific terms of the trust.

For example, as previously discussed, a unit trust in the UK is composed of a trust deed made between the trustee in name and the manager. Corporate trustees are experts in their field, as opposed to the non-expert trustees found in a family context. The intricacy of commercial trust arrangements requires the services of professional trustees, complicating the administration of the trust and introducing further challenges to the trustee's role and to the trust itself. In response to this challenge, contracts (or trust terms) that are capable of introducing flexibility into a trust are used to regulate commercial trustees and administer trusts.

In commercial cases, the courts acknowledge trust terms as the primary regulator of the trustee's role. This is noted as a divergence between traditional trusts and commercial trusts by Lord Toulson in *AIB Group (UK) plc v Mark Redler & Co Solicitors*.[88] English judges are reluctant to interfere with terms that set out the trustee's duties.[89] Courts in the US draw a clearer line between traditional trustees and those operating in the commercial field. They maintain that the obligations of a trustee who holds financial property are exclusively defined by the trust deed.[90] There is even case law, although limited, to the effect that a fiduciary obligation may arise independently of the trust deed where there is a present, rather than theoretical, conflict between the trustee's interests and duties.[91] Both the obligations and the statutory powers granted to a trustee by the Trustee Act 2000 are subject to the trust instrument; this instrument may limit the trustee's discretion.[92]

In short, as analysed in this section, the author proposes that the main differences between the role of trustees in traditional family trusts and trusts for commercial uses are as follows. In most cases, a traditional trustee is a natural person (a friend or family member of the settlor or a person in high repute who is trusted by the settlor), while a commercial trustee is a legal person (ie a corporate trustee). Traditional trustees act gratuitously as amateur trustees; commercial trustees on the other hand are normally professionals who will be remunerated. Traditional trustees are merely expected to hold trust property of land, at first, and then all other family assets in a passive and risk-avoiding way. In contrast, commercial trustees are required to act in an active and risk-taking manner to enhance the value of the trust property, which is mainly a portfolio of financial

[88] *AIB Group (UK) plc v Mark Redler & Co Solicitors* [2014] UKSC 58.

[89] P Rawlings, 'Reinforcing Collectivity: The Liability of Trustees and the Power of Investors in Finance Transactions' (2009) 23(1) *Trust Law International* 14, 32.

[90] See especially the Trust Indenture Act of 1939 (US), §77*ooo*(a)(1); the Delaware Statutory Trust Act 1988; *Meckel v Continental Resources Co* 758 F 2d 811, 816 (2d Cir 1985); *Elliott Associates v J Henry Schroder Bank & Trust Co* 838 F 2d 66, 71 (2d Cir 1988); *Dell'Oca v Bank of New York Trust Co* 71 Cal Rptr 3d 737, 742–43 (Cal App 1 Dist, 2008).

[91] Rawlings (n 89) 15–16.

[92] Trustee Act 2000, s 6(1)(b); A Hudson, 'Trusts and Finance Law' in DJ Hayton (ed), *The International Trust*, 3rd edn (Bristol, Jordan Publishing, 2011) 649.

assets. A trustee's liability appears to differ between that of traditional family trusts (unlimited liabilities) to commercial trusts (limited liabilities). Although limited, a commercial trustee's liabilities and duties are compound and stricter, with a higher standard of care matching with their expanded discretion. A trustee's role is traditionally primarily defined by law but is largely regulated by specific trust terms in commercial contexts.[93]

II. A Commercial Trust is Still a Trust

The changes and challenges that the commercial uses of trusts have brought to the trustee's role call into question whether a commercial trust is still at essence a trust; should it be separated from trusts and regarded as an independent legal vehicle, or would it be better classified into other devices, such as companies or contracts? Four major concerns arise. First, does delegating a trustee's functions between various parties go against the fundamental role of a trustee, and therefore, does it separate commercial trusts from traditional trusts? Second, is a commercial trust better categorised as a company, considering the key role played by the corporate trustee and its overlapping identity as a company? Next, does the frequent and extensive engagement with trust terms and contracts in commercial trustee regulation suggest that a commercial trust is, essentially, a series of contracts? Finally, is trust law still capable of addressing any issues that may arise from commercial trusts?

A. Delegation of Trustees' Responsibilities

Arguably, delegating a trustee's functions between various parties does not undermine the fundamental role of a trustee, nor does it negate the trust essence of a commercial trust. This is because trust law permits the delegation of a trustee's role; in reality, such delegation is required due to the complexity of trust use in a commercial context.

The prohibition of delegation and the appointment of agents has never been seen as satisfactory in private law.[94] Even at the point of commencement, about which it has been said that trustees generally 'have no right to shift their duties on other persons',[95] the trustee's ability to appoint an agent under certain circumstances is well established. The use of specialist agents, such as stockbrokers and solicitors, to carry out purely ministerial functions has always been allowed. Case law affirms this; for instance, *Home v Pringle*[96] noted that it does not matter if

[93] Zhang (n 13) 267.
[94] PD Finn, *Fiduciary Obligations* (London, Lawbook Co, 1977) 20, fn 6.
[95] *Turner v Corney* (1841) 5 Beav 515, 517 (Lord Langdale MR).
[96] *Home v Pringle* (1841) 8 Cl and Fin 264.

the agent is also a trustee, while *Speight v Gaunt* recognised the employment of a broker selected by the beneficiary.[97] In addition, the Trustee Act 2000 permits trustees to delegate their asset management functions to an agent through a policy statement, which 'gives guidance as to how the functions should be excised', to ensure that the assets will be managed in the best interests of trust purposes.[98] As a general rule, set in s 11(1) of the Trustee Act 2000, 'the trustees of a trust may authorise any person to exercise any or all of their delegable functions as their agent'.[99] This ability to delegate a trustee's functions is recognised worldwide.[100] For example, Quebec (a jurisdiction with legal traditions in both common and civil law) allows trustees to enter into a contract with a financial expert as a manager.[101] The functions of the manager and the powers granted to the manager may be quite extensive.[102]

The delegation of a trustee's functions is required by and helps to facilitate the commercial use of trusts. Undeniably, the various commercial uses of trusts will grow in number, potentially becoming even more diversified. The financial objectives prompting the trust use can vary greatly. For example, the purpose behind a trust's use in a commercial conveyancing transaction is very different to its purpose in debt securitisation, giving rise to different considerations.[103] However, most original trustees (eg trustees in name in British unit trusts) are not capable of managing intricate business requirements or an immense investment portfolio, necessitating the delegation of trustee functions. Determining what investments are suitable and whether a portfolio is sufficiently diversified – the main task of a commercial trustee – is hugely complicated. This has led more than ever to trustees delegating their functions to qualified bodies to achieve the trust's purpose.[104] In other words, the delegation of a trustee's functions introduces greater expertise to the role of the trustee, resulting in the refashioning of the trust instrument to expand trustee powers and minimise risks.[105] A trustee can exercise its power to delegate with respect to the entire fund.[106] Thus, delegating a trustee's functions does not contradict the fundamental role of a trustee, nor does it conflict with the commercial trust's essential identity as a trust.

A further question arises from the delegation discussion; namely, whether a trustee is responsible for the actions of assigned parties (or whether the parties are responsible for their own actions). The ordinary rule seems to suggest that

[97] *Speight v Gaunt* [1883] UKHL 1.
[98] Trustee Act 2000, s 15.
[99] ibid s 11(1).
[100] See, eg, Trustee Act 1975 (Bermuda), s 15A and 15B; Trusts Law 1984 (Jersey), art 25.
[101] *Laflamme v Prudential-Bache Commodities Canada Ltd* (2000) SCC 26 (CanLII), [2000] 1 SCR 638 on CanLII.
[102] Lee (n 14) 15: see *Le contrat de gestion de portefeuille de valeurs mobilières* (1994) 25–26.
[103] *Stack v Dowden* [2007] UKHL 17, [2007] 2 AC 432, 69 (Baroness Hale) and 136 (Lord Neuberger).
[104] Wain and Shenkin (n 11) 73 and 76.
[105] Haley (n 9) 542.
[106] Wain and Shenkin (n 11) 76.

the trustee is responsible if the delegated parties are considered to be its agents.[107] However, although the term of agent is adopted in case law and by the Trustee Act 2000, a case-by-case interpretation of the relationship between the trustee and delegated parties (as opposed to fixed regulation) might be more appropriate to the rapidly developing and diversified commercial uses of trusts. Based on this concept, this book proposes that all parties that undertake the functions of a trustee (eg the trustee in name and the manager of a unit trust) should be seen as a whole as the counterpart of the trust beneficiary, and should together be responsible for securing the beneficiaries' interests or ensuring the trust fulfils its objectives. The internal relationships between the trustee and the delegated parties could be determined by the terms of the underlying delegation contracts.

The trustee should ensure that the terms agreed upon by the trustee and the manager are correctly framed in the contract[108] and that the investment manager is sufficiently knowledgeable. It is commonly the trustee that controls trust assets and instructs the investment manager.[109] The trustee must continue to monitor the performance of the investment manager. They should also review the trust investments periodically and determine whether the investments are suitable or whether they require diversification, according to the trust circumstances.[110] The trustee is obliged to take an active engagement in the trust administration in order to preserve and enhance the value of the trust fund. Failure to do so by sitting back and ignoring what is happening is done at their own risk.[111]

When carrying out these duties, it would be more reasonable to expect the manager or other delegated professional bodies to take responsibility for their own expert advice or actions (which are very likely to be beyond the expertise of the trustee in name). In many instances, appointed experts use their own judgement or discretion in their business activities and transactions.[112] Therefore, the trustee in name will not be liable for any loss to the trust arising from a delegation or appointment, if the trustee made such delegation or appointment or permitted the continuation thereof in good faith and without neglect.[113] This is also recognised by case law; for instance, *Ex parte Belchier*[114] acknowledged that 'where trustees act by other hands, either from necessity, or conformable to the common usage of mankind, they are not answerable for losses'.[115]

[107] See especially *Carruthers v Carruthers* [1896] AC 659; *Re Allsop* [1914] 1 Ch 1, 11 (Cozens-Hardy MR): 'A trustee who employs an agent must, according to the ordinary rules of law, be responsible for the acts of the agent'.

[108] *Breen v Williams* (1996) 186 CLR 71, 113 (Gaudron and McHugh JJ); *National Mutual Property Services (Australia) Pty Limited v Citibank Savings Limited* [1998] FCA 564 (Lindgren J); Lee (n 14) 16.

[109] Panico (n 23) 102.

[110] Trustee Act 2000, s 4.

[111] See *Re Lucking's Will Trust* [1967] 3 All ER 726.

[112] RP Meagher and WMC Gummow, *Jacobs' Law of Trusts in Australia*, 5th edn (Sydney, Butterworths, 1986) 404 and 405.

[113] See, eg, Trusts Law 1984 (Jersey), art 25(3).

[114] *Ex parte Belchier* (1754) Amb 218.

[115] ibid 219 (Lord Hardwicke LC).

B. Commercial Use of Trusts does not Make the Trust a Company

Is a commercial trust better classified as a company? It is this author's opinion that the commercial use of trusts does not make a trust a company. A trust is used for commercial purposes before a company appears, and it will continue to exist should the company be no more. Therefore, the commercial trust is distinct and different from a company.

By the seventeenth century, trusts were used in commerce and ultimately became a progenitor of the modern limited liability company.[116] Because of their effectiveness, both long before and long after the corporate form became freely available through statutes of general incorporation in the mid-nineteenth century, trusts were widely used in England and in the US (as a substitute for corporate) to hold the property of unincorporated partnerships and associations. Actually, at the time when the general incorporation statutes first appeared, many large businesses preferred trusts over companies. For instance, when the UK passed its first general incorporation statute in 1844, trusts outnumbered corporations in the UK by a ratio of more than ten to one.[117]

The 'investment trust' in the UK, despite confusing the two separate vehicles of the company and the trust through its misleading name, is in fact evidence that shows that trusts were used for commercial purposes before companies emerged. The investment trusts operated initially as common law trusts to collect capital and invest in non-land assets, and were only categorised as public limited companies, in consideration of their legal status, later in the 1860s following the promulgation of the first Companies Act. The investment trust (more precisely the investment trust company) falls into the scheme of 'investment company' under the European Directive on Undertakings for Collective Investment in Transferable Securitas (UCITS).[118]

The fact that the investment trust company was derived from the common law trust but was defined as a company after the corporate form was introduced makes no suggestion that a modern commercial trust should be categorised as a company. An investment trust company is different from a real commercial trust (eg a unit trust in the UK); their performance can vary significantly.[119]

The key disparity (see chapter two, section I) is that investors in a unit trust have beneficiary interests in the investment funds. That is, the manager of a unit trust is obliged to buy back units when the investors wish to redeem them. This

[116] D'Angelo (n 3) 2.
[117] Morley (n 43) 2146–47.
[118] Directive 2009/65/EC of the European Parliament and of the Council of 13 July 2009 on the coordination of laws, regulations and administrative provisions relating to undertakings for collective investment in transferable securities (UCITS) (recast) [2009] OJ L302/32.
[119] Zhang (n 13) 269.

differs from the practice of investing in a company, where pursuant to the company's capital maintenance rule, investors cannot redeem their investment at will.[120] Investors of an investment trust company are shareholders of a corporation and have no direct interest in the underlying investments.

Neither does the involvement of corporates acting as trustees for commercial trusts make a commercial trust a company; rather, said corporate trustees are engaged because their professional skills (skills that non-expert, natural-person trustees typically do not possess) allow them to manage involuted business arrangements.

Moreover, as a matter of definition, it would be wrong for any legal system to conceptualise the trust as a company or a legal person, since the result will only eliminate the trust as a fundamental legal institution.[121]

C. Commercial Use of Trusts does not Make the Trust a Series of Contracts

For the same reason that components do not determine the essence of a thing, a commercial trust cannot be viewed merely as a series of contracts. Contracts (or trust deeds) are simply components employed to better manage a commercial trust, which remains, in essence, a trust. As Stebbings observed, it is now twice as hard to administer a trust.[122] The function of a trust in a commercial context is markedly different to that of a trust in a family context, or indeed, to that of a trust exposed to less specialised commercial transactions.[123] A commercial trust is employed as a means of enforcing collective action, and the features of the trust institution are thus modified by contract to achieve the commercial objectives.[124] Being a fundamental institution, the trust cannot be another institution such as a sub-category of legal persons or contracts.[125]

Moreover, the application of contracts does not eliminate the trustee's principal duties, nor does it replace them with contractual obligations;[126] it merely provides additional protections to trust parties when the trust administration of the trust is more complex. Duties regulated by the contract or deed must comply with the trustee's core obligations that 'represent the minimum

[120] See Companies Act 2006, pt 18; *Trevor v Whitworth* (1887) 12 App Cas 409.

[121] L Smith, 'Trust and Patrimony' (2009) 28 *Estates, Trusts & Pensions Journal* 332, 332.

[122] C Stebbings, 'Trustees, Tribunals and Taxes: Creativity in Victorian Law' (2007) 70 *Amicus Curiae* 2, 3.

[123] *Re Kayford Ltd* [1975] 1 All ER 604.

[124] Yip (n 36) 358.

[125] Smith (n 121) 349.

[126] For example, clauses of trust instrument may exempt trustees from their liabilities for gross negligence but not for dishonesty, according to *Armitage v Nurse* [1998] Ch 241 and *Walker v Stones* [2001] QB 902; the duty of care may be excluded by the trust instrument, but common law will apply in this case, pursuant to Trustee Act 2000, sch 1(7).

necessary to give substance to the trusts': 'To perform the trusts honestly and in good faith for the benefit of the beneficiaries.'[127] A trust instrument cannot authorise trustees to deliberately or recklessly allow their or a third person's interest to supersede the interest of beneficiaries.[128] Although it may be 'artificial and unreal', as stated by Lord Toulson, to look at a trust in isolation from underlying contractual obligations,[129] it does affirm that a trustee cannot delegate dispositive duties or fiduciary discretions by contracts without express authority in the trust instrument.[130] Even when a trustee is permitted to enter into a transaction by an express provision, this may be invalidated if it conflicts with the trustee's duties.[131]

It therefore becomes apparent that contracts can only be employed when they comply with a trust's rules. These contracts do not and may not replace the trust itself. Denying the essence of the trust and replacing trust duties with contract obligations is inadvisable, as fiduciary duties provide a better protection to beneficiary investors than do contract obligations. A trust, unlike a contract, provides protection against a trustee's personal creditors through the independence of the trust property. Additionally, the beneficiary investor in a trust can trace the trust property and claim against non-bona fide third parties. These activities are not achievable under a contract, which will only bind the parties entering into the contract.

D. The Commercial Trust is not an Independent Legal Scheme Separated from Trusts

A claim that commercial trusts should be treated as an independent legal scheme, separate from trusts as a broader category, requires proof that the current fundamental rule of trusts is unable to regulate commercial trusts. Or, more notably, it requires evidence that no other solution (that requires fewer fundamental changes to be made to the current legal system) is available. The fact is that developments to trust law have consistently addressed any issues arising from the commercial use of trusts. Courts are tempted, and even pressured, to adapt trust law principles to suit commercial objectives; as a result, trust law is always playing catch-up with business developments and legislative intervention.[132]

It cannot be stipulated that the exact same set of rules be applied to different types of trusts, including family and commercial trusts. 'Certain detailed rules

[127] *Armitage v Nurse* [1998] Ch 241, 253–54.
[128] ibid.
[129] *AIB Group (UK) plc v Mark Redler & Co Solicitors* [2014] UKSC 58 [71] (Lord Toulson). The Supreme Court was preoccupied with the rules relating to equitable compensation.
[130] *Re Airey* [1897] 1 Ch 164.
[131] See, eg, *Re Efron's Tie and Knitting Mills Pty Ltd* [1932] VLR 8.
[132] Yip (n 36) 358–59.

applicable to one form of trust do not necessarily have to be applied to other forms of trust if the rationale does not sensibly apply to the latter.'[133] The various types of trusts, justifiably, require treatment that is tailored to their needs.[134] Such modifications, however, do not equate to the argument that commercial trusts should be separated from general trust law and treated as an independent entity. As Lord Neuberger claimed in *Stack v Dowden*, raising different considerations under a commercial trust should not attract a new set of principles.[135]

It is not realistic to make a clear cut between domestic and commercial contexts.[136] 'The reality is that the domestic and commercial lie on a continuum of factual situations'.[137] Although trust principles were sprouted from the context of family and friendship,[138] they have spread branches to commerce and form a fundamental part.[139] Therefore, commercial trusts are still rooted in trust law, and it would be unnecessary or inappropriate to separate commercial trusts from trusts.[140]

III. Conclusion

Despite the changes and challenges of a trustee's role, the fundamental rules of trusts and the core duties of the trustees have been preserved; therefore, a commercial trust still complies with the legal design of a trust. If one claims that a commercial trust is an independent legal vehicle, one is bound to prove that the current rule of trusts is unable to regulate commercial trusts. By contrast, the trust law per se has continually developed to address issues arising in commercial contexts – although this still needs improvement.

[133] *AIB Group (UK) plc v Mark Redler & Co Solicitors* [2014] UKSC 58 [33].

[134] See the totemic decisions in *Target Holdings Ltd v Redferns* [1996] AC 421; *Paragon Finance plc v DB Thakerar & Co* [1999] 1 All ER 400; *AIB Group (UK) plc v Mark Redler & Co Solicitors* [2014] UKSC 58.

[135] *Stack v Dowden* [2007] UKHL 17, [2007] 2 AC 432 [107] (with regard to the issue of domestic context).

[136] See M Yip and J Lee, '"Less Than Straightforward People", Facts and Trusts: Reflections on Context: *Favor Easy Management Ltd v Wu*' (2013) *The Conveyancer and Property Lawyer* 431.

[137] N Hopkins, 'The Relevance of Context in Property Law: A Case for Judicial Restraint?' (2011) 31(2) *Legal Studies* 175, 177.

[138] See Langbein (n 4) 632–43.

[139] See especially The Honourable Sir Anthony Mason, 'Equity's Role in the Twentieth Century' (1997/8) 8 *The King's College Law Journal* 1; S Worthington, 'The Commercial Utility of the Trust Vehicle' in DJ Hayton (ed), *Extending the Boundaries of Trusts and Similar Ring-Fenced Funds* (Alphen aan den Rijn, Wolters Kluwer Law International, 2002) 135.

[140] Zhang (n 13) 270.

6

A Developed Understanding of the Creditor's Interest in Commercial Trusts

A trustee's fiduciary duties and the independence of trust property (ie the separation of trust property from the personal assets of trustees, beneficiaries and settlors) provide a trust with inbuilt protection over the beneficiary's interest. This makes the trust an attractive device for commercial uses compared to other legal vehicles (eg a company, agency or contract). Compared to the beneficiary's interest, the interest of a trust creditor, as the external party of the trust, is less favoured and not as eye-catching. Nevertheless, a study on the topic is still noteworthy, with the aim of providing a comprehensive and in-depth understanding of the changes and challenges that the commercial use of trusts has brought to trusts and trust law. 'A balance needs to be struck between the interests of trust beneficiaries and of creditors, while not neglecting the interests of the trustee as pig in the middle.'[1] Establishing the basis of this research, this chapter first distinguishes the notion of the trust creditor from similar concepts that have been confused or misused in the literature and in practice. It then examines what has been changed in the creditor's role in traditional trusts (which are mainly used to preserve family assets over generations) and what has been maintained and carried over to the evolved commercial use of trusts. The chapter also examines the creditor's remedy, focusing on the question as to whether and to what extent a creditor should be protected when the trustee is in default. It looks into the key theoretical and practical challenges to the realisation of the creditor's interest (ie the two problematic machineries of trustee's indemnity and the trust entity) and proposes a range of solutions that provides a developed understanding of the creditor's interest.

I. Clarification of Similar Concepts

For a better understanding of a trust creditor's interest, it is necessary to first clarify the notion of a trust creditor and differentiate it from similar concepts that have been misused or confused.

[1] *Trust Law Committee Consultation Paper: Rights of Creditors against Trustees and Trust Funds* (1997), para 1.2.

A trust creditor is the creditor of a trust who makes a claim against the trust property. This creditor is different to the personal creditors of trustees, beneficiaries or settlors, who bring personal claims against the assets of the trustees, beneficiaries and settlors, respectively, and have no access to the trust property.

Trust creditors are often confused with a trustee's creditors. This is, presumably, because under a trust the trustee is the person who holds and manages the trust property on behalf of the trust; under common law, trust creditors have no direct access to trust property,[2] and as a result, claim against the trustee (who appears to be in a similar position as the personal creditor of the trustee). This ignores the fact that the trustee wears two hats: one being their fiduciary office and the other concerning their personal affairs. These two roles are distinct, with separate assets held under each.[3] A trust creditor can only claim against trust property; they cannot claim against a trustee's personal assets. Conversely, a trustee's creditor only has access to the trustee's personal assets, with no recourse to the trust property.

Confusion also arises when a beneficiary's personal creditors claim against the capital or income of trust property that has been allocated to the beneficiary. Their actions may make people think that the beneficiary's creditors are also trust creditors, because they seem to have access to the trust property. However, such a claim is possible only when those assets fall into the hands of the beneficiary (being transferred or distributed to the beneficiary in accordance with the trust instrument), and therefore, become the beneficiary's personal assets. That is, the beneficiary's creditors can still claim against the beneficiary's personal property. They cannot claim against the trust property, a quality which distinguishes them from a trust creditor.

Moreover, a trust creditor is often mistaken as (but is different from) a creditor whose interest is secured, by the trust device, in the role of a beneficiary of the trust: for instance, the creditors protected as the beneficiaries of Quistclose trusts, security trusts, or other trusts that are categorised as a type of trust underpinning commercial loan arrangements.[4] Creditors in a separate relationship (eg one that is created when they lend money to others) may adopt trusts to ensure that they themselves are protected from the bankruptcy or insolvency of the borrowers. For example, where a loan is made on the terms that, if the money or assets cannot be used for the purpose for which they have been advanced, a Quistclose trust can be formed; this treats the creditor (lender) as the beneficiary of the trust, thereby ensuring the return of the money. In other words, if the borrower becomes insolvent before spending the money according to the stipulations in the loan agreement, the lender–creditor retains the equitable beneficial interest in the money under the trust, and so is safe from the borrower's insolvency.[5] Similar protection for

[2] L Smith, 'Trust and Patrimony' (2009) 28 *Estates, Trusts & Pensions Journal* 332, 338.

[3] D Waters, L Smith and M Gillen, *Waters' Law of Trusts in Canada*, 5th edn (Toronto, Carswell, 2021) 13.

[4] See ch 2, section I.B for details.

[5] L Tucker, N Le Poidevin and J Brightwell, *Lewin on Trusts*, 20th edn (London, Sweet & Maxwell, 2020) para 8-54.

creditors can also be found in a security trust, which is created to hold security over a debtor's assets for the benefit of their creditors (lenders), considering the creditor as the beneficiary of the trust. These can be found in various situations, such as where trusts hold corporate assets for debenture holders, or where trusts hold real estate for syndicated mortgage lenders, or with trusts that involve project finance and that have a multi-layered debt structure.[6] From these examples, it can be seen that the creditor referred to here is the creditor of a separate relationship (eg a loan), who is protected as a beneficiary of a trust. They are not the creditor of the trust, and therefore have no access to trust property. Those concepts are often confused or misused in discussions on trust creditor protection.

II. Changes to the Creditor's Role and the Creditor's Interest

As discussed in previous chapters, the trust originated in a family context and was adopted primarily to protect landholdings and, later on, all types of family property. The aim was to avoid feudal obstacles and pass on family property over generations. In a traditional family trust, a trustee is usually only expected to hold the trust property, preserve its value and transfer it to the beneficiaries in accordance with the trust terms in a passive and risk-averse way, with minimal active management of the trust property. As a result, there is little room for the trustee to interact with creditors or for the creditor's interest to be involved. In other words, a trust creditor's role in a traditional family trust is simple, even negligible.

Conversely, trusts in commercial contexts have seen evolved use, requiring dynamic and intricate management and investment of trust property. This has resulted in greater involvement by trust creditors, and the creditor's interest and remedy have become complex and significant. Along with a growth in commercial and personal wealth, investor-beneficiaries (who are usually also the settlors of the trust) often seek to invest over the long term, in diversified portfolios, to maximise returns. To secure considerable returns for investors, the management of a trust fund will make use of different financial instruments. These instruments, in turn, rely on creditors to pursue finance or make transactions. Without interaction with creditors, these instruments would not be practical. Thus, that the evolution of trusts in commercial and financial contexts has moved towards a greater dependency on trust creditors. Additionally, trust assets have expanded, moving from family assets to a portfolio of financial assets.[7] The diversification of the assets

[6] See especially DJ Hayton, SCJJ Kortmann and HLE Verhagen (eds), *Principles of European Trust Law* (The Hague, Kluwer Law International, 1999) 6; G Thomas and A Hudson, *The Law of Trusts*, 2nd edn (Oxford, Oxford University Press, 2010) part I, 51 and 52.

[7] PS Davies and G Virgo (eds), *Equity & Trusts: Text, Cases, and Materials*, 3rd edn (Oxford, Oxford University Press, 2019) 25.

attracts multiple creditors in itself, and along with the development of trust property, trustees are granted more discretion so that they can promptly respond to rapidly changing financial markets. The trustees are expected to produce profits through various business activities, including risk-taking behaviours.[8] As a result, more creditors and complex creditor's interest are embraced by those variously inflated activities, and the increasing level of risks brought by the complex activities makes the creditor's remedy more severe in practice. Courts have been concerned with ensuring fair and equal opportunities for all a trust's creditors, aiming to protect their debts[9] and balance the beneficiary's interest so that creditors are not unfairly favoured.[10]

Although more creditors are involved in the commercial use of trusts, and the role and the rules of trust creditor have evolved according to the nature of the trust, the creditor's interest stands as and constitutes an iconic feature of the trust. That is, the creditor of the trust claims against the trust property, and has no access to a trustee's personal wealth. At the same time, the trust property, managed by the trustee in the beneficiary's interest, is protected independently within the trust, making it immune to claims by spouses or personal creditors of the trustee, the beneficiary or the settlor in the event of divorce or bankruptcy (ie providing protection from both family and commercial creditors).[11]

In a trust, the personal creditors of a trustee have no access to the trust property because of the segregated nature of the trust property; that is, the trust property must be separated from the trustee's personal assets. Property held in trust cannot be seized by the personal creditors of the trustees.[12] Should a trustee (an owner of trust property) become bankrupt, the trust property will not be available to their creditors.[13] Consequently, the trust beneficiary's interest in the trust property is held apart from the trustee's personal creditors.[14] When civil lawyers seek to understand why it is that a beneficiary can make claims against third parties for the return of trust assets, or that the personal creditors of a trustee cannot encroach on trust assets to satisfy their claims, they often refer to an analogy that uses the idea of patrimony.[15] The trust beneficiary is seen as a special creditor of the trustee, rather than a creditor of the trust itself.[16] The creditors of

[8] See especially *Cowan v Scargill* [1985] Ch 270 [8]; N D'Angelo, *Commercial Trusts* (Chatswood, LexisNexis Butterworths, 2014) 7 and 160.

[9] See, eg, *E C Investment Holding Pte Ltd v Ridout Residence Pte Ltd and Another* [2010] SGHC 270.

[10] See *Vyse v Foster* (1872) LR 8 Ch App 309.

[11] See, eg, art 2 of the Hague Trust Convention states that 'the [trust] assets constitute a separate fund and are not a part of the trustee's own estate'; art 11 provides: 'The recognition of a trust shall imply that the trust assets shall not form part of the trustee's estate upon his insolvency or bankruptcy.'

[12] *Heritable Reversionary Co Ltd v Millar* (1892) 19 R (HL) 43, [1892] AC 598, 600.

[13] *Sharp v Thomson* 1995 SC 455, 479 (Lord President Hope).

[14] Waters, Smith and Gillen (n 3) 13.

[15] P Matthews, 'The Compatibility of the Trust with the Civil Law Notion of Property' in L Smith (ed), *The Worlds of the Trust* (Cambridge, Cambridge University Press, 2013) 313, 324.

[16] M Benoit, 'The Development of the Concept of Pension Trust under Quebec Civil Law' (1998) 17 *Estates, Trusts & Pensions Journal* 203, 210.

the beneficiary have no access to the trust property until the property is transferred to the beneficiary as the beneficiary's own assets. Likewise, the settlor's personal creditors cannot claim against the trust assets because settlors lose their ownership of the assets when they transfer them to the trustee (unless the settlors retain the right to revoke).[17] One thing that makes a trust superior to a contract is that a trust can offer protection against the personal creditors of the participants, while the contract cannot. The success and unique attraction of the trust, as well as the creditor's interest and remedy, are due, in great part, to this independent protection of trust property.

When discussing the realisation or protection of a trust creditor's interests, key questions that arise and need to be addressed are whether the creditor's interest is still protected when the trustee contracts with the trust creditor in default; to what extent the trust creditor can claim against the trust property when the trustee incurs liabilities beyond their authority; and if a connection between a trustee's liabilities and a creditor's interest is required to have an impact on a creditor's claim.

Deliberations on those questions have resulted in a string of judgments suggesting the need for some degree of ill intent on the part of the trustee and a connection between the trustee's behaviour and the creditor's interest. The discussion in the cases unfortunately appears to confuse trust creditors with the trustee's creditors and is based on the theory of the trustee's indemnity (which, in the author's view, is a misunderstanding of the creditor's interest and remedy that will be criticised in detail in the next section). Thus, this section will analyse the key cases by focusing on what they say about the impact of a trustee's intention or behaviour on the creditor's interest.

An early foundational case is *Balsh v Hyham*.[18] The plaintiff was a trustee for the defendant (the beneficiary) of £1,000 of South-Sea stock. At the desire of the defendant, the trustee borrowed £4,000 from the company by mortgaging the stock. The defendant received the money borrowed. Afterwards, an Act of Parliament (7 George 1, session 2, section 7)[19] was made; this provided that if any of the borrowers paid 10 per cent of what was owed by a certain date, the rest of the debt should be discharged. The beneficiary defendant directed the trustee not to pay the 10 per cent, alleging that he thought the borrowers were not obliged to pay the money borrowed back to the company and that borrowers could elect to forfeit the pledge.[20] The trustee paid the 10 per cent and brought a bill in equity to recover it as laid out for the defendant beneficiary. King LC held that

[17] R Zhang, *A Better Understanding of Common Law Ownership of Trust Property and its Introduction in China Through Comparative Studies* (Guangzhou, World Publishing Corporation, 2019) 6.

[18] *Balsh v Hyham* (1728) 2 P Wms 453, 24 ER 810.

[19] Act of Parliament (7 Geo 1, sess 2, s 7), known as National Debt Act 1721, s 7.

[20] There were some attempts to prove an agreement by the plaintiff trustee and others to pay the money borrowed in compassion to the defendant beneficiary, and in regard to the losses by him sustained, but that proof was deficient.

> within the reason of that rule, where the … trustee has honestly and fairly, without any possibility of being a gainer, laid down money, by which the [beneficiary] is discharged from being liable for the whole money lent, or from a plain and great hazard of being so, the [trustee] ought to be repaid.[21]

This suggests that the actual fraudulence or otherwise of the trustee is to be evaluated when deciding whether the trustee's actions ultra vires will cause the trustee's claim to be denied (and consequently, injure the creditor's interest). A mere exceeding of the trustee's authority will not defeat the creditor's claim in instances where the trustee acted honestly and fairly without any possibility of personal gain, in a way that benefits the trust.[22] This doctrine was followed by the Court of Appeal in *Ex parte Chippendale, Re German Mining Company*.[23]

Regarding the question as to whether a trustee's default should be connected to the creditor's interest, injuring the creditor's claim, *In re Johnson*[24] and *Evans v Evans*[25] seem to suggest that as long as there is a breach of trust or the trustee is otherwise in default, the creditor's interest or claim is correspondingly diminished. *In re Richardson*[26] (decided 31 years after *In re Johnson*) takes this a step further; it distinguishes between paid and unpaid creditors, closing with a solution (one considered more doctrinally coherent and theoretically satisfactory) that states that when the trustee's indemnity is earmarked for the benefit of a creditor whose dealings created the right in the first place, unrelated breaches of trust become irrelevant and have no impact on the creditor's access to trust property.

The doctrine developed by *In re Richardson*, which connects the liabilities of the trustee (ie when the liability is incurred for the benefit of the creditor) and severs the creditor's access to the trust property, is fairer and more reasonable than the previous position. The reason or purpose behind denying a trustee's indemnity or creditor's access is that it protects a beneficiary's interest, thereby being in accordance with a trustee's fiduciary duties. However, it might be the case that, when the trustee behaves wrongly, the injustice caused is not only that the beneficiary is unduly benefited; it is also, and chiefly, that the creditor has suffered a detriment. Taking all three parties in the scenario into account, the beneficiary is not the only one who is legally subject to potential injustices that ought to be avoided; the ability of the beneficiary to extinguish a liability (to the creditor) with a loss (by trustee default) is certainly such an injustice.[27] When a trustee's liability

[21] *Balsh v Hyham* (1728) 2 P Wms 453, 24 ER 810, 810–11.

[22] A Ollikainen-Read, 'Creditors' Claims against Trustees and Trust Funds' (2018) 24(2) *Trusts & Trustees* 177, 185.

[23] *Ex parte Chippendale, Re German Mining Company* (1854) 4 De GM & G 19, 43 ER 415.

[24] *In re Johnson* (1880) 15 Ch D 548, 552.

[25] *Evans v Evans* (1887) 34 Ch D 597, 601.

[26] *In re Richardson* [1911] 2 KB 705.

[27] HF Stone, 'A Theory of Liability of Trust Estates for the Contracts and Torts of the Trustee' (1922) 22 *Columbia Law Review* 527, 529.

is not connected to a creditor's interest or when the creditor has no fault connected to the trustee's wrongdoing, it is unfair to dismiss the creditor's interest. In which case, the creditor not only compensates the beneficiary for the trustee's faults, but also ends up exonerating the trustee. The creditor has given value and received nothing, the beneficiary has been deprived of the amount of the trustee's default (partially or fully compensated by the creditor's given value), and the trustee has paid off their liability to the trust using the creditor's money. The beneficiary may be closer to where they were supposed to be, but the creditor is wronged, and the trustee is allowed to pay off one liability with another.[28] The beneficiary is not enriched (although they have been compensated with the creditor's money): the trustee is.[29] If the trustee is insolvent, the remaining personal claim against the trustee is useless to the creditor.

The *In re Richardson* doctrine offers a more just result to creditors. The trustee's indemnity is earmarked for the payment of an unpaid creditor, for which there is judicial precedent; this is coupled with an appreciation of the factual difference between a beneficial interest and an indemnity.[30] The *In re Richardson* doctrine is also echoed in *Re Staff Benefits Pty Ltd*,[31] in which Needham J confirmed that the trustee's default should be related to the subject matter of the claim if it is to bar the creditor's claim.

III. Challenges to and Proposed Legal Reform of the Creditor's Interest and Remedy

Case law has attempted to address issues related to the creditor's interest; however, a trust creditor is often confused with and referred to as a creditor of the trustee, with the trust creditor's access to the trust property being subordinated to the trustee's indemnity right. In other words, common law has developed a robust level of security for creditors in the form of the trustee's indemnity. Inevitably, questions arise as to whether the trust principles devolved by case law in the eighteenth and nineteenth centuries challenge the creditor's interest and remedy; whether the case law can properly cope with the new uses of trusts in commercial contexts; and whether legislation will develop in this regard (particularly given that when case law actively sprouts, legislative intervention appears to hibernate).

[28] Ollikainen-Read (n 22) 189–90.

[29] This is one reason why the basic US law claim of unjust enrichment of the trust estate is not a suitable solution – aside from the double standard of having to claim that the trust estate can be enriched independently of the trustee despite having no independent legal personality, the trust estate is not actually enriched in these cases. What was a liability by the trustee towards the trust has simply been paid using the creditor's money.

[30] Ollikainen-Read (n 22) 190.

[31] *Re Staff Benefits Pty Ltd* [1979] 1 NSWLR 207, 214.

A. Challenges to the Machinery of the Trustee's Indemnity

A significant problem or challenge that has arisen from the case law is the theory of the trustee's indemnity right.[32] In common law, a trust creditor is viewed as a personal creditor of the trustee and has no direct access to the trust assets.[33] The way for a creditor to claim against trust assets is through the machinery of the trustee's indemnity, which states that a trustee who contracts with creditors in their management of trust business becomes personally liable to those creditors and has a strong indemnity right against trust assets.[34] The creditor of the trust will have to exercise their personal right against the trustee if they are to recover any debts; the trustee will then exercise their right of indemnity to recover this cost from the trust assets. If anything severs that indemnity, the creditor is left only with a claim against the trustee's personal assets (or no claim at all if the trustee is insolvent). This is the case even where the event that severed the trustee's indemnity had nothing to do with the creditor.[35] That is to say, when the trustee has no right of indemnity (for example, when the trustee acts in breach of trust terms),[36] or when the trustee becomes bankrupt, with no personal assets left, the interest of the creditors of the trust cannot be realised.[37]

This (the machinery of the trustee's indemnity that is used to realise the trust creditor's interest), in the author's view, is the result of a misunderstanding. It confuses the creditors of a trust with a trustee's personal creditor and misinterprets the pathway that trust creditors take to claim against the trust property through a trustee because the trustee is the titleholder of that property. The creditor's remedy is subject to the trustee's indemnity, and thus the creditor's interest is eliminated when the trustee's indemnity is void or when the trustee has no or insufficient personal property.

First, the machinery of the trustee's indemnity confuses trust creditors with a trustee's personal creditors. As clarified before, the creditor of the trust claims

[32] The right of indemnity of a trustee is a right to be reimbursed out of the trust property for moneys properly paid out of the trustee's own pocket or a right to be exonerated from paying out his own money through the power to pay due debts out of the trust property (whether capital or income) in the first place (see *Re Blundell* (1888) 40 Ch D 370, 376). The right of reimbursement or the right of exoneration will extend to the whole range of trust assets except for that part of such assets excluded from being used for the trust activity giving rise to the relevant liability (see especially *Fraser v Murdoch* (1881) 6 App Cas 855; *Dower v Gorton* [1891] AC 190).

[33] Smith (n 2) 338.

[34] See especially *Muir v City of Glasgow Bank* (1879) 4 App Cas 337; *In re Johnson* (1880) 15 Ch D 548, 552.

[35] See *Investec Trust (Guernsey) Ltd v Glenalla Properties Ltd* [2018] UKPC 7, [2019] AC 271 (PC) [59]; Ollikainen-Read (n 22) 179–80; B Shah, 'Trustee's Indemnity and Creditors' Rights' (2013) 19(1) *Trusts & Trustees* 79.

[36] A trust instrument may limit the trustee's indemnity to a particular part of the trust property or oust trustee's indemnity against the trust property. See especially Trustee Act 1925, s 69(2); *RWG Management Ltd v Commissioner for Corporate Affairs* [1985] VR 385, 395; *Ex parte Chippendale, Re German Mining Company* (1854) 4 De GM & G 19, 52.

[37] *Equity Trust (Jersey) Ltd v Halabi* [2022] UKPC 36, [2023] AC 877 (PC) [212].

against the trust property, regardless of the status of the trustee's personal property. This is different to the route taken by a trustee's personal creditor, whose claim is against the trustee's personal assets. Therefore, the bankruptcy of a trustee's personal assets has no impact on the trust creditor's interest or remedy.[38] In fact, a trust does not fail for want of a trustee – this is a fundamental rule of trusts.[39] Even though a trustee is essential to a trust, a trust does not fail simply 'because no trustee is designated or because the designated trustee declines, is unable, or ceases to act, unless the trust's creation or continuation depends on a specific person serving as trustee'.[40] In English law, for example, one or more new trustees may be appointed by writing 'in the place of the trustee so deceased remaining out of the United Kingdom, desiring to be discharged, refusing, or being unfit or being incapable, or being an infant, as aforesaid'.[41] If nobody is willing to carry out the trust, the court can, in certain circumstances, appoint a public or judicial trustee to discharge the trust. As a last resort, the court can act on an ad hoc basis as a trustee itself.[42] Upon the death of the sole or last surviving trustee, the trust property devolves upon the trustee's personal representatives.[43] Therefore, trusts continue to exist even when a trustee is dead or has become bankrupt, as does the trust property. The trust creditors' interest in the trust property is consequently unaffected; they simply need to wait for a new trustee to be appointed to facilitate their access to the trust property.

Second, the machinery of the trustee's indemnity misinterprets the pathway (ie through a trustee) via which a creditor's claim can be realised against trust property as the basis or derivation of the creditor's interest. It might be true that trust creditors cannot place a direct claim on the trust but have to claim against the trustee. However, this is only because the trustee is the person who holds and manages the trust property on behalf of the trust.[44] As Lord Hodge noted in the

[38] A trustee may be personally liable to a trust creditor, in which case the trust creditor is also a personal creditor of the trustee. However, the two roles are still distinct, with separate assets and liabilities under each role: a creditor has access only to the trust property only as the trust creditor and can only claim against the trustee's personal property when in the role of a trustee's personal creditor.

[39] This rule has exceptions. Some trusts require specific trustees. In this unusual case, it is a prerequisite to the existence of the trust that only a specific, named trustee is to hold the office. In such a case, it is of the essence of a trust that the trustees selected by the settlor, and no one else, act as the trustees of it. See *Re Lysaght* [1966] 1 Ch 191, 194 (per Buckley J). If those trustees cannot or will not undertake the office, the trust must fail. Moreover, in such a case, a trust will fail where the potential trustee disclaims the trusteeship. In those rare situations, the trust is treated as never having come into effect. This is said to have been void *ab initio*.

[40] Restatement (Third) of the Law of Trusts, § 31 (2001) (US).

[41] Trustee Act 1925, s 36(1).

[42] G Watt, *Equity and Trusts Law Directions*, 7th edn (Oxford, Oxford University Press, 2021) 254.

[43] Tucker, Le Poidevin and Brightwell, *Lewin on Trusts* (n 5) 441.

[44] A trust has no legal personality, and so its obligations can only be owned to trust creditors by the trustee. The trustee is empowered or permitted to pay for trust creditors out of the trust property because the obligations are incurred in the performance of the trustee's office. See S Agnew and K Pukis, 'Trustees' Indemnities – Is Timing Everything?' (2018) 24 *Trusts & Trustees* 989; J Hudson and C Mitchell, 'Trustee Recoupment: A Power Analysis' (2021) 35 *Trust Law International* 3.

Privy Council case of *Investec Trust (Guernsey) Ltd v Glenalla Properties Ltd*:[45] 'A trust is not a legal person. Its assets are vested in trustees, who are the only entities capable of assuming legal rights and liabilities in relation to the trust.'[46] It does not mean that the trust creditor's interest is derived from or subject to the trustee's indemnity or personal assets. A trustee has managerial control of the trust property as its titleholder, but the trustee is obliged to use the property for the benefit of the beneficiaries and is not permitted to access the property other than in accordance with the trust terms. The trustee's indemnity right is not the essence or the origin of the creditor's interest; it is only the external appearance and the pathway for the trust creditor's remedy. The indemnity right should neither define nor deny the trust creditor's interest or remedy.

The machinery of the trustee's indemnity right is a theory adopted only in common law. In civilian jurisdictions, the patrimony theory (which is widely used to accommodate trusts) clearly indicates that a trust creditor is claiming from a trust patrimony. The trust patrimony consists of the trust property owned by the trustees as a whole and any obligations the trustee has incurred through the administration of the trust property.[47] If that patrimony is empty, the trust creditor must go without, as the private patrimony of the trustee is not available. The civilian tradition accepts that the assets and liabilities of a trust patrimony, although held by the same person (ie the trustee), are separate from the trustee's private patrimony. The trust patrimony is distinct from the trustee's private patrimony in law and should be kept distinct through the proper labelling of funds and suitable accounting practices.[48] Any sales or exchanges of trust property are allocated to the trust patrimony. The trust patrimony is accessible to the trust creditors without affecting the trustee's personal assets. If the trust property is transferred in breach of the trust, the value received by the trustee automatically becomes part of the trust fund for the simple reason that when the trust property is transferred, the trustee is seen as receiving any proceeds into the trust, as opposed to into the trustee's private patrimony. This is also the case in respect to any profits that a trustee makes in breach of the principle that a trustee must not act as *auctor in rem suam* (someone who acts in their own interests).[49] When there is a separate trust fund, the bankruptcy of a trustee's private patrimony cannot cause the end of the trust. Trust property should not be used when winding up a company acting as trustee, only when winding up the trust.[50] A trust continues even when all trustees are dead or have become insolvent, as does the creditor's interest.

[45] *Investec Trust (Guernsey) Ltd v Glenalla Properties Ltd* [2018] UKPC 7, [2019] AC 271 (PC).

[46] ibid [59].

[47] See discussion in ch 3, section I.

[48] KGC Reid, 'Patrimony Not Equity: The Trust in Scotland' (2000) 8 *European Review of Private Law* 427, 432.

[49] *Discussion Paper on the Nature and the Constitution of Trusts* (Scot Law Com DP No 133, 2006), para 2.19.

[50] See especially *Re Byrne Australia Pty Ltd (No 2)* [1981] 2 NSWLR 364; *Re Matheson* (1994) 121 ALR 605, 615.

Even in common law jurisdictions, the argument that a trust creditor has no direct access to trust property has been revised; laws have been changed so as to give creditors a direct access to trust assets. As noted by Smith, the clearest example is in the US.[51] The creditors of a trust in the US have direct access to the trust assets by claiming against the trustees, not relying on the trustees' indemnity rights but rather on the division of capacities and of assets. Similar to the civil law concept of special patrimony, trustees in the US hold segregated personal capacity and trust capacity, which is called the 'fiduciary capacity' in the Uniform Trust Code,[52] or the 'representative capacity' in the Restatement (3d) Trusts.[53] The Trust Law Committee in England issued a consultation paper on the topic in 1997[54] and a report with recommendations for reform in 1998.[55] The report insists on a creditor's direct right of recourse to the trust fund 'to grant such a security by virtue of the trust instrument and any statutory powers'.[56] The consultation paper and report were a part of the English Law Commission's 9th and 10th (subsequently abandoned) programmes.[57] The Trust Law Committee also affirmed in its 2023 Discussion Paper on Trustee Indemnities and the Priority Ranking of Claims against Trust Property[58] that the trustee is empowered or permitted to directly transfer trust property to trust creditors.[59] 'The New Zealand Law Commission has also included [the change] in its review of the law of trusts, with recommendations for reform that have now led to legislative proposals.'[60] One piece of legislation proposed by the New Zealand Parliament in section 80 of the Trusts Bill (2017)[61] suggests that creditor claims against trust assets should be allowed in certain cases: either where the trustee has a right of indemnity,[62] or where the creditor has given value, and the trust has benefited and the creditor has acted in good faith.[63]

[51] L Smith, 'Scottish Trusts in the Common Law' (2013) 17 *Edinburgh Law Review* 283, 305.

[52] Uniform Trust Code (US), § 1010.

[53] American Law Institute, *Restatement of the Law Third: Trusts*, 4 vols, vol 4 (2012) (American Law Institute 2003–2012), ch 21.

[54] *Trust Law Committee Consultation Paper: Rights of Creditors against Trustees and Trust Funds* (1997).

[55] *Trust Law Committee Report: Rights of Creditors against Trustees and Trust Funds* (1998).

[56] *Trust Law Committee Consultation Paper: Rights of Creditors against Trustees and Trust Funds* (1997), para 3.9.

[57] Ollikainen-Read (n 22) 177.

[58] *Trust Law Committee Discussion Paper: Trustee Indemnities and the Priority Ranking of Claims against Trust Property* (2023). In addition to the trustee's indemnity right, this paper also discussed two other issues: the relationship between retired and current trustees and the resolution of priority disputes between trustees seeking indemnity and/or other parties with claims against trust property.

[59] ibid para 8 (iii): '[B]ecause these are duties incurred in the performance of the trustee's office she is empowered or permitted to pay for them out of the trust property, either by transferring trust property to the relevant third party directly, or by paying the third party herself and then treating trust property as her own to the extent required to make good her loss.'

[60] Ollikainen-Read (n 22) fn 4 Law Commission (NZ), 'Court Jurisdiction, Trading Trusts and Other Issues' 2011, ch 7, with a bill introduced to the New Zealand Parliament on 1 August 2017, pt 4(2).

[61] Trusts Bill 290-1 (2017) (New Zealand), s 80.

[62] ibid s 80(1)(a).

[63] ibid s 80(1)(b)(i)–(iii). Good faith is defined as knowledge of matters that limit the trustee's indemnity (s 80(3)). The claim is limited to the extent of value given (s 80(4)(a)).

In Jersey,[64] Guernsey, Florida, the Turks and Caicos Islands, and South Africa, it is recommended that the creditor have an original primary right of direct recourse to the trust funds 'by suing the current trustee in his representative capacity as trustee if the creditor knowingly dealt with a trustee,[65] acting as such, in circumstances where the creditor was not thereby dishonestly assisting in a breach of trust'.[66] For example, article 32 of the Trusts (Jersey) Law 1984 states that:

> (1) Where a trustee is a party to any transaction or matter affecting the trust –
>
> (a) if the other party knows that the trustee is acting as trustee, any claim by the other party shall be against the trustee as trustee and shall extend only to the trust property;
>
> (b) if the other party does not know that the trustee is acting as trustee, any claim by the other party may be made against the trustee personally (though, without prejudice to his or her personal liability, the trustee shall have a right of recourse to the trust property by way of indemnity).
>
> (2) Paragraph (1) shall not affect any liability the trustee may have for breach of trust.[67]

Following the trend seen in the legislation, the literature has also sided with the amendment to allow a creditor direct access. For instance, Singaporean scholars have noted that the trustee's indemnity right leaves multiple risks for the trust creditors – risks that could be avoided if the creditors were able to directly claim against the trust property.[68]

Even in the jurisdictions that have stayed with the machinery of trustee's indemnity right, the creditor's subrogation to the trustee's indemnity is recognised, allowing a creditor to bring a direct claim against the trust property to realise their interest. That is, a creditor may claim against the assets of the trust by stepping into the shoes of the trustee (henceforth referred to as subrogation) and claiming the benefit of their right of indemnity.[69] In effect, the trustees are considered as holding their indemnity right on trust for the creditor. As Sir George Jessel MR

[64] See Trusts (Jersey) Law 1984.

[65] It is possible that the trustees, in not disclosing that they were trustees, were really acting for themselves and not for the trust, but when a loss arises, they attempt to indebt the loss to the trust estate. In this case, where the creditors did not originally know they were dealing with the trustees as trustees, they cannot claim against the trust as trust creditors (unless the creditors have notified each of the beneficiaries of full capacity who are entitled to intervene in the creditors' action against the trustees). See *Trust Law Committee Consultation Paper: Rights of Creditors against Trustees and Trust Funds* (1997), para 4.7.

[66] *Trust Law Committee Consultation Paper: Rights of Creditors against Trustees and Trust Funds* (1997), para 4.4.

[67] Trusts (Jersey) Law 1984, art 32.

[68] See, eg, H Tjio, 'Merrill and Smith's Intermediate Rights Lying between Contract and Property: Are Singapore Trusts and Secured Transactions Drifting away from English Law towards American Law?' (2019) *Singapore Journal of Legal Studies* 235, 245.

[69] See especially *In re Richardson* [1911] 2 KB 705, 715; *Octavo Investments Pty Ltd v Knight* (1979) 144 CLR 360, 371.

stated in *In re Johnson* (where the doctrine of the creditor's subrogation right is considered to have originated[70]):

> Where a trustee is authorised by a testator, or by a settlor – for it makes no difference – to carry on a business with certain funds which he gives to the trustee for that purpose, the creditor who trusts the executor has a right to say 'I had the personal liability of the man I trusted, and I have also a right to be put in his place against the assets; that is, I have a right to the benefit of indemnity or lien which he has against the assets devoted to the purposes of the trade.'[71]

Academic debates have considered whether a trust creditor is required to put a trustee into formal insolvency proceedings before subrogating the trustee's right of indemnity, with particular attention being paid to the situation in a commercial context, where the trustee is a legal person.[72] *E C Investment Holding Pte Ltd*[73] was a trail-blazing judgment for the common law world, arguing that trustees do not have to become insolvent for a trust creditor to subrogate the trustee's right to directly claim against the trust property. This development was significant and beneficial to both the creditor's interest and remedy. It grants creditors a subrogation right to place a direct claim on trust property and negates an unnecessarily stringent condition (ie the insolvency of the trustee). The rule set up in *E C Investment Holding Pte Ltd* provides fairness and equality to all creditors regardless of the nature of the trustee they are contracted with.[74] Moreover, the subrogation of trustee's indemnity grants trust creditors priority over other unsecured creditors,[75] and in insolvency cases, those who obtain the subrogation right first rank ahead of those who come after. For this reason, the need for a trustee's insolvency creates a race for creditors to subrogate and secure their debts first; the results of this race, consequently, will lead to different treatments among trust creditors.

Although the possibility of subrogating the trustee's indemnity right provides a trust creditor with some extent of protection, the machinery of the trustee's indemnity is still problematic, so legal reform is required. The indemnity machinery fails to provide full protection to trust creditors, in the same way that its counterpart grants creditors a direct independent recourse to trust property. This is because

[70] An earlier case of *Ex parte Garland* (1804) 10 Ves Jun 111, 32 ER 786 is held to be irrelevant because it did not determine the nature of the creditor's interest. *Ex parte Edmonds* (1862) 4 De GF & J 488 simply proceeded on the assumption that 'creditors of the trade are entitled to the benefit of the right of the trustee's indemnity and thus become creditors of the fund to which the executor or trustee has a right to resort' (p 498). Therefore, the first case considered to directly discuss the nature of the creditor's access to the trust assets in the language used today is *In re Johnson* (1880) 15 Ch D 548.

[71] *In re Johnson* (1880) 15 Ch D 548, 552.

[72] See, eg, HW Tang, 'Creditors, Trust and Insolvency' (2014) 20(4) *Trusts & Trustees* 383.

[73] *E C Investment Holding Pte Ltd v Ridout Residence Pte Ltd and Anor* [2010] SGHC 270.

[74] Where a trustee's insolvency is required for a legal-person trustee, different treatments apply to trust creditors who interact with natural-person trustees where insolvency is not a case and creditors who transact with legal-person trustees.

[75] Ollikainen-Read (n 22) 180. This is because the trustee's indemnity provides a proprietary right within an unascertained fund, and payment of the indemnity is what ascertains the fund.

creditors are authorised with the subrogation right only when the trustee's indemnity exists,[76] and the indemnity right only exists when debts are properly incurred (ie stemming solely from trust business that the trust deed authorises the trustee to carry out).[77] In other words, if there is no trustee with an indemnity right through which to claim, there is no creditor claim to realise.[78] The only recourse the creditor has is against the trustee personally.[79] The subrogation right the creditor receives is only a derivative right to the trustee's indemnity.

In terms of the nature of a derivative right to the trustee's indemnity, the title of the creditor to be put in the place of the trustee, so to speak; it is a title that receives nothing where nothing is due to the trustee.[80] The creditors cannot be in a better position than the trustees themselves;[81] their subrogation right, where possible, only grants them access to the trust fund to the extent of the indemnity and is subject to all the limitations set out for the trustee's indemnity.[82] If the trustees are at fault, or should they owe money to the trust, their right of indemnity is correspondingly diminished or extinguished.[83] If the trustee has wronged the trust estate (eg if the trustee has taken more money out of the assets than is needed to pay the debts, and instead of applying this to the payment of debts has put it into their own pocket), there is no equity on the creditor's claim to subrogate the trustee's indemnity, because the beneficiary is not taking the benefit.[84] As Sir George Jessel MR stated in *In re Johnson*:

> [The creditors are given an] additional benefit [ie the right to have recourse to trust assets] so as to avoid a supposed injustice; but the injustice to be avoided is the injustice of the [beneficiary] walking off with the assets which have been earned by the use of the property of the creditor: but where the [beneficiary] does not get that benefit, there is no injustice as between him and the creditors, and there is no reason for the court [to interfere] to give [the creditors] a larger right than that they bargained for, namely, their personal right against the trustee.[85]

[76] See *In re Leslie; Leslie v French* (1883) 23 Ch D 552.

[77] See MS Donald, 'The "Proper" Approach to a Trustee's Right to Indemnity out of Trust Assets' (2014) 8 *Journal of Equity* 283.

[78] *In re Leslie; Leslie v French* (1883) 23 Ch D 552.

[79] Ollikainen-Read (n 22) 188.

[80] *In re Johnson* (1880) 15 Ch D 548, 552.

[81] *Evans v Evans* (1887) 34 Ch D 597, 601 (per Cotton LJ).

[82] *Trust Law Committee Consultation Paper: Rights of Creditors against Trustees and Trust Funds* (1997), paras 2.23–2.24.

[83] See especially *Kemtron Industries Pty Ltd v Commissioner of Stamp Duties* [1984] 1 Qd R 576, 587; *Re Suco Gold Pty Co* (1983) SASR 99, 109; *Jennings v Mather* [1901] 1 KB 108, 113–14; *Stephenson v Barclays Bank Co Ltd* [1975] 1 All ER 625, 637. The trustee's entitlement to be indemnified out of trust property for payments actually made and liabilities incurred in the due administration of the trust entitles the trustee to retain the trust property or an appropriate part of them until their claim for reimbursement or exoneration has been satisfied.

[84] See especially *In re Johnson* (1880) 15 Ch D 548, 552; *Re Frith* [1902] 1 Ch 342; *Re British Power Traction & Lighting Co* [1910] 2 Ch 470. This reflects the principle that a defaulting trustee cannot claim any beneficial interest before making good their default, eg *Doering v Doering* (1889) 42 Ch D 203; *Re Dacre* [1916] 1 Ch 344, 347.

[85] *In re Johnson* (1880) 15 Ch D 548, 555–56.

A creditor's claim can be defeated by an unconnected liability that the trustee has in regard to the trust. A previous and unconnected breach of trust can negate the creditor's subrogation (ie their recourse to trust property).[86]

In other words, under the machinery of trustee's indemnity, the trust creditor's remedy is dependent on the trustee's goodwill or good behaviour. In fairness, no one ought to be able to sever a creditor's right of relief without wrongdoing by that creditor. The indemnity machinery also imposes on the trust creditor an additional burden to check trust instruments, to assess a trustee's existing indebtedness to the trust (ie whether it exceeds what is likely to be due to the creditor), or even to defend a trustee's honesty or good behaviour to secure and realise their (creditor's) interest.[87] Those extra burdens create difficulties and introduce unfairness to the creditor's situation, especially in instances where the creditor interacts with numerous trusts and trustees. This unfairness is due to the fact that what has been agreed in the trust instruments and the nature of a trustee's behaviour is beyond the creditor's control or knowledge. The creditor cannot know whether the trustee is in default and does not normally have access to the trust's internal accounts. The burden placed on creditors to make inquiries about whether their debtors are, in fact, trustees and whether these trustees are in default goes against the utility of the trust as a modularity device, in that the parties' obligational complexity is kept internal while outsiders can simply deal with the trustee as the property holder.[88] This is considered by the Trust Law Committee to be the most difficult and unsatisfactory hurdle for a trust to surmount.[89] It puts the creditors, who are already in a less favourable position in a trust, in an unfairly passive and disadvantageous situation. Although courts have attempted to develop compromises (for instance, by allowing an indemnity where the trustee's breach is made to benefit the trust without personal gain),[90] and it is possible to cope with this problem by requesting that a trustee disclose information on the trust terms and their behaviour when interacting with creditors, the creditors are still not liberated from the trustee's behaviour. The situation becomes complicated, going against the simplicity and efficiency that are key advantages of a trust.

[86] See especially *Jacubs v Rylance* (1873–74) LR 17 Eq 341; *Doering v Doering* (1889) 42 Ch D 203 (where the trustee had also become entitled to a beneficial interest); *In re Towndrow* [1911] 1 Ch 662. The principle that was established by the case law was revised by the *Trust Law Committee Report: Rights of Creditors against Trustees and Trust Funds* (1998). Paragraph 3.4 states: 'we recommend that the indebtedness of a trustee that is not connected with the contract with the creditor should not prevent such creditor having a right to be indemnified out of the trust fund (although preventing the trustee from having such a right of indemnity)'.

[87] *Trust Law Committee Consultation Paper: Rights of Creditors against Trustees and Trust Funds* (1997), para 3.4.

[88] See H Smith, 'Property as the Law of Things' (2012) 125 *Harvard Law Review* 1691.

[89] *Trust Law Committee Report: Rights of Creditors against Trustees and Trust Funds* (1998), para 3.9. 'Without detailed inquiries, which the trustees and the beneficiaries (wanting privacy) may well resent, how can C [creditor] know whether T [trustee] is in breach of his duty to diversify investments or to supervise the agent dealing with T or to take account of a particularly relevant consideration, or has failed to measure up to the standard of care required to be exhibited in contracting with C.'

[90] See especially *Evans v Evans* (1887) 34 Ch D 597; *Jennings v Mather* [1901] 1 KB 108; and *Vacuum Oil Company Proprietary Limited v Wiltshire* (1945) 72 CLR 319.

As the Trust Law Committee has said, 'reform is necessary because nineteenth century case law creates problems for wary creditors, let alone unwary creditors, and disadvantages creditors who deal with trustees rather than absolute beneficial owners: some levelling of the playing field seems needed in modern conditions'.[91] It is important that the common law grants the creditors of the trust a direct, non-derivative access to trust property simply because they are the creditor of that property. Although such a claim must be made through the trustee (as the title-holder of the trust property), it has nothing to do with the trustee's indemnity right or their personal assets. This reform also helps to facilitate consistency in trust law between common law and civil law, and consequently promotes the use of trusts in commercial contexts and international markets, where familiar rules and expected outcomes are considered to be advantageous.

B. Challenges to the Machinery of Trust Entity

Another problematic machinery relating to the trust creditor's interest and remedy is the trust entity theory. This theory has become particularly apparent through the increasing use of trusts for commercial purposes, especially given that professional trustees are involved. Its argument takes the other extreme to the machinery of the trustee's indemnity; it states that a trust behaves (from a legal perspective) as if it were a private limited corporation and its trustees are merely the directors of that corporation.[92] This machinery creates a trust entity and treats the indemnity right as a lien: assignable and enforceable independently of the trustee's rights of legal ownership.[93] Where a creditor is an assignee of the trustee's 'lien', there appears to be nothing to stop the creditor from claiming against the trust assets directly and following the assets from one set of hands to another, treating the trustee at the time as nothing more than an agent or manager of the property. As such, the creditor's right is no longer dependent on the trustee's personal right of access, and the trust behaves like a limited liability company rather than as an enterprise based on the trustee's duty-engrafted rights as the holder of a legal title.[94]

[91] *Trust Law Committee Consultation Paper: Rights of Creditors against Trustees and Trust Funds* (1997), preface.

[92] See *In re Johnson* (1880) 15 Ch D 548, 552; Ollikainen-Read (n 22) 177–78.

[93] Ollikainen-Read (n 22) 188. The lien reasoning in *Jennings v Mather* [1901] 1 KB 108 and subsequent Australian cases was aimed at protecting the creditors when the trustee was no longer in office and therefore no longer held legal title to the property.

[94] ibid 191. 'The description of the trustee's right as a lien grants a creditor the ability to follow the pool of assets independently of the trustee. This is because a lien is an assignable property right – it can be held just as well by a creditor as the trustee himself, and no reference need be made to the trustee's personal liability or limited right to access the assets. The mechanism of creditor access changes from the trustee being personally liable and satisfying that liability from the trust assets in accordance with the trust's terms, to the creditor contracting (i) through the trustee, (ii) with the trust estate, (iii) for a lien on the trust assets. Thinking of the trustee's indemnity as a lien therefore severs the creditor's dependence on the trustee's right. An assignee of this lien has a claim directly against the pool of assets in the trust, just as we would expect in the case of limited liability companies' (191–92).

This book argues that, although the trust entity machinery releases the trust creditor's interest from the trustee's indemnity, it wrongfully interprets a trust as a corporation and ignores the fact that, even though the trust is an independent legal instrument that is different to an agency, corporation or contract, it does not have its own juristic personality and thus requires that another person (usually a trustee) hold and manage the property on its behalf. Therefore, the creditor's access to the trust property will be made through the trustee as the titleholder of the trust property, rather than as a lien that is independent of the trustee's legal ownership.

A trust is not a corporation. As discussed in previous chapters, trusts existed before corporations.[95] Trusts were used in commerce and, by the seventeenth century, had become a progenitor of the modern limited liability company.[96] When the general incorporation statutes first appeared, many large businesses preferred trusts over companies. Both long before and long after the corporate form became freely available through statutes of general incorporation in the mid-nineteenth century, trusts were widely used in common law (eg in England and the US) as a substitute for a corporation, holding the property of unincorporated partnerships and associations.[97]

Moreover, from a theoretical perspective, it would be wrong for any legal system to conceptualise a trust as a corporation or legal person, because the result will only eliminate the trust as a fundamental legal institution.[98] To be a fundamental institution, trusts cannot be another institution such as a sub-category of legal persons or contracts.[99]

The legal person theory that considers the trust as a legal person and itself the owner of the trust property has been strongly rejected. For example, in its consultation paper and report on rights of creditors against trustees and trust funds, the Trust Law Committee clearly affirms that a trust has no legal personality.[100] The Scottish Law Commission, although recognising the feasibility of granting legal personality to trusts, is concerned that a legal person trust's operational disadvantages far outweigh any presentational advantages.[101] The legal person theory would cut Scotland off from international practice and future developments in trust law; this is because the concept of a legal device (wherein a property is owned by one

[95] For example, investment trusts operated initially as common law trusts for the aggregation of capital invested in non-land assets, but later they were categorised as public limited companies when the first Companies Act was passed in the 1860s.

[96] D'Angelo (n 8) 2.

[97] J Morley, 'The Common Law Corporation: The Power of the Trust in Anglo-American Business History' (2016) 116(2) *Columbia Law Review* 2145, 2146–47.

[98] Smith (n 2) 332.

[99] ibid 349.

[100] *Trust Law Committee Consultation Paper: Rights of Creditors against Trustees and Trust Funds* (1997), para 2.2; *Trust Law Committee Report: Rights of Creditors against Trustees and Trust Funds* (1998), para 2.2.

[101] *Discussion Paper on the Nature and the Constitution of Trusts* (Scot Law Com DP No 133, 2006), paras 1.3–1.4.

person on behalf of another) was at the time being developed at European[102] and international levels.[103] This method would also complicate things because, even if the trust were a legal person, it would still have to exercise its active legal capacity through agents (presumably, trustees). Trustees would, therefore, continue to owe fiduciary obligations to beneficiaries and to the trust.[104] In modern financial markets, time constraints on transactions create significant difficulties; considerable risks will be presented should a person not appreciate that they are dealing with a trustee.[105]

A trustee is not just the director of a trust. In most jurisdictions (both common and civil law) and in both family and commercial contexts, a trustee is granted the legal title to the trust property.[106] This is different to the title of director or manager of a company, as such titles hold no ownership of the company's assets.[107] As a result, a creditor is not an assignee of the trustee's lien. Misunderstandings in this regard are based upon the false premise that the trustee is acting as an agent for the trust.[108] If the trustee has a lien over trust property, it is hard to explain who or what right that lien is held against. One may argue that it is an equitable lien against the beneficiary's right to the trust property; however, the beneficiary does not have a direct claim to the trust property,[109] so the right cannot be held against the beneficiary's property rights. If the trustee's lien were to be held against the beneficial title generally, the problem is then how a lien would operate against an equity.[110]

In short, the machinery of trust entity has made progress in terms of releasing creditor's remedy from trustee's indemnity right, but it goes too far by considering a trust as a corporation, thus placing the trustee in the position of director of the corporation. A trust is not a corporation nor a legal person. It is the trustee, not the trust, who holds the trust property. Therefore, the creditors of the trust can make non-derivative claims against the trust property, but only through a trustee (as the legal owner of the trust property and under its 'fiduciary office' hat).

[102] See, eg, the Hague Trust Convention and the work of the Coordinating Group on Trust Law.

[103] *Discussion Paper on the Nature and the Constitution of Trusts* (Scot Law Com DP No 133, 2006), para 2.43.

[104] ibid para 2.41.

[105] *Trust Law Committee Consultation Paper: Rights of Creditors against Trustees and Trust Funds* (1997), para 3.2.

[106] The traditional common law concept of dual ownership of trust property establishes a distinction between the trustee's legal ownership of the trust assets and the beneficiary's equitable title to those same assets. Legal ownership provides the trustee with the legal rights and powers associated with the trust property. Those rights and powers must act in accordance with the trustee's personal obligation, ie to exercise legal ownership of trust property pursuant to the trust terms and thus to ensure the benefit of the beneficiaries. In civil law jurisdictions, ownership is indivisible and absolute. Most countries grant exclusive ownership to the trustee, except for Quebec Law, which defines the nature of the trust as a patrimony by appropriation through the Civil Code of Quebec. Under Quebec Law, neither the trustees nor the beneficiaries have any real right to the property, but full administration of the property (with corresponding obligations) is conferred on the trustee.

[107] See Companies Act 2006.

[108] *Trust Law Committee Report: Rights of Creditors against Trustees and Trust Funds* (1998), para 3.12.

[109] See especially *Gartside v Commissioners of Inland Revenue* [1968] AC 553 and *Sainsbury v IRC* [1970] Ch 712.

[110] Ollikainen-Read (n 22) 192.

C. Proposed Legal Reforms to the Creditor's Interest and Remedy

The two problematic machineries of trustee's indemnity (the argument that a trustee's indebtedness destroys a creditor's access to trust property) and trust entity (the conferring of a legal personality on a trust) do, in fact, present a dilemma. The liability of the trustee damages the creditor's interest because the creditor claims through the trustee. When a creditor's claim is independent of the trustee, it is the trust that holds the assets; the trustee is merely a manager. Namely, 'either the creditor is subject to the injustices of the unconnected liability rules, or the trust is a legal entity'.[111]

However, there is a solution to both machineries: a legal reform of the creditor's interest and remedy. This book suggests that trust creditors be offered direct, non-derivative access to trust property, thereby recognising their position, legally and financially, as creditors of the trust and the trust property. This direct claim would still be made through a trustee, as the titleholder of the trust property, but could be made irrespective of the trustee's indemnity right or the insolvency of its personal assets. Since the creditor's claim is not derived from any trustee rights (eg the indemnity right), the creditor's direct interest in the trust property and its remedy would remain independent and unaffected, even when the trustee exercised their fiduciary power improperly or exceeded the trust instrument, so long as the creditor was not previously aware of this. The creditor's access to the trust property would be limited to the extent to which that creditor enriched and benefited the trust property, and would be deprived if the creditor failed to act in good faith, contracted without consideration, or had knowledge of the trustee's default.[112]

As the Trust Law Committee recommended in its 1998 report *Rights of Creditors against Trustees and Trust Funds*:

> [W]hen an individual contracts 'as trustee' or 'as executor' or 'as administrator' or 'as personal representative' with another person, the individual shall not be personally liable to such person beyond the value of the trust fund or the deceased's estate at the time the other person requests payment; but, exceptionally, where the individual knows of a liquidated amount that is due or will become payable on a contingency and yet reduces the value of the trust fund, by making distributions to beneficiaries or by

[111] ibid 188.

[112] In the context of claims to make third parties liable for knowing receipt or dishonest assistance, Millett J (in *El Ajou v Dollar Land Holdings plc* [1993] EWCA Civ 4, [1993] 2 All ER 685, 713) and Lord Nicholls (in *Royal Brunei Airlines Sdn Bhd v Philip Tan Kok Ming* [1995] UKPC 4, [1995] 2 AC 378, [1995] 3 All ER 97, 107–08) appear to allow third parties to assume a trustee has wide investment powers. Indeed, Lord Nicholls states that '[b]eneficiaries cannot reasonably expect that all the world dealing with their trustees should owe them a duty to take care lest the trustees are behaving dishonestly' (*Royal Brunei Airlines Sdn Bhd v Philip Tan Kok Ming* [1995] UKPC 4, [1995] 2 AC 378, [1995] 3 All ER 97, 108). It is prima facie dishonest for a trustee deliberately to incur liabilities improperly.

> incurring further obligations that are not reasonably necessary for the preservation of the trust assets, such individual shall also be personally liable to the extent of the reduction in value.[113]

This is an advanced way of understanding the creditor's interest and remedy. It applies both to traditional family trusts and commercial trusts, sits well in civil law (particularly with the patrimony theory that has adapted to accommodate trusts), and matches with the new legislative amendments in common law jurisdictions such as the US.

IV. Conclusion

Laws related to the creditor's interest are the unprepossessing child of the trust family when compared to the more interesting 'siblings' of trustee's role or beneficiaries' interest. This chapter attempts to fill the lacuna in the literature and legislation on this subject. It distinguishes the concept of the trust creditor from misused concepts (eg the trustee's creditor) and resolves the misunderstandings surrounding the creditor's interest caused by this confusion. Upon examining the changes and challenges the commercial use of trust and surrounding case law have brought to the trust creditor's interest and remedy, this chapter proposes solutions to these discovered challenges and develops a coherent understanding of the creditor's interest that fits into civil law and aligns with the new developments in common law.

This book denies the machinery of the trustee's indemnity right, which confuses the trust creditor with the trustee's creditor and unfairly bases the trust creditor's interest and remedy on the trustee's indemnity right. The trustee's indemnity machinery is only a pathway taken in common law; it is different to civil law practice, and even in common law jurisdictions (eg in the US), the law has been revised to confer direct access to trust property to trust creditors. This book also rebuts the machinery of trust entity (a dilemma surrounding the trustee's indemnity theory), which defines the trust as a private limited corporation and thus places the trustee in the simple position of the director of the corporation. The trust entity machinery confuses trust with corporation, and unnecessarily and wrongfully grants juristic personality to the trust. In denying the two main problematic theories, this book proposes a unified understanding of the creditor's interest, thereby identifying the most practical way to realise and protect that interest; that is, to provide the trust creditors (who are a bona fide third party for value with no knowledge of any connected defaults by the trustee) with direct, non-derivative access to the trust property. In doing so, this book supports recognising the creditors of trust property and appreciating that the claim is to be made through the trustee (not the trust itself) as the titleholder of the trust property, irrespective of the trustee's indemnity right or the insolvency of its personal assets.

[113] *Trust Law Committee Report: Rights of Creditors against Trustees and Trust Funds* (1998), para 3.14.

7

The Future of Trusts

Although it originated as a product of equity, the trust is now no longer exclusive to common law or family contexts. Together with the development of commercial activities and the international financial market, trusts are now often used for commercial purposes (indeed, this has become the main use of trusts today) and, as a result, they have been accommodated in civilian jurisdictions. The commercial use of trusts has introduced changes and challenges to trust law and to the rights and obligations of trust participants (eg beneficiaries, trustees and trust creditors). This does not separate a commercial trust from the traditional form, as the fundamental rules of trusts (eg the independence of trust property and the trustee's fiduciary duty) still apply. However, traditional approaches and a unified set of rules imposed on both family and commercial trusts are no longer fit in all circumstances. Therefore, a legal reform of trust law is required and this is considered to be a crucial part of the future of trusts.

This chapter develops an overview of the legal reform of trust law in the UK. It suggests an evolutionary development of statutory law that provides special rules for commercial trusts, instead of a revolutionary reform of the entire normative system that separate commercial from traditional trusts. It claims that currently proposed alternative solutions (eg case law, foreign law, international law and contracts) cannot take the place of a developed domestic legislation.

I. Proposal for the Legal Reform of Trust Law

The legislation of trusts in England has not been comprehensively reviewed since 1925. In contrast, many other offshore and onshore jurisdictions, including New Zealand,[1] Singapore,[2] Jersey[3] and Scotland,[4] have modernised their trust laws

[1] See Trusts Bill 290-1 (2017) (New Zealand).

[2] See Business Trusts Act 2004 (Chapter 31A) (Singapore).

[3] See Trusts (Jersey) Law 1984.

[4] Scotland has conducted a momentous review and reform of its trust law. See especially *Report on Trust Law* (Scot Law Com No 239, 2014); *Discussion Paper on Liability of Trustees to Third Parties* (Scot Law Com DP No 138, 2008); *Discussion Paper on the Nature and the Constitution of Trusts* (Scot Law Com DP No 133, 2006).

and have been creative in their maintenance of a healthy trust market.[5] Civil law notaries and commercial lawyers have become increasingly aware of the use of trusts to provide ring-fenced financial arrangements in their civilian jurisdictions. Pressure from these notaries and lawyers led to the Hague Conference on Private International Law, during which various countries took steps towards the preparation of a convention[6] recognising trusts in civil law and international markets.[7] The development of trusts and trust law in other jurisdictions (both common and civil law) and at regional and international levels has made the need for the legal reform of trust law in the UK, especially in England, more urgent.

Various different reform suggestions, both revolutionary and evolutionary, through the retrospective remedy of rectification or remedy of rescission,[8] have been submitted. The Society of Trust and Estate Practitioners, the National Association of Pension Trusts, the Association of Pension Lawyers, and the Charity Commission have all supported the idea of a more fundamental reform (while favouring the modification and clarification of existing law).[9] The Association of Corporate Trustees and the Law Society's Land and Succession Committee, in contrast, are strongly against fundamental reform, with the view that minor reforms, coupled with the precautions set out in the Financial Law Panel paper, *Financial Dealings with Trustees*,[10] will provide a satisfactory solution.[11]

This book does not fully side with any of the above-stated views. Instead, it argues that, although a revolutionary reform that separates commercial from traditional trusts and that requires the reorganisation of the entire normative system is unnecessary and wrong, the precautions in the Financial Law Panel's paper are insufficient. Instead, it suggests that the development of legislation supplementing the special rules regarding commercial trusts is what is required in the UK (and notably in England). Such evolutionary yet cautious reform would make trust law nimbler and more efficient. It would help to modernise UK trust law and enhance the competitiveness of the country's trust services in both national and

[5] See *Thirteenth Programme of Law Reform* (Law Com No 377, 2017), para 2.24.

[6] The Hague Convention on the Law Applicable to Trusts and on their Recognition (Hague Trust Convention) (The Hague, 1 July 1985).

[7] DJ Hayton, 'Thoughts on Future Trust Law Developments' (2016) 22(9) *Trusts & Trustees* 1002, 1002.

[8] See Hayton (n 7) 1012. There are two types of legal rectification with different objectives: the retrospective remedy of rectification and the remedy of rescission. The remedy of rectification is granted more restrictively than the remedy of recession. Rectification for mistake is restricted to rectify the effect of a mistake, as opposed to the consequences of a mistake in a broad sense that is rectified by recession for mistake. A major difficulty is the ambiguity of the terms 'effect' and 'consequence'. The doctrine of rescission for mistake enables the mistaken consequences to be rescinded for a fresh start to be made, while the doctrine of rectification enables wording to be rectified from the outset so as to produce the effect or meaning then intended by the signatory. Thus mistaken consequences can only be rescinded, not rectified.

[9] *Trust Law Committee Report: Rights of Creditors against Trustees and Trust Funds* (1998), paras 4.1–4.2.

[10] *Financial Law Panel Paper: Financial Dealings with Trustees* (1997).

[11] *Trust Law Committee Report: Rights of Creditors against Trustees and Trust Funds* (1998), para 4.3.

global markets, as well as providing a response to the international development of trust law.[12]

There is no need for revolutionary reform, and it would be wrong to state that a commercial trust is not a trust. As discussed in previous chapters, the changes and challenges commercial use has brought to trusts and trust law do not separate commercial from traditional trusts. This is because the essence and fundamental principles of trust (eg the independence of trust property and the trustee's fiduciary duty) still apply to commercial trusts, and court decisions and case law have developed in such a way as to manage the changes and challenges they have been presented with (albeit not always successfully). Indeed, the essential principles of trusts are what make the trust an attractive and pragmatic instrument for commercial use.

While appreciating that a commercial trust is still a trust and so requires the application of fundamental trust principles, a unified set of rules should not be forced to apply to trusts in both a family and commercial context. The starting point for a legal reform of trust law is a shift in mindset – one that acknowledges that a commercial trust has special qualities and merits specific provisions distinct from the current rules set out to serve a traditional family trust.

Existing trust legislation in the UK, particularly in England, mainly focuses on regulating trustees' rights and obligations; provisions for settlors, beneficiaries and trust creditors are mostly absent. Even legislation relating to the actions of trustees is significantly lagging behind. The regulation of trustees' powers and appointments is still relegated to the Trustee Act 1925, which accompanied the land reform legislation that took place in the 1920s. Provisions for trustees' duties are contained in the Trustee Act 2000. Although the 2000 Act is relatively modern and covers parts of a trustee's investment powers (in part II of the Act), its stipulations are still restricted and inadequate, falling far behind the varied and increasingly prevalent commercial use of trusts in practice.[13]

Given the above, legal reform of UK (primarily English) trust legislation to provide special rules for commercial trusts and address the vehicle's unique changes and challenges is required. As noted by Bryan, specialist rules must be developed (or at the very least, settled equitable principles must be modified) so that the business objectives of the trust can be properly effectuated and established trust principles can be adapted to the contemporary reality faced by the beneficiary of a commercial trust (whose expectations are very different to those of the traditional object of a settlor's bounty).[14] Special rules for commercial trusts should be developed to reflect this newly evolved role and to provide more flexible

[12] *Thirteenth Programme of Law Reform* (Law Com No 377, 2017), para 2.24.

[13] For example, see ss 36(3), 37 and 38 of the Trustee Act 2000, the power of investment under the 2000 Act does not apply to occupational pension schemes, authorised unit trusts or common investment or common deposit schemes for charities.

[14] See M Bryan, 'Recipient Liability under the Torrens System: Some Category Errors' (2007) 26(1) *University of Queensland Law Journal* 83.

and liberal parameters than those offered by traditional trust laws.[15] Targeted remediation and regulation should be implemented through the action not only of the courts but also of the legislatures.[16] Statutory development is particularly needed to address the challenges that arise regarding matters to do with commercial trusts: the concept of a commercial trust; the beneficiary's interest; the trustee's rights and obligations and their delegation (eg the delegation of a trustee's role in a unit trust between a trustee in name and a manager); and the trust creditor's interest and remedy.

The first and arguably most important clarification that a reformed legislation of trust should make relates to the concept of a commercial trust; that is, what constitutes a commercial trust, what is the essence of a commercial trust, and what are the main forms or types of commercial trust according to their different uses. This is particularly important, because the notion of what a commercial trust is may vary between different jurisdictions, and misunderstandings may result in denial that a commercial trust is a trust, or confusion with other legal vehicles such as companies or contracts. The future of the trust as an independent legal scheme requires the clarification of the term itself; it needs to be distinguished from similar commercial instruments. If this does not happen, or if the legislation fails to do this, the concern is that 'the trust will cease to have any real distinction from other legal ideas'.[17] Only when this cornerstone (ie the concept of the commercial trust) is established, can specific rules regarding trustees, beneficiaries and other trust participants be methodically regulated.

More meticulous and professional rules should be developed for commercial trusts than for traditional family trusts, because commercial trusts necessitate more complex activities and a growing number of professional trustees and skilled lawyers and bankers are involved in commercial trusts. Contractual liabilities are increasingly being incurred by trustees (or their delegates) on behalf of trusts; they may be borrowing money, purchasing on credit, or entering into transitions in financial markets. Commercial trustees (especially those in investment trusts) face a double-sided personal exposure: first, to the trust's equity investors (normally the settlor-beneficiaries of the trust) as a fiduciary, and second, to external contract counterparties (the creditors of the trust) as the principal (being the titleholder of trust property on behalf of the trust).[18] Nowadays, to manage their risk position vis-à-vis both the equity investors and external parties, consideration is given to ways in which trustees use contractual techniques to maximise their power and minimise their required duties.[19]

A variegated trust structure has developed to address the trustee's various investment powers. It is foreseen that the trust will be increasingly used for investment

[15] Hayton (n 7) 1002.
[16] See Bryan (n 14) 83.
[17] DJ Hayton (ed), *The International Trust*, 3rd edn (Bristol, Jordan Publishing, 2011) 838.
[18] N D'Angelo, *Commercial Trusts* (Chatswood, LexisNexis Butterworths, 2014) 220.
[19] ibid 158.

purposes, and so its legislation will experience necessary reform (although the duties and liabilities of trustees may depend on the terms of the trust in question and the relationship between the relevant parties). A classic rule of the trustee's investment duty is established in *Harvard College v Amory*,[20] in which Justice Putman asserted that all that can be required of a trustee when investing is that they conduct themselves faithfully and exercise sound discretion.[21] Specifically, trustees must be faithful and not invest the trust funds in their own property nor place themselves in a position of conflict. Trustees should treat trust beneficiaries impartially regarding both income and capital.[22] They should exercise sound and positive discretion (ie they should make prudent and discreet choices in relation to all aspects of investment management). Acting prudently does not require investors to avoid risk; no investment is risk-free. Rather, investors are required to manage risks through adequately diversified portfolios, minimising investment costs and avoiding speculation.[23] Speculation is considered *ipso facto* imprudent and thus is not permitted.

The rules established in *Harvard College v Amory* help to guide modern commercial trustees in the absence of a detailed statutory law. However, it is an US case, and so some of its rules are not completely favoured by UK governmental institutions. This reaffirms the importance of developing English legislation. For example, the Law Commission for England and Wales recommended that, in the longer term, HM Revenue and Customs and HM Treasury should enter into discussions with the trust industry regarding the feasibility of total return investment (ie investment that ignores the distinction between income and capital), so far as it is consistent with current tax policy.[24] With respect to the trustee's power of speculation, the Trust Law Committee holds a different view to that of the case law, stating that a trustee's powers in the financial markets, especially investment powers, may be exercised to allow the use of derivatives, either for the purpose of controlling and limiting risk or for speculative reasons.[25]

In summary, instead of a revolutionary reform that separates commercial from traditional trusts, this book supports the idea of an evolutionary reform that supplements trust law with special provisions concerning commercial trusts (either in the form of a uniform trust act or as a special law of commercial trusts). This approach would be both sufficient and efficient, and this book considers it to be the future of trusts. The objective of such legal reform is to accommodate the

[20] *Harvard College v Amory* (1830) 26 Mass (9 Pick) 446.

[21] ibid 461.

[22] G Watt and P Todd, *Cases & Materials on Equity & Trusts*, 10th edn (Oxford, Oxford University Press, 2016) 393.

[23] Modern portfolio theory originated with the work of Harry Markowitz. See H Markowitz, *Portfolio Selection: Efficient Diversification of Investments* (Yale, Yale University Press, 1959).

[24] *Capital and Income in Trusts: Classification and Apportionment* (Law Com No 315, 2009), para 5.104.

[25] *Trust Law Committee Consultation Paper: Rights of Creditors against Trustees and Trust Funds* (1997), para 1.1.

reasonable commercial expectations of the participants in a modern commercial trust while preserving the substantial benefits accrued through the trust device and the fundamental principles of trusts. Such a solution would continue to permit the use of a trust as an attractive commercial instrument, while remedying its flaws through targeted and incremental changes by the legislature, assisted by the courts. This legal reform would help to identify and affirm the nature of a commercial trust (ie that it *is* a trust); preserve the core trust principles that make a trust attractive for commercial use (eg inbuilt protection for the beneficiary); provide a better understanding of trusts; resolve the myths surrounding and the misuse of trusts; and develop solutions to any challenges that might arise.

II. Rebuttal of Alternative Solutions to the Reform of Trust Law

One might argue that, given that the commercial uses of trust are still evolving, the legal reform of trust law is neither urgent nor required, as any reformed statutory law would in the end result in legal hysteresis because of the stability and expectancy requirements placed upon statutory law. Alternatively, it might be argued that continuing to leave the emerging changes and challenges to the auspices of 'more flexible' case law is totally fine. This book objects to this assertion, as case law has misunderstood several issues (eg it has mistaken the trustee's indemnity as the basis for the trust creditor's remedy). Additionally, long-standing legislative inaction has resulted in numerous instances of confusion and the misuse of commercial trusts; for example, there have been doubts as to whether a commercial trust is still a trust and instances where the commercial trust has been misinterpreted as a corporation. For these reasons, although case law has developed to resolve issues that have arisen, a reform of statutory law in relation to commercial trusts is still required to consolidate the vehicle's nature and fundamental principles and to provide a legislative response to the already considerably evolved commercial uses of trust in practice. As Hayton states, 'so for the future the fear is continued drift; the hope is for a clear concept and an enlightened manner of its application. The plea is that we realise what is happening before, as things seem, it is too late.'[26] Immediate statutory reform would be beneficial, as it would maximise the chances for the early adoption and implementation of solutions, in turn helping to direct or correct developments in case law. Law in general should only be changed by a process of gradual development, rather than by violent new advances or retreats, revolutions or ruptures; a danger to judicial probity arises in instances where the court deliberately sets out to alter the law. Giving judges uncontrolled discretionary power would, in effect, intrude into the role played by other arms of

[26] Hayton (n 17) 889.

government.[27] 'To err is human. To reform is divine.'[28] A developed statutory law might, therefore, be the most reliable code of conduct for legal practitioners.

In addition to case law, an alternative solution has also been raised: using foreign laws to address commercial issues in the UK. For example, Hayton indicates:

> Choice of a foreign governing law can be supported by exclusive trust jurisdiction clauses, whether to ensure that a court will have the necessary expertise if litigation arises or to make it more difficult or expensive to litigate in a distant country, particularly if it requires security for costs from non-local litigants. It is my belief that more use of a foreign governing law and of changes of governing law to a more flexible foreign governing law will be a feature of future developments in the practice of trust law for wealthy clients justifying bespoke trusts.[29]

While, in the absence of suitable domestic regulation, foreign laws might sometimes help to address trust issues that arise in the UK, this is neither a long-term solution nor the optimal choice. The real need and priority here is the presence of an internal authority and the development of domestic legislation; foreign laws are and should be considered as only transitional relief or as the last resort in the absence of a domestic law. As Hayton notes, foreign governance laws only apply to 'trust[s] with significant English elements'[30] and it can be dangerous to apply foreign legislation when the pitfalls around doing so are overlooked.[31] No jurisdiction can or should be based on foreign laws. In fact, implementing foreign laws to resolve trust matters in the UK (particularly in England) is a forced choice that calls attention to the lack of domestic legislation and the urgency of legal reform.

In addition to foreign laws, international law[32] is also referred to as a legal resource in the UK and used to resolve trust issues.[33] However, this does not always work, because the direct application of the Hague Trust Convention or other international laws requires that there be compatibility between the international law in question and domestic law (ie that there be significant English elements in the Hague Trust Convention's approach to trusts). The Hague Trust Convention, differing from the English approach, adopts a neutral means of regulating trusts, encompassing a broad jurisdictional scope by incorporating both common and civil law.[34] The Hague Trust Convention is considered to be

[27] See JD Heydon, 'Judicial Activism and the Death of the Rule of Law' (2003) 23(2) *Australian Bar Review* 110.

[28] JA Cooper, 'Empty Promises: Settlor's Intent, the Uniform Trust Code, and the Future of Trust Investment Law' (2008) 88 *Boston University Law Review* 1165, 1210.

[29] Hayton (n 7) 1003.

[30] ibid 1004.

[31] ibid 1003.

[32] Primarily the Hague Convention on the Law Applicable to Trusts and on their Recognition (Hague Trust Convention) (The Hague, 1 July 1985).

[33] See Recognition of Trusts Act 1987. This Act was reproduced in SIF Group 128 (Trusts and Liferents, Scotland) and Group 98:4 (Property, England & Wales: Trusts).

[34] See Hague Trust Convention, art 2: 'For the purposes of this Convention, "the term trust" refers to the legal relationships created – *inter vivos* or on death – by a person, the settlor, when assets have been placed under the control of a trustee for the benefit of a beneficiary or for a specified purpose.

an amazing comparative mediation between different legal cultures, acting as a bridge between the common–civil law divide.[35] Indeed, instead of being adopted by a single jurisdiction to address its domestic issues, private international law has been developed in such a way that recognises the different laws produced by various nations deserve a wide measure of respect.[36]

For these reasons, some international instruments recognise the use of mechanisms related to (but not identical to) trusts.[37] For example, usufructs seen in Louisianan law are expressly mentioned in the Common Reporting Standard (CRS).[38] The CRS is an international rule developed by the Organisation for Economic Co-operation and Development (OECD)[39] that applies to trusts used for tax planning purposes. Under the CRS and the Foreign Accounts Tax Compliance Act (FATCA)[40] banks and trustees in over 100 jurisdictions have to file an annual report regarding any foreign resident controlling persons or equity interest holders of qualifying trusts holding financial accounts within their territory.[41] The CRS is aimed at tackling cross-border tax evasion activities and has led to trusts having a high degree of global regulatory transparency. As is the case with the Hague Trust Convention, the CRS has been developed to facilitate international communication and collaboration, instead of being used by a single jurisdiction to resolve domestic issues. Therefore, international rules and conventions have not been developed as alternatives to domestic laws in the UK, and their implementation does not negate the demand for a reform of UK (notably English) statutory trust law.

A trust has the following characteristics – a) the assets constitute a separate fund and are not a part of the trustee's own estate; b) title to the trust assets stands in the name of the trustee or in the name of another person on behalf of the trustee; c) the trustee has the power and the duty, in respect of which he is accountable, to manage, employ or dispose of the assets in accordance with the terms of the trust and the special duties imposed upon him by law.' See also M Lupoi, 'The Shapeless Trust' (1995) 1(3) *Trusts & Trustees* 15; F Noseda, 'Equitable Ownership, Butter and Donkeys: Setting out a Vision for the Future of the Hague Trust Convention' (2022) 28(10) *Trusts & Trustees* 924, 934.

[35] Noseda (n 34) 925.

[36] Hayton (n 7) 1005. The various national laws should be given effect unless they are manifestly incompatible with a jurisdiction's public policy. For example, in *Re Fitzgerald* [1904] 1 Ch 573, the English Court of Appeal held that the assignment to a London moneylender of a Scots non-assignable alimentary life interest under a trust and as security for a loan provided no security to the lender. It would, however, have done so under an English trust, because English life interest cannot be non-assignable.

[37] Noseda (n 34) 935.

[38] The Common Reporting Standard (CRS), developed in response to the G20 request and approved by the Organisation for Economic Co-operation and Development (OECD) Council on 15 July 2014, calls on jurisdictions to obtain information from their financial institutions and automatically exchange that information with other jurisdictions on an annual basis. It sets out the financial account information to be exchanged; the financial institutions required to report; the different types of accounts and taxpayers covered; as well as common due diligence procedure to be followed by financial institutions. The purpose of CRS is to combat tax evasion and protect the integrity of tax systems.

[39] The Organisation for Economic Co-operation and Development (OECD) is an intergovernmental organisation with 38 member countries, founded in 1961 to stimulate economic progress and world trade. It is a forum whose member countries describe themselves as committed to democracy and the market economy, providing a platform to compare policy experiences, seek answers to common problems, identify good practices, and coordinate domestic and international policies of its members.

[40] Foreign Accounts Tax Compliance Act, § 6038D (2010) (US).

[41] See Common Reporting Standard, art VIII.

Another alternative solution that has been proposed to settle trust issues in England is the contract. Contracts are widely used in commercial trusts in various situations, for instance, in instances where a trustee's role has been delegated among professionals via a trust deed (eg between the trustee in name and the manager in a unit trust), where the investment and/or management of trust fund has been arranged by contracts, and where trust creditors are engaged and have transacted with a trust through contracts. Such increased involvement of contracts and contractual obligations in trusts have led to a misunderstanding that the trust relationship could be sufficiently regulated by contract; that is, that trust law has itself assumed a subsidiary status and thus no longer has an urgent need for reform. It might be the case that, nowadays, internal relationships in or disputes concerning commercial trusts are resolved through multiple means that might include contracts, arbitration and/or mediation.[42] Additionally, a trust document is understood to reflect a contract, and contractarian principles form a fundamental pillar of trust law.[43] However, the involvement of contracts in trusts does not make the trust a series of contracts (as the components of a thing do not determine its essence).[44] And, as an independent legal scheme, a trust is still subject to trust law as its primary and fundamental legal resource. Therefore, a legal reform of trust law (most significantly, a reform of the outdated trust acts) is of great importance.

In short, although the suggested alternative solutions (case law, foreign law, international law and contracts) all play a certain role in resolving issues arising from the commercial trust, they are only adopted as transitional relief or as a last resort and cannot replace domestic law. Thus, the need for statutory reform of trust law in England (or, more broadly, throughout the UK) is still at the forefront of the discussion. The demand for legal predictability and stability fosters the development of statutory trust law; any such development should acknowledge the limits[45] and risks caused by the greater rigidity and complexity of legislation compared to case law, as what appear to be default guidelines governing trust investment management would morph into rigid requirements. Should this happen, a range of common estate-planning and commercial techniques would lose much of their allure.[46]

III. Conclusion

The trust has gained widespread acceptance in modern financial markets, a fact attributable to its tax advantages and favourable legal status. After analysing

[42] See examples as in Guernsey, Bahamas and Florida.
[43] Cooper (n 28) 1182.
[44] Detailed discussion can be found in ch 5, section II.C.
[45] For example, new law normally only has prospective effect; the remedy of rectification is unique in having retrospective effect.
[46] Cooper (n 28) 1170.

the evolvement of the trust from a traditional family instrument to the modern commercial vehicle, the trust's introduction into civil law as a result of its commercial advantages and the changes and challenges the commercial use of trusts has presented to trust participants, this book has concluded with a final chapter that looks ahead to the future of the trust. It submits that a legal reform of trust law, particularly statutory law, is imperative after the long dormancy of trust acts. Although alternative resources, including case law, foreign laws, international rules and contracts, have been employed to resolve issues arising from commercial trusts, they cannot supplant domestic statutory trust law nor negate the need for its reform in the UK, and in England in particular.

Conclusion

The trust has become a popular instrument at the heart of complex commercial dealings. It serves as an extremely useful mechanism for achieving fair play in a variety of fast-changing, highly sophisticated environments, such as investment, insolvency, securitisation and shareholding. The diversified uses and increasing prominence of trusts in business and commerce have a strong impact on the nature of trust law. Commercial trust law is an ever-evolving area of research.

Based on comprehensive studies of case law, legislation, theories and literature, this book rethinks the traditional legal approaches of trusts and generates new doctrinal insights into the evolved role of trusts for commercial uses, its principal forms developed in common law and its legal transplant in civilian jurisdictions. It examines the changes and challenges the commercial uses of the trust have brought to the rights and obligations of beneficiaries and trustees, and it provides advice on trust law reforms by juxtaposing historical, interdisciplinary, comparative, theoretical and doctrinal methodologies.

The analysis of this book provides greater legal certainty for commercial trusts and fills the gap in legal research on UK commercial trusts, which is of great research significance for both scholars and legal practitioners. The author hopes that this work will provide some insights on the future of trust law and direct both the scholarly debate and legislative agendas on the subject of commercial trusts towards a better development.

Bibliography

Agnew, S and K Pukis (2018), 'Trustees' Indemnities – Is Timing Everything?' 24 *Trusts & Trustees* 989.

Baker, J (2019) *An Introduction to English Legal History*, 5th edn (Oxford, Oxford University Press).

Batiza, R (1957) 'The Evolution of the Fideicomiso (Trust) Concept under Mexican Law' 11 *Miami Law Quarterly* 478.

Bean, JMW (1968) *The Decline of English Feudalism, 1215–1540* (Manchester, Manchester University Press).

Beinart, C (1980) 'Trusts in Roman and Roman-Dutch Law' 1(1) *Journal of Legal History* 6.

Benoit, M (1998) 'The Development of the Concept of Pension Trust under Quebec Civil Law' 17 *Estates, Trusts & Pensions Journal* 203.

Bryan, M (2007) 'Recipient Liability under the Torrens System: Some Category Errors' 26(1) *University of Queensland Law Journal* 83.

Cameron, E and others (2018) *Honoré's South African Law of Trusts*, 6th edn (Cape Town, Juta and Company Pty Ltd).

Carn, ME (2015) 'Distinguishing Traditional from Commercial Trusts: A Dangerous Precedent or Necessary Complication?' 21 *Trusts & Trustees* 868.

Chalmers, J (2009) 'Ownership of Trust Property in Scotland and Louisiana' in VV Palmer and EC Reid (eds), *Mixed Jurisdictions Compared: Private Law in Louisiana and Scotland* (Edinburgh, Edinburgh University Press) 132.

Chen, D (2003) *Trust Law and the Innovation of Trust System in China* (Shanghai, Lixin Accounting Publishing House).

Chesterman, MR (1984) 'Family Settlements on Trust: Landowners and the Rising Bourgeoisie' in GR Rubin and D Sugarman (eds), *Law, Economy and Society, 1750–1914: Essays in the History of English Law* (Abingdon, Professional Books) 124.

Coing, H (1973) *Treuhand kraft privaten Rechtsgeschäfts* (Munich, Beck).

Cooper, JA (2008) 'Empty Promises: Settlor's Intent, the Uniform Trust Code, and the Future of Trust Investment Law' 88 *Boston University Law Review* 1165.

Corbett, MM (1993) 'Trust Law in the 90's: Challenges and Change' 56(2) *Journal of Contemporary Roman-Dutch Law* 262.

Cornish, W and others (2010) *The Oxford History of the Laws of England: Volume XII: 1820–1914 Private Law* (Oxford, Oxford University Press).

Cushing, HA (2018) *Voting Trusts: A chapter in Recent Corporate History* (Charleston, BiblioBazaar).

Cutts, T (2012) 'The Nature of Equitable Property: A Functional Analysis' 6 *Journal of Equity* 44.

Dale, B (1988) 'Varying Trustees' Investment Powers' 5 *The Conveyancer and Property Lawyer* 380.

D'Angelo, N (2014) *Commercial Trusts* (Chatswood, LexisNexis Butterworths).

Davies, PS and Virgo, G (2019) *Equity & Trusts: Text, Cases, and Materials*, 3rd edn (Oxford, Oxford University Press).

Donald, MS (2014) 'The "Proper" Approach to a Trustee's Right to Indemnity out of Trust Assets' 8 *Journal of Equity* 283.

Du Toit, F (2013) 'Jurisprudential Milestones in the Development of Trust Law in South Africa's Mixed Legal System' in L Smith (ed), *The Worlds of the Trust* (Cambridge, Cambridge University Press) 257.

Emerich, Y (2013) 'The Civil Law Trust: A Modality of Ownership or An Interlude in Ownership?' in L Smith (ed), *The Worlds of the Trust* (Cambridge, Cambridge University Press) 21.

English, D (2014) 'The Fiduciary Duties and Powers of a Trustee under the Uniform Trust Code' 20 *Trusts & Trustees* 52.

Fairpo, A and Salter, D (2019) *Revenue Law: Principles and Practice*, 37th edn (Edinburgh, Bloomsbury Professional).
Finn, PD (1977) *Fiduciary Obligations* (London, Lawbook Co).
Fortin, G (1999) 'How the Province of Quebec Absorbs the Concept of the Trust' 18 *Estates, Trusts & Pensions Journal* 285.
Gao, L (2010) *The Misunderstood Trust: Principles on Trust Law* (Shanghai, Fudan University Press).
Garton, J, Probert, R and Bean, G (2020) *Moffat's Trusts Law: Text and Materials*, 7th edn (Cambridge, Cambridge University Press).
Geach, WD and Yeats, J (2007) *Trusts: Law and Practice* (Wetton, Juta).
Graziadei, U Mattei and L Smith (2005), 'Commercial Trusts in European Private Law: The Interest and Scope of the Enquiry' in M Graziadei, U Mattei and L Smith (eds), *Commercial Trusts in European Private Law* (Cambridge, Cambridge University Press).
Graziadei, M, Mattei, U and Smith, L (eds) (2005) *Commercial Trusts in European Private Law* (Cambridge, Cambridge University Press).
Gretton, GL (1996) 'Trust and Patrimony' in H MacQueen (ed), *Scots Law into the 21st Century: Essays in Honour of W A Wilson* (Edinburgh, W Green/Sweet & Maxwell) 182.
—— (1997) 'Constructive Trusts' 1 *Edinburgh Law Review* 281.
—— (2000) 'Trusts Without Equity' 49 *ICLQ* 599.
—— (2000) 'Trusts' in KGC Reid and R Zimmermann (eds), *A History of Private Law in Scotland* (Oxford, Oxford University Press) 480.
Guan, J (2008) *Trust Law and Practice in China* (Beijing, China Law Press).
Haley, M (2017) 'Section 61 of the Trustee Act 1925: A Judicious Breach of Trust?' 76(3) *CLJ* 537.
Harris, R (2009) *Industrializing English Law: Entrepreneurship and Business Organization, 1720–1844* (Cambridge, Cambridge University Press).
Hart, WG (1899) 'What is a Trust?' 15 *LQR* 294.
Hayton, DJ (2002) 'English Trusts and Their Commercial Counterparts in Continental Europe' in DJ Hayton (ed), *Extending the Boundaries of Trusts and Similar Ring-Fenced Funds* (London, Kluwer Law International) 23–58.
—— (2010) 'The Uses of Trusts in the Commercial Context' in A Kaplan (ed), *Trusts in Prime Jurisdictions*, 3rd edn (London, Globe Law and Business) 611.
—— (ed) (2011) *The International Trust*, 3rd edn (Bristol, Jordan Publishing).
—— (2016) 'Thoughts on Future Trust Law Developments' 22(9) *Trusts & Trustees* 1002.
Hayton, DJ, Kortmann, SCJJ and Verhagen, HLE (eds) (1999), *Principles of European Trust Law* (The Hague, Kluwer Law International).
Hayton, DJ, Pigott, H and Benjamin, J (2002) 'The Use of Trusts in International Financial Transactions' 1 *Journal of International Banking & Financial Law* 23.
He, X (1987) 'Studies of Trust Law' 1 *Chung Hsing Law Review* 1.
Heydon, JD (2003) 'Judicial Activism and the Death of the Rule of Law' 23(2) *Australian Bar Review* 110.
Ho, L (2003) *Trust Law in China* (Hong Kong, Sweet & Maxwell Asia).
—— (2004) 'The Reception of Trust in Asia: Emerging Asian Principles of Trust?' *Singapore Journal of Legal Studies* 287.
—— (2012) 'Trust Laws in China: History, Ambiguity and Beneficiary's Rights' in L Smith (ed), *Re-imagining the Trust: Trusts in Civil Law* (Cambridge, Cambridge University Press) 183.
Ho, L, Lee, R and Jin, J (2013) 'Trust Law in China: A Critical Evaluation of its Conceptual Foundation' in L Ho and R Lee (eds), *Trust Law in Asian Civil Law Jurisdictions: A Comparative Analysis* (Cambridge, Cambridge University Press) 80.
Hohfeld, WN (1917) 'Fundamental Legal Conceptions as Applied in Judicial Reasoning' 26 *Yale Law Journal* 710.
Honoré, T (1997) 'Obstacles to the Reception of Trust Law? The Example of South Africa and Scotland' in AM Rabello (ed), *Aequitas and Equity: Equity in Civil Law and Mixed Jurisdictions* (Jerusalem, The Hebrew University of Jerusalem) 793.

—— (2003) 'Trusts: The Inessentials' in J Getzler (ed), *Rationalizing Property, Equity and Trusts: Essays in Honour of Edward Burn* (Oxford, Oxford University Press) 1.
Hopkins, N (2011) 'The Relevance of Context in Property Law: A Case for Judicial Restraint?' 31(2) *Legal Studies* 175.
Hudson, A (2011) 'Trusts and Finance Law' in DJ Hayton (ed), *The International Trust*, 3rd edn (Bristol, Jordan Publishing) 649.
Hudson, J and C Mitchell (2021), 'Trustee Recoupment: A Power Analysis' 35 *Trust Law International* 3.
Huo, Y (2003) *Discussions of Trust Law* (Beijing, China University of Political Science and Law Press).
Kahan, M (2002) 'Rethinking Corporate Bonds: The Trade-off between Individual and Collective Rights' 77 *New York University Law Review* 1040.
Keeton, G (1971) *Modern Developments in the Law of Trusts* (Belfast, Northern Ireland Legal Quarterly).
Langbein, JH (1995) 'The Contractarian Basis of the Law of Trusts' 105 *Yale Law Journal* 625.
—— (1997) 'The Secret Life of the Trust: The Trust as an Instrument of Commerce' 107 *Yale Law Journal* 165.
—— (2004) 'The Rise of the Management Trust' 143 *Real Property, Trust and Estate Law Journal* 52.
—— (2005) 'Questioning the Trust Law Duty of Loyalty: Sole Interest or Best Interest?' 114 *Yale Law Journal* 929.
Langbein, JH, Lerner, RL and Smith, BP (2009) *History of the Common Law: The Development of Anglo-American Legal Institutions* (New York, Aspen Publishers).
Leavitt, JA (2020) *The Voting Trust: A Device for Corporate Control* (New York, Columbia University Press).
Lee, WA (2001) 'Trustee Investing: Homes and Hedges' 1(1) *Queensland University of Technology Law and Justice* 3.
Lepaulle, P (1951) 'La notion de « trust » et ses applications dans les divers systèmes juridiques' in Institut International Pour l'Unification du Droit Privé, *Actes du Congrès international de droit privé tenu à Rome en juillet 1950*, vol 2 (Rome, L'unification du droit).
Li, Q (2000) 'The Legal Nature and Basic Principles of Trust' 3 *Chinese Journal of Law* 118.
Loretz, D (2016) 'Liechtenstein Trusts and Foundations: Creation and Operation' in A Kaplan (ed), *Trusts in Prime Jurisdictions*, 4th edn (Surrey, Globe Law and Business) 287.
Lupoi, M (1995) 'The Shapeless Trust' 1(3) *Trusts & Trustees* 15.
—— (2000) *Trusts: A Comparative Study* (Cambridge, Cambridge University Press).
Maitland, FW (1936) *Equity: A Course of Lectures*, 2nd edn (Cambridge, Cambridge University Press).
Malumian, N (2009) *Trusts in Latin America* (Oxford, Oxford University Press).
Markowitz, H (1959) *Portfolio Selection: Efficient Diversification of Investments* (Yale, Yale University Press).
Matthews, P (2013) 'The Compatibility of the Trust with the Civil Law Notion of Property' in L Smith (ed), *The Worlds of the Trust* (Cambridge, Cambridge University Press) 313.
Matthews, P and others (2022) *Underhill and Hayton Law of Trusts and Trustees*, 20th edn (London, LexisNexis Butterworths).
Maurice, 'The Office of Custodian Trustee' (1960) 24 *Conveyance and Property Lawyer* 196.
McAuley, M (2012) 'Truth and Reconciliation: Notions of Property in Louisiana's Civil and Trust Codes' in L Smith (ed), *Re-imagining the Trust: Trusts in Civil Law* (Cambridge, Cambridge University Press) 119.
McFarlane, B and Stevens, R (2010) 'The Nature of Equitable Property' 4 *The Journal of Equity* 44.
McGhee, J et al (eds) (2022) *Snell's Equity*, 34th edn (London, Sweet & Maxwell).
McKendrick, E (1993) (ed), *Commercial Aspects of Trust and Fiduciary Obligations* (Oxford, Oxford University Press).
Meagher, RP and Gummow, WMC (1986) *Jacobs' Law of Trusts in Australia*, 5th edn (Sydney, Butterworths).
Meier, G and Schmidt, O (2010) 'Liechtenstein' in A Kaplan (ed), *Trusts in Prime Jurisdictions*, 3rd edn (London, Globe Law and Business) 275.

Milsom, SFC (1981) *Historical Foundations of the Common Law*, 2nd edn (Oxford, Oxford University Press).
Moloney, N (2008) *EC Securities Regulation* (Oxford, Oxford University Press).
Morley, J (2016) 'The Common Law Corporation: The Power of the Trust in Anglo-American Business History' 116(2) *Columbia Law Review* 2145.
Ni, S (2012) 'Commercial Trusts and Companies as Business Organisations: Through Comparative Studies' 6 *Securities Law* 410.
Nolan, R (2004) 'Property in a Fund' 120 *LQR* 108.
—— (2006) 'Equitable Property' 122 *LQR* 232.
Noseda, F (2022) 'Equitable Ownership, Butter and Donkeys: Setting out a Vision for the Future of the Hague Trust Convention' 28(10) *Trusts & Trustees* 924.
Oakley, AJ (2015) *Parker and Mellows: The Modern Law of Trusts*, 9th edn (London, Sweet & Maxwell).
Ollikainen-Read, A (2018) 'Creditors' Claims against Trustees and Trust Funds' 24(2) *Trusts & Trustees* 177.
Oosterhoff, AH, Chambers, R and Mclnnes, M (2019) *Oosterhoff on Trusts*, 9th edn (Toronto, Carswell).
Panico, P (2009) 'Trustee Investment Powers in International Trust Law' 15(2) *Trusts & Trustees* 96.
—— (2017) *International Trust Laws*, 2nd edn (Oxford, Oxford University Press).
Penner, JE (2022) *The Law of Trusts*, 12th edn (Oxford, Oxford University Press).
Pettit, PH (2012) *Equity and the Law of Trusts*, 12th edn (Oxford, Oxford University Press).
Pollard, D (2013) *The Law of Pension Trusts* (Oxford, Oxford University Press).
Powles, E and Mazzier, S (2009) 'The New Rule against Perpetuities: Hidden Traps for Commercial Trusts' 8 *Journal of International Banking & Financial Law* 486.
Qi, D and Yan, L (2005) 'The Study of Modern Trust Function' 4 *Journal of Shaoyang University Social Science* 44.
Ramjoin, M (2008) *Text, Cases and Materials on Equity and Trusts*, 4th edn (Oxon, Routledge Cavendish).
Rawlings, P (2009) 'Reinforcing Collectivity: The Liability of Trustees and the Power of Investors in Finance Transactions' 23(1) *Trust Law International* 14.
Reid, KGC (1999) 'National Report for Scotland [G]' in DJ Hayton, SCJJ Kortmann and HLE Verhagen (eds), *Principles of European Trust Law* (The Hague, Kluwer Law International) 67.
—— (2000) 'Patrimony Not Equity: The Trust in Scotland' 8 *European Review of Private Law* 427.
—— (2012) 'Conceptualising the Chinese Trust: Some Thoughts from Europe' in L Chen and CH van Rhee (eds), *Towards a Chinese Civil Code: Historical and Comparative Perspectives* (Leiden, Martinus Nijhoff Publishers) 209.
Rudden, B (1944) 'Things as Thing and Things as Wealth' 14 *OJLS* 81.
Shah, B (2013) 'Trustee's Indemnity and Creditors' Rights' 19(1) *Trusts & Trustees* 79.
Sin, KF (1997) *The Legal Nature of the Unit Trust* (Oxford, Oxford University Press).
Sitkoff, RH (2004) 'An Agency Costs Theory of Trust Law' 89 *Cornell Law Review* 621.
Smith, H (2012) 'Property as the Law of Things' 125 *Harvard Law Review* 1691.
Smith, L (2009) 'Trust and Patrimony' 28 *Estates, Trusts & Pensions Journal* 332.
—— (2013) 'Scottish Trusts in the Common Law' 17 *Edinburgh Law Review* 283.
Stebbings, C (2002) *The Private Trustee in Victorian England* (Cambridge, Cambridge University Press).
—— (2007) 'Trustees, Tribunals and Taxes: Creativity in Victorian Law' 70 *Amicus Curiae* 2.
Stephenson, 'Co-trustees or Several Trustees?' (1942) 16 *Temple ULQ* 249.
Stone, HF (1922) 'A Theory of Liability of Trust Estates for the Contracts and Torts of the Trustee' 22 *Columbia Law Review* 527.
Su, D (2006) 'Trusts and Taxes' 11 *Times Finance* 7.
Sun, X (2008) *Property Law* (Beijing, China Law Press).
Swirski, C, Stewart, A, Underhill, L and Marcel V (2016) 'Investment Trusts: Tax' *Practice Law* 2.
Tang, HW (2014) 'Creditors, Trust and Insolvency' (2014) 20(4) *Trusts & Trustees* 383.
Tang, J and Chao, R (1990) *Financial Trust and Financial Market* (Tianjin, Tianjin science and Technic Press).

Televantos, A (2021) *Capitalism Before Corporations: The Morality of Business Associations and the Roots of Commercial Equity and Law* ((Oxford, Oxford University Press).
Mason, Sir Anthony (1997/8) 'Equity's Role in the Twentieth Century' 8 *The King's College Law Journal* 1.
Thomas, G and Hudson, A (2010) *The Law of Trusts*, 2nd edn (Oxford, Oxford University Press).
Thompson, HL (1998) 'Impact of the New Law on Trustee's Investment Powers' 4(8) *Trusts & Trustees* 16.
Tjio, H (2019) 'Merrill and Smith's Intermediate Rights Lying between Contract and Property: Are Singapore Trusts and Secured Transactions Drifting away from English Law towards American Law?' *Singapore Journal of Legal Studies* 235.
Trukhtanov, A (2007) 'The Irreducible Core of Trust Obligations' 123 *LQR* 342.
Tucker, L, Le Poidevin, N and Brightwell, J (2020) *Lewin on Trusts*, 20th edn (London, Sweet & Maxwell).
Virgo, G (2023) *The Principles of Equity & Trusts*, 5th edn (Oxford, Oxford University Press).
Wain, M and Shenkin, M (2009) 'Trustee Investment Powers and the Use of Asset Managers' 15(2) *Trusts & Trustees* 72.
Wang, L (2016) *Property Law Research*, 4th edn (Beijing, China Renmin University Press).
Wang, Z (2021) *Principles of Personal Claims*, 4th edn (Beijing, Beijing University Press).
Waters, DWM (1995) 'The Institution of the Trust in Civil and Common Law' 252 *Recueil de Cours* 113.
Waters, DWM, Smith, L and Gillen, M (2021) *Waters' Law of Trusts in Canada*, 5th edn (Toronto, Carswell).
Watkin, TG (2007) 'Changing Concepts of Ownership in English Law During the Nineteenth and Twentieth Centuries: The Changing Idea of Beneficial Ownership Under the English Trust' in M Dixon and GLLH Griffiths (eds), *Contemporary Perspectives on Property, Equity and Trusts Law* (Oxford, Oxford University Press) 139–61.
Watt, G (2021) *Equity and Trusts Law Directions*, 7th edn (Oxford, Oxford University Press).
Watt, G and Todd, P (2016) *Cases & Materials on Equity & Trusts*, 10th edn (Oxford, Oxford University Press).
Wen, S and Feng, X (2005) 'Ownership of Trust Property: On the Improvement of China's Legislation' 2 *Wuhan University Journal* 203.
Wilson, S (2015) *Todd & Wilson's Textbook on Trusts & Equity*, 12th edn (Oxford, Oxford University Press).
Wilson, WA and Duncan, AGM (1995) *Trusts, Trustees and Executors*, 2nd edn (Edinburgh, Green for the Scottish Universities Law Institute).
Woloszyn, JJ (1975) 'A Practical Guide to Voting Trusts' 4(2) *University of Baltimore Law Review* 245.
Wood, PR (2013) 'Commercial Trusts in an International Context' 19 *Trusts & Trustees* 267.
Worthington, S (2002) 'The Commercial Utility of the Trust Vehicle' in DJ Hayton (ed), *Extending the Boundaries of Trusts and Similar Ring-Fenced Funds* (Alphen aan den Rijn, Wolters Kluwer Law International).
Wu, H, Jia, X and Cheng, S (2003) *Trust Law: Legal Regulations of the Development of China Trust Market* (Shanghai, Lixin Accounting Press).
Yip, M (2016) 'The Commercial Context in Trust Law' 5 *The Conveyancer and Property Lawyer* 347.
Yip, M and Lee, J (2013) '"Less Than Straightforward People", Facts and Trusts: Reflections on Context: *Favor Easy Management Ltd v Wu' The Conveyancer and Property Lawyer* 431.
Yu, H (2010) 'China's Reception of the Dual Ownership of Anglo-American Trust' 3 *Modern Law Science* 159.
—— (2011) *How to Localise the British and American Law on Trust Property in China* (Beijing, China University of Political Science and Law Press).
Zhang, R (2015) 'A Comparative Study of the Introduction of Trusts into Civil Law and its Ownership of Trust Property' 21(8) *Trusts & Trustees* 902.
—— (2015) 'Trust Law of China and Its Uncertainties: Examination of the Rights and Obligations of Trust and Ownership of Trust Property' 10:1 *National Taiwan University Law Review* 45.

—— (2017) 'The New Role Trusts Play in Modern Financial Markets: The Evolution of Trusts from Guardian to Entrepreneur and the Reasons for the Evolution' 23(4) *Trusts & Trustees* 453.
—— (2019) *A Better Understanding of Common Law Ownership of Trust Property and its Introduction in China Through Comparative Studies* (Guangzhou, World Publishing Corporation).
—— (2020) 'A Developed Understanding of the Beneficiary's Interest in Commercial Trusts through a Comparative Study of Chinese Law' 27(3) *Maastricht Journal of European and Comparative Law* 343.
—— (2021) 'Changes and Challenges of the Role of a Trustee in a Commercial Context: Does This Separate Commercial Trusts from Trusts?' 42 *Business Law Review* 262.
—— (2022) 'Principal Forms of Commercial Trusts in the UK and the Rethinking of Traditional Approaches' 28(8) *Trusts & Trustees* 787.
Zhou, X (1996) *Comparative Studies of Trust Law* (Beijing, China Law Press).
—— (2012) *Trust Legislation: Theories and Practice* (Beijing, China Legal Publishing House).

INDEX

www.ingramcontent.com/pod-product-compliance
Ingram Content Group UK Ltd.
Pitfield, Milton Keynes, MK11 3LW, UK
UKHW021906150926
475560UK00003B/217

9 781509 974054